I0092124

The Anthropocene
and the Undead

Lexington Books Horror Studies

Series Editors: Lorna Piatti-Farnell, Auckland University of Technology, and Carl Sederholm, Brigham Young University

Lexington Books Horror Studies is looking for original and interdisciplinary monographs or edited volumes that expand our understanding of horror as an important cultural phenomenon. We are particularly interested in critical approaches to horror that explore why horror is such a common part of culture, why it resonates with audiences so much, and what its popularity reveals about human cultures generally. To that end, the series will cover a wide range of periods, movements, and cultures that are pertinent to horror studies. We will gladly consider work on individual key figures (e.g. directors, authors, show runners, etc.), but the larger aim is to publish work that engages with the place of horror within cultures. Given this broad scope, we are interested in work that addresses a wide range of media, including film, literature, television, comics, pulp magazines, video games, or music. We are also interested in work that engages with the history of horror, including the history of horror-related scholarship.

Titles in the Series

The Anthropocene and the Undead: Cultural Anxieties in the Contemporary Popular Imagination, edited by Simon Bacon
Gothic Mash-Ups: Hybridity, Appropriation, and Intertextuality in Gothic Storytelling, edited by Natalie Neill
Japanese Horror: New Critical Approaches to History, Narratives, and Aesthetics, edited by Fernando Gabriel Pagnoni Berns, Subashish Bhattacharjee, and Ananya Saha
Violence in the Films of Stephen King, edited by Michael J. Blouin and Tony Magistrale
Dark Forces at Work: Essays on Social Dynamics and Cinematic Horrors, edited by Cynthia J. Miller and A. Bowdoin Van Riper

The Anthropocene and the Undead

Cultural Anxieties in the Contemporary Popular Imagination

Edited by
Simon Bacon

LEXINGTON BOOKS
Lanham • Boulder • New York • London

Published by Lexington Books
An imprint of The Rowman & Littlefield Publishing Group, Inc.
4501 Forbes Boulevard, Suite 200, Lanham, Maryland 20706
www.rowman.com

86-90 Paul Street, London EC2A 4NE

Copyright © 2022 by The Rowman & Littlefield Publishing Group, Inc.

All rights reserved. No part of this book may be reproduced in any form or by any
electronic or mechanical means, including information storage and retrieval systems,
without written permission from the publisher, except by a reviewer who may quote
passages in a review.

British Library Cataloguing in Publication Information Available

Library of Congress Cataloging-in-Publication Data

Names: Bacon, Simon, 1965- editor.
Title: The anthropocene and the undead : cultural anxieties in the contemporary popular
    imagination / edited by Simon Bacon.
Description: Lanham : Lexington Books, [2022] | Series: Lexington Books horror studies
    | Includes bibliographical references and index. | Summary: "This book explores the
    interconnectedness of the cultural zeitgeists around the anthropocene and the undead
    showing how the latter reveals increasing cultural anxieties over who and what
    constitutes humanity in the twenty-first century and whether it has a place in any
    possible post-Anthropocene futures"—Provided by publisher.
Identifiers: LCCN 2021062996 (print) | LCCN 2021062997 (ebook) | ISBN
    9781793625823 (cloth) | ISBN 9781793625830 (epub)
Subjects: LCSH: Zombie films—History and criticism. | Zombies in motion pictures. |
    Human ecology in motion pictures. | Horror tales—History and criticism. | Zombies in
    literature. | Human ecology in literature. | Posthumanism in literature. | Ecocriticism.
Classification: LCC PN1995.9.Z63 A58 2022 (print) | LCC PN1995.9.Z63 (ebook) |
    DDC 791.43/6164—dc23/eng/20220215
LC record available at https://lccn.loc.gov/2021062996
LC ebook record available at https://lccn.loc.gov/2021062997

Contents

Acknowledgments

With such a turbulent time in the run-up to this collection coming out because of the ongoing pandemic I would like to thank all the authors involved in the project for managing to get their essays written and getting this book over the line and out into the world. I would also like to thank Judith at Lexington for all her help and patience during the production and completion of this book. Most importantly I want to thank my wife Kasia for her unending help, patience, and support and without whom none of this would get done or be worth doing. Also, our two not-so-little monsters Seba and Majki who always manage to provide some light relief and distraction no matter how stressful things get. And last but not least the constant support (and sernik Magdi) of Mam i Tata Bronk.

Introduction

The Anthropocene and the Undead

Simon Bacon

The Anthropocene most typically describes the ongoing period when human-ity, and human activity, has become the driving force of planetary history. No longer a minimal part of a larger ecosystem but a decisive part of its direc-tion and its success or failure. The end of World War II and the newfound awareness of military capability is any easy point from which to start such a viewpoint, though it can also be "defined to have started when there is any discernible human influence on the local environment, through modification of local ecosystems and shifts in local biodiversity" (Mahli 2017, 12). That said, the start of the Industrial Revolution and its relationship to Empire and capitalism are possibly more indicative of the start of a course of action from which there was less and less chance of returning from—it is unsurprising, and rather apt for this volume, that this period was bookended by such semi-nal undead (eco)monsters as Frankenstein's Monster (*Frankenstein*, Shelley, 1818) and Count Dracula (*Dracula*, Stoker, 1897) who are energized by the influence of Modern man's quest for domination and power while equally revealing the "gaping maw" (Smith and Hughes 2016, 5–6) of nonhuman landscapes that lay behind such endeavors. This sees a change in human-ity's relation to the environment where the environment beyond civilization becomes increasingly wild and dangerous, representing a separation from a world we are no longer inherently joined to by a shared evolutionary history—H. G. Wells makes much of this in *War of the Worlds* as being the only factor that saves humanity from destruction by the Martians[1]—but have become unwelcome aliens in our own home.

    This linkage between the Anthropocene and undead, as noted above, is not coincidental and as shall be shown here the entanglement of the two sees much of how we conceptualize and experience one being done so in terms implicit in the other. As shall be argued here, the connection between them

1

runs far deeper than the oft cited connection to the popularity of the zombie genre. In many respects the Anthropocene itself can be read as being undead, both in concept and practice. This is partially due to the indefinite nature of the Anthropocene itself, in what specifically signals its beginning and even its end, and how that might transition into a "post-Anthropocene." More so, as with many other topics in the early twenty-first century not everyone believes that it is in fact occurring and that we are living through times that are to be expected in a planetary ecosystem that was previously seen to be extremely volatile—some have argued the planet has been in a process of cooling for the past three million years and the recent rise in temperature is actually a good thing (Maasch 1997, Chandler 2007, and Badtach 2015). Indeed, there even seems to be much confusion over exactly what to call this period of geological history, or "cene." Anthropocene is usually interpreted as denoting human impact on the planet, though as noted later in this volume by Andrew Wilson, it more specifically talks to "mankind"[2] and the kinds of colonial endeavor linked to patriarchal domination linking it to ideas around the "Capitalocene" (Moore 2017). This sees the patriarchal push to monetize all aspects of human life and our interactions with the environment and each other, seeing a turning point around the time of the industrial revolution which initiates an inevitable trajectory to the kinds of consumerist excess of the early twenty-first century. Which then gives rise to terms that can be seen to more specifically reflect the affective experience of our current moment in history as seen in terms such as "Technocene" (Martins 2018) that describe both global societies growing dependence on technology but also the economic ecology around it with its inherent discriminations; Justin McBrian's (2016) "Necrocene" voicing the anxiety around the accumulation of extinction events across the globe; Heather Davis' (2015, 235) notion of the "Plasticene" that centers on the ongoing crisis and indestructibility of plastics in the world—an undead menace in the oceans and beyond; and even the "Virocene" (Fernando 2020) that has been given added resonance due to the ongoing COVID-19 outbreak and humanities' inability to effectively deal with it. Other terms speak more to the idea of transition itself and more closely reflect the current time of indecision yet might also point to time beyond the Anthropocene, if that is what it actually is. Here then are terms like "Entropocene" (Robbins 2017) that consider the environment as acting in line with the laws of thermodynamics and will slowly entropy, and decline, to reach a constant, base value; such a "winding down" is also seen in Elana Gomel's use of the word "Limbotopia", in this volume, to delineate a form of zombie-like shambling or interminable dying and which seems almost naturally to lead toward Edward O. Wilson's description of the "Eremocene" or "the Age of Loneliness" (2014), where increasing extinction leaves humanity more and more alone in its inevitable demise. Of course many of these terms, and unsurprisingly given the often human-centric idea of the Anthropocene, only view the ongoing situation in what the outcome might be for humanity and so theorists like Donna Haraway (2016) have tried to necessarily widen the framework so that it considers all forms of life as equal and create ways of being and living responsibly in the present moment as part of an ongoing body of life; Jeffrey J. Cohen continues in this vein proposing the "Disanthropocene" that sees our life in the moment but in relation to an infinite future where the true scale of humanities self-importance is put into appropriate scale alongside our interference and entanglement with the environment around us (2016); this is given more focus in ideas such as the "Symbiocene" (Everard 2016) which both calls for and envisions a future of greater entanglement and symbiosis between humanity, other life-forms and the environment. These are by no means all of the possible categories that the present or possible futures can be described with creating a moment of almost infinite indeterminacy where we live in a time that is neither one thing or the other, everything or nothing; forever caught between the real and the imagined, superstition and reason. As noted by Nils Bubandt in this volume this is exactly the kind of state as described as defining the undead which is neither alive nor dead, caught interminably between worlds (Showalter 1992, 179). As Bubandt further notes, in this volume, we are still living in the time of the "Holocene" where superstition still walks among the living and the dead will not let go of their hold on the present.

Unsurprisingly central to a consideration of the Anthropocene, related terms, and the undead is time as they all speak to a tension or disparity between human time and what might be called planetary or infinite time—or what could even be seen as the difference between human life and immortality. Inherent within this is the notion of scale and in terms of the Anthropocene this brings in the idea of "hyperobjects" as proposed by Timothy Morton (2013). Morton talks of hyperobjects as those which are in all aspects massive in comparison to humans, such as time, space, distance, and scale. Galaxies and planets are seen as being such objects as they create and exist in time and space in a very different way than humans do—we do not generally bend time around ourselves as such massive entities do. However, he also views things such as Styrofoam and plastics as being hyperobjects as once they are created they can never degrade on their own. The intersection of these two examples works quite well in regard to humanity as they describe both our insignificance and the impact that we can have yet have no understanding of. Indeed, comprehension becomes tantamount in considering hyperobjects, and by extension, the Anthropocene. Hyperobjects are necessarily incomprehensible to humanity due to their scale, so that the human lifespan and even the Anthropocene itself are so small in comparison to say the life of the Earth itself as to be insignificant (Morton 2013). In similar vein the undead, once created, share many of the same properties as hyperobjects—or indeed plastic; they are immortal, they sense and interact with their surroundings in ways beyond the merely human, and they are virtually indestructible so that they experience space and time very differently to humanity.

Important within this is also the connection between the past, present, and future. For humans this is a very real linear progression; birth, life, death; ancestors, contemporaries, and descendants. For bodies that are dimensionally massive in comparison this is considerably less so, if not insignificant. Stoker's Count Dracula who is hundreds of years old experiences time in this manner finding the notion of human life and death almost quaint (Stoker 1993, 35). The later film *Dracula* by Tod Browning from 1931, takes this further with the Count becoming excited by the idea of death: "To die, to be *really* dead, that must be glorious!" to which he adds, "There are far worse things awaiting man than death" (Browning 1931, emphasis in original). The inference being that eternity has made living meaningless to him and the ongoing resurrections of the Count in films, books, and many others—Christopher Lee as Dracula rose and then "died" again seven times in Hammer films alone—suggests that time will never end for the undead vampire.[3] The brevity of human life then seems something of thrill to him. Of note within the idea of the undead, and as seen in Count Dracula in particular is how his existence outside of time disrupts the linear progression of human history so that the past never dies but remains into the present—a present that is continually moving into the future. Stoker's novel most clearly shows this in the vampire taking his Old-World superstition and powers with him into London, the modern heart of the Empire, where he causes havoc.

Within this there is much of the hauntological, though not quite the kinds of ghosts or traces as mentioned by Derrida in *Specters of Marx* (2006) or those of nostalgia noted by Mark Fisher ("McNeil 2011"), but something more active and malignant that looks to negate a future for a return to the past. This sees, what we might term, undead memory literally consuming the present, feeding on its life and vitality, so that the unfolding present simply replicates what has gone before. Obviously, this does not create a simulacrum of history but rather a return to previous ways of viewing and interpreting the world and consequently any actions or reactions to environmental, cultural, and political events. Political populism is an obvious example but responses to the Anthropocene can be equally consumed with undead memories. This can be seen in the ongoing denial of the import of unfolding events and their collective and accumulative meaning or in how conceptions of the Anthropocene place the importance maintaining current human behavior and/ or the centrality of monetary value to any kind of solution (green capitalism). Undead memories here then also speak to a purposeful contraction or fixing of time and a purposeful denial of the kinds of temporal scale that Fisher observes, and which again highlights humanities self-importance. Implicit within this view is the absence of any real vision of what a future beyond the present might look like—an eternal present has no future only continuation of the same. Much of this reflects some of the categories given to the current geological, historical period we are living in mentioned above and particularly those that refuse to accept a vision of the future, even a posthuman future that does not have humans or humanity being central to it. The Capitalocene, the Anthropocene, and climate change denialism being ones most likely to be backward-looking in their conceptual frameworks viewing any kind of future as either a direct continuation of the (undead)past or a modification of it that is, to all purposes, only a more appealingly packaged version of what came before.

As noted previously, the idea of the undead past "living" in the present acts as a kind of haunting, a spectral presence that destabilizes the contemporary world we live in. In many ways the persistence of the past can be seen to Gothicize the present, turning it into what Mélanie Joseph Vilain calls an "inauthentic and ruined place" (2021, 106), an environment that is increasingly disjointed and anxiety ridden—in many respects the recent pandemic has increased this sense and exacerbated the underlying tensions that were already present. This Gothicization in relation to the current geological situation can be seen to have two main sources: the undying presence of the past, as already mentioned, and the repressed or unrecognized anxiety that something is deeply wrong with the world. In many ways the former is used to try and obscure the latter, in that the recourse to older forms of viewing the world and our place within it often covers over how that relationship has gone catastrophically awry and that the escalating examples of extinction events and erratic and extreme weather occurrences are not a sign that we need to change the fundamental nature of our lives on Earth. This knowing repression of the increasingly obvious evidence that the planet itself is responding negatively to our continued interactions with it changes the nature of our encounters with the environment, each other, and indeed every aspect of our daily lives. And while we try to maintain an air of obliviousness to these changes the environment we once thought of as safe or "homely" is becoming less so. The alienation we can feel to our surroundings, or the uncanniness that occurs when a known environment suddenly acts strangely is becoming increasingly felt in a world where flooding, fires, and tornadoes occur in places they have not done so previously or in extremes that have broken all previous records.

This change in relationship to, or perspective on, our surroundings, or the nonhuman world that we live in is important here, as Amitav Ghosh observes "these changes are not merely strange in the sense of being unknown or alien; their uncanniness lies precisely in the fact that in these encounters we recognize something we had turned away from: that is to say, the presence and proximity of non-human interlocutors" (Ghosh 2021, 40). Uncanniness is similarly important in the sense it is the human mind trying to recognize the world around it yet being unable to. These macroscale events necessarily affect the microscale environments around us as well so that objects, family, our homes, even ourselves are no longer the same as they were so that we can, individually or collectively, become "strangers to ourselves" (Kristeva 1991). With every aspect of ourselves and our lives being thrown off kilter by this purposeful misrecognition of ourselves and our place in the wider ecosystem, an aporia opens up, an unbridgeable abyss between what we think we know and what is actually happening—in many ways this is captured by Morton's idea of scale and the immense disparity between the human and the planetary. The exact nature of this unbridgeable gap often gives shape to the anxieties and feelings of unhomeliness we experience in the face of the nonhuman interlocutors that Ghosh speaks of, an ecological, nonhuman, other that is simultaneously a source of comfort in our daily existence yet a wild, blank abyss waiting to consume us (Smith and Hughes 2016, 5–6). The uncanny here, often fueled by our repressed anxieties over what we innately sense is a growing catastrophe, gives affective impetus to our unhomely relationship to the environment constructing it as a world of undead doppelgängers that both reflect our own character while revealing the nature of its effects on the Earth. The real-world evidence of this and the negative effects of the Anthropocene—in particular humanity's exploitation and mismanagement of its "home"—is seen in the more direct Gothicization, or "ruination" of the environment around us producing toxic wastelands, melting icecaps, and mass extinctions, turning it into a dark undead specter of its former fecundity. This, in turn, manifests the Gothic cultural world of the zombie horde, insatiable vampires, and the vengeful undead seeing it not just being a product of the imagination but a reflection of the nightmare reality that mankind has created.

One of the things which adds to the increasing unhomeliness that humanity feels in the world is due to the fact that the flora and fauna of the Earth are not standing idly by and while many species have suffered and disappeared from the planet, others are adapting and finding new ways to continue and thrive. Among those are the more extraordinary examples of microbes managing to live within the toxic waste produced by the petrochemical and other such industries (see the chapter by Aaron Bradshaw in this volume) both as hybrids of existing species but also ones that are uniquely suited to living in extreme environments. While large scale industrial or mining works might seem exceptional cases there are those much closer to home that are seeing species adapt and survive within human-created environments. The urban space of cities has become extremely beneficial to species that are predominantly considered as pests and vermin such as cockroaches, mice, rats, and pigeons. Similarly types of fungus, plants, and pollinating insects have found convenient new sites within metropolises within which to thrive. Further, many larger species have found ways to adapt to the presence of humans or take advantage of other species inability to survive in the changing environment around them (Baraniuk 2017).[4] Within this is an indication of a kind of symbiosis or adaptation between humanity and the life forms around it as we increasingly disturb and intrude on their habitats, they find ways to survive and adapt in ours.

This also begins to describe a porosity between the human "body"—the internal and external space we more intimately inhabit and which contains us—and the nonhuman species around us. On human terms at least, this can be seen to be a further example of Gothicization both of the area immediately around us and our bodies. This is not just in how we adapt our own lives to accommodate other life forms but how they transform our biological structure to become part of us. Something of this can be seen in the case of Lyme disease and the ticks that carry it. The ticks, due to climate change, are migrating from their former habitats and hosts to new ones and because of the proximity of human are choosing them as a new means of survival and allowing them to quickly adapt and evolve in the changing environment around them (Waits 2020). Infected ticks then pass on Lyme disease to their hosts which can dramatically alter their biological and psychological make-up (see the chapter by Sarah Lewison in this volume). This can be further seen in examples such as the recent pandemic and the SARS-CoV-2 or COVID-19 virus which has migrated from mammals to human hosts and is mutating at a rate which suggests it will continue to survive while there are densely populated human societies to infect—not unlike influenza. Indeed, the increase in pandemic scale diseases since 2000 suggests that not only is the current stage of the Anthropocene creating the perfect conditions for such migrations to occur but that any kind of human future will necessarily include such ongoing hybridizations, as Elana Gomel calls it "a brave new world" of "hopeful monster[s]" (Gomel 2021, 227).

The Gothicization of the human body, a process labeled as creating the abhuman body which is "continually in danger of becoming not-itself, becoming other" (Hurley 2004, 3), seems an appropriate environmental response to the kinds of human exceptionalism that is arguably at the core of mankind's mistreatment of the planetary ecosystem. Further, it serves to prove that no matter how much we feel humans are separate from the world around us—the original example of Cartesian misdirection where the mind is a separate entity from the body/environment around it—we are and always will be intimately entangled with it. In fact, much of what has brought the idea of the Anthropocene into the popular imagination is the very real and affective ways that the changing environment impacts on people's lives across the globe from weather conditions and air quality through to microbes and viruses that leave traces of their passing in our bodies or dramatically alter the structures, membranes, and organs it comes into contact with. In this way we all possess abhuman bodies and the Gothicization of ourselves and the world we are part of shows clearly how mankind has continually and consistently misrecognized its place in the planetary ecosystem. This misrecognition, the abyss mentioned earlier, is then the source of the undead horde that rampages through the Anthropocene, manifesting the increasingly frantic attempts to deny where we really are in the ecological hierarchy. These undead, which arise from a past that we will not allow to die and from a denial of the state of the environment around us are not so much a form of eco-revenge or insatiable historical ghouls, but metaphorical night terrors meant to wake us from the ecological nightmare we have fashioned in our own image. The decomposing, decaying, oozy animated corpses of the undead are to remind us of our own abhuman bodies and that the idea of the Symbiocene is not a vision of the future but the ongoing history of human evolution on the Earth.

FROM NOW TO THEN: THE FUTURE OF THE ANTHROPOCENE

The book itself is divided up into five sections that trace something of a progression from where we are now—in terms of how the Anthropocene as a product of colonial, capitalist, patriarchal endeavor, which shapes our ideas of who we can be and how we attempt to configure and contain the increasingly undead environment around us—and slowly shifting toward a reconsideration of our relationship to both time and the planetary ecosystem which further suggests what a post-Anthropocene, posthuman future might mean. The collection then opens with "Part I: Undead Identity in the Anthropocene" which considers the, often, undead role of masculinity and particular kinds of identity positions that reinforce and reify the conditions that have created the Anthropocene. The chapters here describe how such masculine traits are inherent within conceptions such as the Capitalocene and the attempts to return to an undead past that denies the extent of what is occurring around us. More so, they offer reflections not only on how such masculinity impacts on other identity positions, such as "father," "daughter," "mother" and alongside this the way in which notions of femininity and equality are shaped by such a system. The section begins with Kyle William Bishops', "(Un)Death of the Father: Self-Sacrificing Paternity in Modern Zombie Narratives," that focuses on the rise of the figure of the protective father figure in recent apocalyptic movies. More particularly Bishop examines the films *The Road* (Hillcoat: 2009), *Maggie* (Hobson: 2015), *Train to Busan* (Yeon: 2016), and *Cargo* (Howling and Ramke: 2017), and how they represent a paternal masculinity that is coming to the realization of the untenable nature of the world they live in and/or have created and must negotiate new ways with which to interact with it. This is followed by "Undeath, Theatricality, and the Anthropocene in DC Moore's *Common* (2017)," by Gheorghe Williams that shifts focus to theatrical performance and a historically set play that speaks to the early twenty-first century. Here, the main female protagonist, Mary, only finds power in the patriarchal world around her by returning from the dead—dying to her womanhood and being reborn as a "(s)mothering" masculine force—reinforcing the ideologies of privilege, capitalism, and dominion over nature that have created the world we currently live in. Closing the section is Johan Höglund's "*Maggie* in the Necrocene," which returns to the film featured in the first chapter but offers a closer reading of the narrative. Höglund unpicks the narratives' patriarchal frameworks to suggest ways that undead identify positions, specifically that of the daughter Maggie, which might subvert the unfolding Necrocene depicted in the movie and offer alternatives to inevitable extinction. "Part II: Undead Spaces and 'Zones' of the Anthropocene" shifts to how spaces of control and containment are constructed to separate "dangerous" or polluted environments from those that are classified as "pure"—this comes from Mary Douglas' *Purity and Danger* (1966) where maintaining the integrity of a society is primarily achieved by monsterizing that which is outside of it, but also undesirable elements within it. Purity here signifying the modern, civilized world that is in control of the environment around it and so is untouched by monstrous entities such as the Anthropocene, superstition, the supernatural, and more specifically any suggestion of the undead. Nils Bubandt, in "The Uncanny Valley of the Anthropocene: Short Stories about the Undead under the Brightest of Lights," charts out the ways in which the supernatural and the Anthropocene share common ground in their respective framings of what can be considered as undead. More specifically in the ways that the undead are neither one thing or the other but manifest a space of uncertainty and ambiguity consequently allowing for different ways to frame and understand the ongoing experience of the Anthropocene. Next is "Mutants and Tourists: Horror Film, Sacrifice Zones, and *Chernobyl Diaries* (2012)," by Steffen Hantke that also references real-world events but as channeled through an imaginary cinematic narrative. The site of the Chernobyl nuclear disaster is the focus here though many years after the event and when unauthorized tourists are making secret excursions into the exclusion zone around the still radioactive site. The zone acts as both one of containment, to protect the world beyond from the radioactive fallout, but also as a "sacrifice" zone where the living and the "undead"—those that are no longer considered human—are brought into contact with each other to gauge what occurs. Something similar is featured in "A Panic on the 4th of July: Municipal Malfeasance, Mutation, and Monstrosity in Barry Levinson's *The Bay* (2012)" by Rebecca Stone Gordon but which moves the action from Eastern Europe to North America and shows that the escape of what should be excluded is not an exception, as configured in the *Chernobyl Diaries*, but an everyday occurrence even in the heartland of Western consumerism. Of note in both films discussed in these last two chapters is the use of handheld cameras to bring a faux authenticity to obviously imaginary events creating a similar "undead" blurring between categories as earlier laid out by Bubandt. Following this is "Part III: The Anthropocene and the End of 'Time'" that moves from spatial environments to temporal ones and in particular the different ways in which we can experience time from the human to the planetary and beyond. This section opens with Elana Gomel and "'Dying All the Time': The Future as the Extended Present and the Zombification of History in the Anthropocene," who focuses on recent zombie films and how the shambling undead body constructs a very particular experience of time. The zombie body, as fleshy manifestation of the current state of the Anthropocene and humanity as it repeatedly fails to deal with it creates, what Gomel calls, a kind of "Limboscene" where nothing ever resolves or completes but just aimlessly continues. Next is "Avenging the Anthropocene: Returning the Dead to Life while Destroying the Planet in *The Avengers* Films" by Kevin J. Wetmore Jr. which considers the representation of death in the films of the Marvel Cinema Universe and in particular those centered on the Avengers. As noted by Wetmore, the superheroes are themselves undead in their inability to remain dead for any significant period of time, at least until their war with Death himself (Thanos). More significantly in their final battle Death kills a third of the world's population including superheroes, which is intended to save the world and the wider universe from extinction level overpopulation. However, in reversing this, and reestablishing the heroes as undead, they and the millions that died with them, return to an environment and resources that are now significantly depleted ensuring the inevitability of ecological collapse and a very real end of time. The final chapter in this section, "'To Remember Forever to Forget': *Into Eternity* and the Anti-Anthropocene," by Kristopher Woofter and Mikaela Bobiy switches to a documentary film about an underground excavation that is intended to bury Finland's nuclear waste. However, this very human endeavor is one that will be judged on a planetary scale as it will be 100,000 years before it is considered safe. This brings into direct contact the kinds of difference in scale that Morton speaks about and what can be done now to ensure that humans in 20,000-, 50,000-, or 75,000-year time will not mistakenly open the caverns thinking there is something precious rather than deadly contained there. "Part IV: The Disantnropocene: Is Not All about Us" moves from the future of time to that of humanity and considers more closely the idea that humans are integrally entangled with all other life on Earth. Here we are intimately bound to and with other species to adapt to Anthropocene and post-Anthropocene environments. Andrew J. Wilson in "'You're Next!': The Enemy Within and the End of the Anthropocene as Seen in Adaptions of 'Who Goes There?' and *The Body Snatchers*" examines the series of films related to and adapted from *The Thing From Another World* (Nyby: 1951) and their representation of humanities relationship to the natural world. Here the invasion thematics that have informed The Thing become increasingly directed toward the enforced biological hybridity of the human body as it evolves into the future. Something of this continues in "Non-Consensual Eco-sex a Guided Meditation to the Permeable Membrane," by Sarah Lewison also focuses on biological sexual abuse but changes to a real-world example rather than an imaginary one. Lewison describes the migration of ticks to new habitats and hosts and the effects of Lyme disease that a percentage of them carry and pass on to their "victims." Lyme disease can cause significant and long-term effects on those that have it describing an unusual form of biological hybridity and eco-revenge. Aaron Bradshaw's, "Back from the Dead: Tailings Ponds in the Albertan Oil Sands Mining Operations" examines another real-world example, but this time of an environment poisoned by human activity, but one where life still manages to develop and thrive. However, while this "greening" of a ruined landscape is viewed in terms of sustainability and management of the human world, the actual timescale involved shows it as an environment that we will never know revealing a world that is intended to thrive without our presence. The final section in the collection, "Part V: The Post-Anthropocene, the Symbiocene, and Undead Futures" takes us to the cusp of new futures and beyond describing an ecology coping with what humans have left behind and new forms of hybridity that see humanity evolving into unexpected bodies and configurations to suit their changing environment. First here is "Post-Anthropocenic Undying Futures: The Ecocritical Dystopian Posthuman in Lai's *The Tiger Flu* and Bacigalupi's 'The People of Sand and Slag'," by Conrad Scott that speaks of an environmental step forward but also one backwards as new generations of humans adapt and evolve to survive in the broken world they have created. Unusually here though, while the shape of humanity has changed its purpose has not and it is still determined to monetize the world around it creating ever more poisonous ecologies to cope with see the Anthropocene as a never-ending trauma. The focus begins to shift in "'Cause tonight is the night| When two become one': *Stranger Things*, Parasitism, Assimilation, and the Abject" by Daisy Butcher who examines the popular television series *Stranger Things* which features two very different realms on the Earth; the human and that of a dark ecology. The "dark side" here is one that is fueled by an ecological jouissance that will forcibly invade the civilized world and violently penetrate human bodies to birth a new and future species. The collection closes with a different view of the Earths future and one that is more clearly posthuman. "After the End: The Post-Anthropocene Future of *Endzeit*," by Lars Schmeink returns to a zombie-like narrative but one which shares something of the undead supernatural described by Nils Bubandt. The narrative shows the end of humanity as we become reintegrated back into the natural world around us. However, this is not the violent eradication of human life as seen in *Stranger Things* but rather an acceptance of our place in the world and that the future is not necessarily either ours to determine or to continue to influence. The visions of the future described in these final works show our present selves as spectral, undead presences in the future; neither truly of it nor totally absent. Humanity will become an undead memory shambling into the unending future identified only by the traces of ourselves that survive in the pieces of plastic that will never degrade and random strings of DNA that have long become parts of other bodies.

NOTES

1. Welles' *War of the Worlds* appeared in serialized form the same year that *Dracula* was published.

2. "Mankind" here is used to comment on the fact that much of the human activity cited as causing the Anthropocene can be seen to have been caused by inherently and interdependent patriarchal endeavors such as colonialism, capitalism, exploitation, and the creation and sustaining of male dominated social and economical hierarchies. This is in contrast to the word "humanity" which is used to denote human peoples as a whole.

3. Stoker himself has originally intended to call his novel *The Dead Undead* referring to the Counts nature of being neither alive nor dead.

4. See Baraniuk 2017. It should be noted that even with the numbers of some species increasing they are far outnumbered by the unprecedented number of other kinds of flora and fauna becoming extinct.

WORKS CITED

Baraniuk, Chris. 2017. "The Animals Thriving in the Anthropocene." *BBC Future*. 1 August. https://www.bbc.com/future/article/20170801-the-animals-thriving-in-the -anthropocene. Accessed September 28, 2021.

Bastach, Michael. 2015. "Greenpeace Co-Founder: We're In One Of The Coldest Periods In Earth's History." *Daily Caller*. 16 October. https://dailycaller.com /2015/10/16/greenpeace-co-founder-were-in-one-of-the-coldest-periods-in-earths -history/. Accessed September 27, 2021.

Browning, Tod (dir.). 1931. *Dracula*. Universal City: Universal Pictures.

Chandler, David L. 2007. "Climate myths: It's been far warmer in the past, what's the big deal?" *New Scientist.* 16 May. https://www.newscientist.com/article/dn11647 -climate-myths-its-been-far-warmer-in-the-past-whats-the-big-deal/. Accessed September 27, 2021.

Cohen, Jeffrey Jerome. 2016. "Environing." Theorizing the Contemporary, *Fieldsights.* 6 April. https://culanth.org/fieldsights/environing. Accessed 28 September 2021.

Davis, Heather. 2015. "Toxic Progeny: The Plastisphere and Other Queer Futures" *PhiloSOPHIA* 5(2) (Summer): 232–250.

Derrida, Jacques. 2006. *Specters of Marx* [1993], trans. by Peggy Kamuf. London: Routledge Classics.

Douglas, Mary. 1966. *Purity and Danger: An Analysis of Concepts of Pollution and Taboo.* London: Routledge and Kegan Paul.

Everard, Mark. 2016. *The Ecosystems Revolution.* London: Palgrave.

Fernando, Jude L. 2020. "The Virocene Epoch: The Vulnerability Nexus of Viruses, Capitalism and Racism," *Journal of Political Ecology* 27(1), 635–684. doi: https:// doi.org/10.2458/v27i1.23748

Ghosh, Amitav. 2021. *Uncanny and Improbable Events.* London: Penguin.

Gomel, Elana. 2021) "The Epidemic of History: Contagion of the Past in the Era of the Never-Ending Present." *Embodying Contagion: The Viropolitics of Horror and Desire in Contemporary Discourse*, edited by Sandra Becker, Megen de Bruin-Molé and Sara Polak. Cardiff: University of Wales Press, 219–234.

Haraway, Donna J. 2015. *Staying with the Trouble: Making Kin in the Chthulucene.* Durham: Duke University Press.

Hurley, Kelly. 2004. *The Gothic Body: Sexuality, Materialism, and Degeneration at the Fin de Siècle.* Cambridge: Cambridge University Press. doi:10.1017/ CBO9780511519161.001

Joseph-Vilain, Mélanie. 2021. *Post-Apartheid Gothic: White South African Writers and Space.* Lanham: Fairleigh Dickenson University Press.

Kristeva, Julia. 1991. *Strangers to Ourselves*, trans. by Leon S. Roudiez. New York: Columbia University Press.

Maasch, Kirk A. 1997. "The Big Chill." Nova Online. https://www.pbs.org/wgbh/ nova/ice/chill.html. Accessed September 27, 2021.

Mahli, Yadvinder. 2017. "The Concept of the Anthropocene." *Annual Review of Environment and Resources*, 42:1, 77-104.

Martins, Hermínio. 2018. *The Technocene: Reflections on Bodies, Minds, and Markets.* London: Anthem Press.

McNeil, Joanne. 2011. "Past and Present in 'Strange Simultaneity': Mark Fisher Explains Hauntology at NYU." *Rhizome.* 18 May. https://rhizome.org/editorial /2011/may/18/hauntology/. Accessed September 28, 2021.

Moore, Jason W. 2017. The Capitalocene, Part I: On the Nature and Origins of Our Ecological Crisis, *The Journal of Peasant Studies.* http://dx.doi.org/10.1080 /03066150.2016.1235036

Morton, Timothy. 2013. *Hyperobjects: Philosophy and Ecology after the End of the World.* Minneapolis: University of Minnesota Press.

O'Brien, Justin. 2016. "Accumulating Extinction: Planetary Catastrophism in the Necrocene." *Anthropocene or Capitalocene? Nature, History, and the Crisis of Capitalism*, edited by Jason W. Moore. Oakland: PM Press, 116–137.

Robbins, Jeffrey H. 2018. The Entropocene. *Proceedings of the 61st Annual Meeting of the ISSS*, Vienna, Austria, (1). Retrieved from https://journals.isss.org/index.php /proceedings61st/article/view/3232. Accessed September 28, 2021.

Showalter, Elaine. 1992. *Sexual Anarchy: Gender and Culture at the Fin de Siecle*. London: Virago.

Smith, Andrew and William Hughes (eds). 2016. "Introduction." *Ecogothic*, edited by Andrew Smith and William Hughes. Manchester: Manchester University Press, 1–14.

Stoker, Bram. 1993. *Dracula* [1897]. London: Wordsworth Classics.

Wilson, Edward O. 2014. *A Window on Eternity: A Biologist's Walk Through Gorongosa National Park*. New York: Simon & Schuster.

Waits, Audrey. 2020. "Infections on the Move." *WWF*. 14 April. https://arcticwwf .org/newsroom/the-circle/on-the-move-migration-in-the-arctic/infections-on-the -move/. Accessed September 28, 2021.

Part I

UNDEAD IDENTITY IN THE ANTHROPOCENE

Chapter 1

(Un)Death of the Father

Self-Sacrificing Paternity in Modern Zombie Narratives

Kyle William Bishop

The environmental crises arising from the anthropocentric era are indelibly the result of long-standing patriarchal hierarchies, gendered social and cultural structures that have led directly to the oppression of the planet and a tragic failure of earthly stewardship. Whereas humanity *should* have been "raising" and "protecting" the natural environment for the past centuries, it has instead *neglected* the care of the Earth, manifesting ideologically more as a "dead-beat dad" than anything else. What the world needs, now more than ever, is to redefine the patriarchy in more paternalistic terms. Existing patriarchal systems must become more mindful and caring vis-a-vis the natural environment if the planet is to survive the Anthropocene, and, perhaps surprisingly, one can find examples of this kind of "heroic fatherhood" in narratives featuring the living dead. Zombies are understandably and often inextricably linked to environmental disaster and climate change,[1] manifesting as a type of "herald" of the end of the Anthropocene, but some recent zombie films use their apocalyptic settings to tell stories of responsible parenting, stories of self-sacrifice from which all of humanity can learn, especially in terms of their natural obligations and stewardship.

The heroic father figure tasked with the protection of a young child or adolescent charge is hardly a new trope to a variety of genres, but it appears to have become more popular in recent years. Take, for example, the second season of Marvel's *The Punisher* (Lightfoot: 2017–19)—which recounts Frank Castle's (Jon Bernthal) particularly violent efforts to keep precocious Amy Bendix (Giorgia Whigham) safe from a host of nefarious criminals, assassins, and psychopaths—or the ongoing adventures of Star Wars' *The Mandalorian* (Favreau: 2019-present), in which a lone gunslinger (Pedro

Pascal) takes it upon himself to protect a mysterious alien child and deliver him to his own people. Both of these examples draw heavily from the tradition of the Japanese manga *Lone Wolf and Cub*, created by writer Kazuo Koike and artist Goseki Kojima in 1970, in which a skilled assassin must protect his young son from harm in the midst of a violent path toward revenge.

While the protective father figure has thus become an almost ubiquitous trope in a number of genres (super hero, science fiction, action/adventure, fantasy, etc.), the opposite has usually been true in the horror genre.[2] While such narratives are replete with "monstrous mothers"—thanks in large part to the long-standing, misogynistic idea of the "monstrous feminine" (see Barbara Creed's 1993 foundational work)—even a cursory review of the oeuvre of Stephen King reveals a panoply of "monstrous fathers," perhaps most famously realized in the psychopathic paternal character of Jack Torrence from *The Shining* (1977).[3] Likely building upon such foundational mythologies as Cronus, who infamously ate his own children, a fear of the powerful paternal force remains a prevailing part of the human psyche.[4] Within the twentieth-century tradition of the zombie narrative, one sees not only an absence of protective father figures, but a general dearth of children as well. As Steven J. Kirsh writes in his introduction to his 2019 monograph *Parenting in the Zombie Apocalypse*, "the Zombie Apocalypse will be unkind to everyone, but it will be especially cruel to children" (5).

Only in recent years have zombie narratives begun to explore the possibility of heroic fathers and father figures, valiant protagonists who risk everything to keep their own offspring or similar young charges safe. Whereas many of these heroic fathers are portrayed somewhat as superheroes—such as the seemingly unstoppable juggernaut Rick Grimes from Robert Kirkman's *The Walking Dead* comic series (2003–19) or the rugged survivalist Joel in the 2013 Naughty Dog video game *The Last of Us*—more recent filmic iterations of the figure are far more mundane, and, thus, more relatable to an audience of similarly average fathers. In particular, the films *Maggie* (2015), *Train to Busan* (2016), and *Cargo* (2017) all feature "everyman" protagonists who stop at nothing—and often sacrifice everything—to protect their children (curiously, in these examples, all daughters) from the ravaging infestation of a zombie apocalypse, with varying degrees of success and with notably different outcomes.

I contend that, building on the narrative tradition of Cormac McCarthy's *The Road* (2006), post-apocalyptic tales in general, and zombie narratives in particular, have begun to provide paternal fans of the genre safe spaces in which to explore a progressive, nontoxic masculinity that presents fatherhood, child rearing, and a nurturing nature as not only possible but also preferable to more traditional depictions of (hypermasculine) paternity—what Kathleen Mullan Harris and S. Philip Morgan call the "new father" in their 1991 study on paternal involvement (531). By humanizing the zombie threat—either via a terminally ill child or an incurably infected father—these kinds of films represent a softer, more sensitive exploration of the apocalypse, one more in line with the values and priorities of writers, producers, directors, and fans of zombie narratives who are now (potentially, if not likely) facing the issues and challenges of parenthood themselves. Furthermore, these narratives function as particularly contemporary allegorical tales of environmental responsibility, redefining the patriarchy at a micro level—fathers who love and care for their charges—and perhaps even the macro level—environmental stewardship associated with the anthropocene—as well.[5]

NONTOXIC FATHERHOOD

In 2012, I was invited to join a new Facebook group called "Redefining Fatherhood," a virtual community for progressive, paternalistically minded men who self-identify as fathers in one capacity or another. According to group administrator Michael Paradiso-Michau, the group

> exists as a platform for communication among dads of all sorts who really care about their roles as fathers, supporters, partners, engaged citizens, and concerned advocates for their family's and children's flourishing. In this changing and sometimes confusing world, male social roles, morals, and expectations change all the time, thus altering what "fatherhood" means. That is why this group is being called "Redefining Fatherhood" because "modern" (think: stereotypical 1950s USA) parenting styles are not the only way of being a dad; there is [sic] a variety of parenting options available. We endeavor to give voice (and ear) to questions, concerns, joys, [and] troubles, and in the meantime create and sustain a community of mutual support ("About This Group").

This proactive collective and its focus on the redefinition of "modern fatherhood" isn't the only social network option available to new/experienced, young/old, progressive, experimental, or struggling fathers; even a cursory search for the term "fatherhood" in other Facebook groups yields 83 results, including such communities as "Fighting for Fatherhood" (2019), "The Brotherhood of Fatherhood" (2020), and the "Franklin Glen Fatherhood Alliance for Rearing and Togetherness" (2021). Clearly, fathers in our current age are actively seeking insights, support, and ways in which they can more ably fulfill their paternal responsibilities, becoming Harris and Morgan's "new fathers," who have "moved beyond the traditional role[s] of breadwinner and disciplinarian" and who share "more equally in all aspects of parenting" (1991, 531).

A progressive interest in the active role fathers should play in the physical *and* psychological development of their children is of course nothing new, but it *is* relatively recent. In 1990, for example, the nonprofit "National Center for Fathering" was founded by Ken Canfield and Judson Swihart, an organization that currently hosts the website fathers.com, a hub for religious-centric research, articles, facts, and encouragement on fatherhood ("Our History"). The site includes a weekly newsletter, archives of research on fatherhood, blogs, and a digital library of articles to support engaged fathers. Additionally, the "National Fatherhood Initiative" was founded in the United States in 1994, based on the scholarly efforts of social scientist Don Eberly, a nonprofit organization that became dedicated in 2001 to the creation and dissemination of "high quality fatherhood skill-building resources, curricula, and training," largely through their website fatherhood.org ("About Us: National Fatherhood Initiative"). This site claims to provide "everything you need to serve fathers," including instructive blog posts, informative brochures, and access to the "Father Engagement Academy" ("Everything You Need").

Additional efforts in developing a more engaged and revised version of fatherhood, now in the twenty-first century, have begun to flourish, including more organizations, websites, social networking communities, research, and self-help books. The Australian charity the "Fathering Project," to spotlight just one example, was founded in 2013 by Bruce Robinson, and it provides engaged fathers with current research into effective fathering, a library of "tips and resources" for fathers, and a "Dads Group program" that works within the Australian school system ("About Us: Our History"). This nonprofit organization is led by professionals from various fields who have "a huge passion for the impact that fathering can have on [a] community" ("About Us"). The Fathering Project's website repeatedly emphasizes how "effective fathering" leads to both children with "happier, healthier futures" and parents who can do their best "for the benefit of kids" ("The Fathering Project"). Increasingly, it seems, society is recognizing that "fatherhood" means more than just siring offspring; it should also include responsibility for the intentional care of those children.

Sarah J. Schoppe-Sullivan and Jay Fagan (2020) recently published a comprehensive review of the "fathering research" conducted in the twenty-first century for the *Journal of Marriage and Family*. They note both an increase in professional and governmental investigations into the state of fatherhood and fathering practices in the past twenty years (178–79), along with new changes in public policy to support stay-at-home fathers and responsible fathering (179). Additionally, they cite studies that show fathers in the 2010s spent substantially (2–3 times) more time engaged in "developmental child-care activities" than fathers in the 1980s (176). Schoppe-Sullivan and Fagan pinpoint an increased interest not only in more intentional paternal behaviors but also a link between fathering and familial environment, arguing a "greater focus on fathers in context during the past decade . . . fueled by the publication of several influential works on fathering since the year 2000, including *Package Deal* ([Nicholas] Townsend, 2002) and *Situated Fathering* ([William] Marsiglio, [Kevin Roy, and Greer Litton Fox], 2005), which emphasized environmental supports for and barriers to engaged fathering" (178). A market clearly exists for self-help books for fathers (likely new and young fathers seeking guidance and education) with a particular focus on creating an environment conducive to healthy child rearing—albeit not exactly advocating the value of parenting amidst a zombie apocalypse.

Back in 2011, pioneering zombie scholar Peter Dendle chronicled the changes to the filmic zombie monster demanded by the so-called Millennial Generation. He focuses in particular on the alleged lack of attention spans in those born in the 1980s (179), claiming that characteristic as an explanation for the faster, smarter, and more biologically plausible zombies seen in films from the early twenty-first century (176-77). These Millennial zombie fans— those who came to love the new-and-improved zombies of the so-called Zombie Renaissance—are all now of child-rearing age, and it stands to reason that many of the male fans (some now in their 40s) are fathers. Based on the trends documented above, I contend many consumers of zombie films and other narratives *also* belong to the kind of communities that are invested in active, engaged, and supporting fathers and father figures. It therefore stands to reason that as zombie narratives evolved to adapt to a new generation of fans in the 2000s, they would continue to adapt as those fans continued to age and transition into fathering roles.

(SUPER)HERO FATHERS

Children in tales of horror naturally up the stakes and increase the narrative tension. From the poor little girl murdered by Boris Karloff's monster in *Frankenstein* (1931) to the tormented young siblings in *Poltergeist* (1982), children represent the most vulnerable of victims and therefore should increase the physiological manifestations of fear and anxiety in any caring and sympathetic viewer. Yet few twentieth-century zombie films feature children, and those unfortunate enough to find themselves in such narratives don't fare particularly well. George A. Romero's foundational zombie film, *Night of the Living Dead* (1968), for example, features not only a monstrous father figure (Karl Hardman) but also a monstrous child (Kyra Schon), a child whose devolution into a zombie arises directly from the failure of her father to protect her. In a more comedic example, a zombified baby can be found at the center of Peter Jackson's *Braindead* (1992), a film that nonetheless horrifies with its brutal depiction of a monstrous child and the inept efforts of a feckless caregiver and father figure (Lionel Cosgrove). Only in recent years do we encounter a swath of children in zombie films, a development that makes sense for the post-apocalyptic subgenre as innocent, defenseless children provide the protagonists increased motives for survival.

Two particularly notable zombie narratives of the twenty-first century both feature stories focused at their hearts on the embattled relationships between fathers and children struggling to survive post-apocalyptic wastelands teeming with zombic threats. In Kirkman's comic series, law-enforcement officer and father Rick Grimes must risk everything—repeatedly—to keep his son Carl safe. He begins his epic, 193-issue story as a competent and honest lawman, one clearly trained in the use of firearms and the management of violent threats. Yet he is also fundamentally the father of Carl throughout the entire run of the comic series, and he consistently establishes his paternal duties as his primary motivation. Rick soon becomes a single father, and as he transforms into the leader of an increasingly growing civilization of survivors, Rick must become a kind of *Übermensch*, an "action hero" (Pielak and Ramirez 2017, 130), and even something of a monster himself. Rick uses guns, knives, and even his teeth to destroy anyone— or anything— that threatens Carl, and he overcomes injury, illness, dismemberment, and betrayal to make a brave new world for his offspring.[6] While a great example of determined paternity, Rick is nonetheless unrealistically extraordinary, an exaggeration of the idealized *pater familias*.

The award-winning video game *The Last of Us* also features a super-heroic single father (figure) who struggles to protect others on an increasingly dangerous quest for survival. Players of the game primarily control Joel (Troy Baker) as their in-game avatar, a character who begins the narrative as an average, working-class man, husband, and father. Tragically, despite anything players may attempt to do, Joel loses his daughter Sarah (Hana Hayes) during the onset of an apocalyptic zombie outbreak. The game's story then jumps ahead twenty years, and Joel now possesses the superhuman attributes one would expect of the chief protagonist of an action video game—he runs, jumps, fights, uses various weapons, takes damage, and recovers quickly like a superhero.[7] Joel (and the player) soon finds himself enlisted to become the protector of and father figure to a young girl, Ellie (Ashley Johnson), whom he must protect at all costs as they traverse an increasingly hostile landscape (indeed, even if Joel survives an encounter, the game ends if ever Ellie is killed). A sense of fatherhood is central to the game, but although Joel begins the game as an average man, he becomes an exaggerated superhero like Rick Grimes.

Although not remotely a zombie narrative, Cormac McCarthy's novel *The Road* certainly feels like one, as the story relates the harrowing journey across a post-apocalyptic wasteland taken by a lone survivor and his son. Along with the 2009 cinematic adaptation, directed by John Hillcoat, the tale of *The Road* is essentially a story of paternity, one focused on an important transitionary protagonist. According to John Jurgensen of the *Wall Street Journal*, "the backstory of Mr. McCarthy's novel is deeply personal, springing from his relationship with his 11-year-old son, John (2009)." In a 2007 interview with Oprah Winfrey, "McCarthy said the inspiration came . . . when he was in a hotel room . . . with his young son who was asleep. In the middle of the night, he stared out the window wondering what the city might look like in 50 or 100 years. 'I thought about my little boy' and made some notes, he said" (qtd. in Conlon 2007). The Man, played with touching pathos in the movie by Viggo Mortensen, is clearly a hardened survivor, one capable of making difficult decisions and committing shocking acts of violence to keep his young son (Kodi Smit-McPhee) safe. But in contrast to Rick and Joel, the Man is relatively average, someone who demonstrates no specialized knowledge or skills (although he is a very good shot with a gun) and who struggles to survive despite being starving, weak, and terminally ill.

The film adaptation of *The Road* clearly links fatherhood—the first word of spoken dialogue is "Papa"—with humanity's unexplained decimation of the natural environment. After an opening flashback sequence, the visual style of *The Road* becomes washed out, sepia toned, and muted, cinematography that mirrors the bleak, dying landscape. Throughout the film, ominous crashing noises can be heard on the soundtrack—thunder, earthquakes, falling trees, and so on—all signs of the death throes of the planet and the general state of the human survivors. The Man is similarly dying, but he continues to survive, not for himself but for his son, and implicitly for the future of the human race (and thus, hopefully, the planet itself). While no superhero, the Man is nonetheless ferociously driven: he loves his boy and exhibits a very strong will to live. In addition to the scenes of environmental catastrophe, the narrative also focuses on the Man's tender efforts to nurture the Boy, enjoying the unfamiliar pleasure of drinking a Coke with him, protecting him at all costs, and even showing him how to kill himself should that need arise. Despite the bleak story, the two nonetheless "carry the fire," and the narrative's resolution promises some hope for the future, especially for the Boy.

In many ways, then, *The Road* marks an important shift for apocalyptic fiction generally and the portrayal of survivalist fathers specifically. In the past five years alone, we have seen an increase of zombie films that feature average male protagonists, often single fathers, whose survivalist instincts are secondary only to their protective obligations. While this new, kinder, and gentler hero has his origins in films such as *28 Days Later* (Boyle: 2002), the self-sacrificing "everyman" father hero has reached maturation in the more recent narratives *Maggie*, *Train to Busan*, and *Cargo*. These films—all written and directed by young artists in their child-rearing years[8]—heavily emphasize compassion over violence, paternal duty over personal salvation, and self-sacrifice over glory. A notable number of the "new" zombie narratives are thus about fatherhood, films that offer fans with alternatives to the kinds of toxic masculinity that continue to plague modern society.

EVERYMAN FATHER HEROES

The groundbreaking horror film *28 Days Later* provides one of the first examples of the "everyman" father hero in zombie cinema—with both a literal father and an adoptive father figure. On the one hand, both Frank (Brendan Gleeson) and Jim (Cillian Murphy) are far from superheroes, but on the other, they unflinchingly put themself at risk to protect Frank's young daughter Hannah (Megan Burns). Frank may be little more than an overweight, middle-aged man, but when he becomes infected, he immediately distances himself from Hannah, declares his love for her before saying goodbye, and makes sure he dies before he might attack, infect, or kill her. Jim begins the story as thin, sickly, and terrified, but by the climax of the film, he fights tooth and nail to keep both Hannah and Selena (Naomie Harris) safe from a group of sex-starved soldiers. Paternity isn't nearly as central in *28 Days Later* as it will be in later narratives, but the sympathetic focus might begin here—at least in terms of zombie films.

Some of the father-figure heroes in recent zombie films have become even more average and realistic—and, more often than not, these men are fathers of imperiled *daughters*, not sons.[9] *Maggie*, for example, directed by Henry Hobson, is a remarkable film about a tender and touching father/daughter relationship—a film that, in my opinion, deserves more critical attention, not only because it slowly and subjectively documents the transformation of a human victim into a zombie, but also because of its moving portrayal of family dynamics amidst a horrifying infection and unavoidable death. In addition to featuring what I consider to be Arnold Schwarzenegger's greatest dramatic performance to date, *Maggie* shows zombies in a very sympathetic light—victims, not monsters—almost in a way similar to how zombies were portrayed in the earliest examples of zombie films. For the purposes of this analysis, its similarity in tone and style to *The Road* is significant—washed out cinematography, gray colors schemes, a general desolate landscape, and the sounds of storms and rumbles of thunder in the background. The story is thus both fundamentally about the paternal relationship between a father and daughter but also grimly post-apocalyptic.

When *Maggie* begins, the zombie apocalypse has already been raging for a few months, a fact driven home by establishing shots of deserted city streets, abandoned cars, derelict gas stations, and ever-present smoke plumes on the horizon. In the tradition of *Night of the Living Dead*, much of what the audience learns about the zombie outbreak in *Maggie* comes from the media: the film opens with Schwarzenegger's taciturn Wade listening to an NPR broadcast about the "necroambulis" virus, a worldwide infection that (implicitly) is killing both humans *and* their crops.[10] Governments are encouraging farmers to burn their fields in hopes of saving future plantings, an objective correlative that prefigures the civic "final solution" to dealing with humans infected by the virus. As both the natural world and the human condition are clearly collapsing, so too crumble societal infrastructures. Those infected who reach the eighth week of transmission must report to "quarantine camps" where, it soon becomes clear, they are "humanely" euthanized. Essentially death camps, the anthropocenic "cure" for the virus becomes a desperate purgation, one that awaits all unfortunate enough to suffer "The Turn," including Maggie (Abigail Breslin), the film's eponymous protagonist.

In perhaps the most curious parallel to *The Road*, the first spoken word of *Maggie* is "dad," an utterance that unequivocally declares the film's focus to be about paternity as much as zombies and apocalyptic collapse. Schwarzenegger plays Wade as a caring and deeply emotional father who must come to terms with his daughter's senseless infection and terminal diagnosis. Audiences learn that he has spent two weeks prior to the beginning of the filmic narrative searching for his runaway daughter, but beyond this paternal devotion, he is also established to be a nurturer and a responsible steward: he is a farmer who grows acres of crops, he has lovingly replanted his deceased wife's garden with daisies (Maggie's true namesake), and he even stubbornly refuses to give up his old pickup truck, a machine he tirelessly tends to and repairs. Even though Schwarzenegger remains a large and powerful figure, in this film he portrays a simple, gentleman. Playing against his action-hero type, Schwarzenegger's Wade has only the care and protection of Maggie as his motivation and focus, even somewhat neglecting his new wife (Joely Richardson) and their two children.

Maggie begins the film infected and already unavoidably doomed; instead of protecting her from death, then, Wade's paternal efforts focus on making her final weeks happy ones, protecting her from overzealous authority figures and ensuring that her ultimate death be as merciful and peaceful as possible. He spends the film defending his daughter, reminiscing with her, and preparing for her death. He refuses to let local authorities take Maggie away to the quarantine camp, and he lets the rest of his family leave so he can tend to Maggie more safely by himself. Yet Wade's love for his daughter doesn't blind him to the tragic reality of their situation—Wade's resolve is progressively demonstrated over the course of the narrative, as he first burns his dying crops, then mercifully euthanizes his infected neighbors, and finally shoots a caged fox that has been injured by Maggie. Wade is clearly prepared to perform the most terrible of duties for his daughter; and although he cannot save Maggie from death, he treats her lovingly and humanely until the end, making her final moments happy ones.[11]

An interest in averagely skilled, working-class, paternalistic fathers is not limited to zombie films from the United States; similar concerns are manifesting internationally, as in the South Korean film *Train to Busan*, from critically acclaimed director Sang-ho Yeon. While the tone and style of the film is much different from *Maggie*, this high-speed, action-packed horror movie is nonetheless also grounded in an unexplained anthropocenic environmental disaster. The opening sequence of the film shows a truck passing through some kind of decontamination procedure, with traffic cones, men in hazmat suits, and a sprayed chemical treatment. One of the workers explains to the driver that there has been "a minor leak in the Biotech District." The driver then hits (and clearly kills) a deer on the rural road. After he drives away, the deer ominously stirs, convulsing, bucking, and cracking its joints as it gets back to its feet, now with milky white eyes. Having an animal appear as the first "zombie" implies that *Train to Busan* will be a more environmentally impactful zombie apocalypse than most other films.

This irresponsible mismanagement of the natural world is mirrored in the film's protagonist, Seok-woo (Gong Yoo), a fund manager whose obsessive work ethic has destroyed his marriage and is damaging his relationship with his young daughter Soo-an (Su-an Kim). Soo-an insists on going to stay with her mother in Busan, due to her father's inattention: he works all the time and doesn't really know what is going on in his daughter's life. Seok-woo has callously missed Soo-an's school recital, at which she was unable to perform the song "Aloha Oe" through her tears—the song she had learned especially for him—and he gives her a Wii for her birthday, even though he had recently given her one for Children's Day. In light of such undeniable dereliction, Seok-woo reluctantly agrees to accompany Soo-an on the train to Busan, and the narrative thus shifts focus to include not only Seok-woo's moral journey but his physical journey as well. In *Maggie*, we see a father who remains fiercely devoted to his daughter from beginning to end; in *Train to Busan*, the father only becomes fiercely devoted *in* the end, thanks to the harrowing "hero's journey" of the train trip.[12]

Train to Busan continues to link the idea of environmental disaster with fatherhood throughout the flow of the narrative. As with *Maggie*, viewers gain vague clues about the growing catastrophe from the media, this time from a news headline on Seok-woo's computer screen: "Mysterious Fish Deaths at Jinyang Reservoir." Further, on the way to the train station the next morning, Seok-woo is startled by a convoy of emergency response vehicles and police—he looks with dread at a high-rise fire in the distance as Soo-an catches a piece of the ash that has begun to fall on their car like snow. Despite these ominous signs, the two make it onto the train for what they think will be an uneventful, short journey (the film is almost presented in real-time), but a final passenger follows them—a young woman infected with the unexplained zombic pathogen. Needless to say, the infection quickly spreads through the closed system of the train, and as threats, violence, and death increase, Seok-woo must join forces with expecting father Sang-hwa (Ma Dong-seok) to risk his life for the protection of others.

Seok-woo must overcome his selfish identity to save his daughter, and he becomes a noble father in the process; however, it proves to be a long, hard (and tragically terminal) journey. During the initial outbreak, Seok-woo rushes past Sang-hwa when the latter is trying to help a zombie victim, and then he closes a connecting door on Sang-hwa and Seong-kyeong (Jung Yu-mi) as they flee for their lives. Seok-woo only opens the door and saves the young couple at the last moment because Soo-an insists; unlike her father, she is always kind and selfless. Sang-hwa proves to be a more traditional hero—large, muscular, and selfless—and Seok-woo (gradually) learns from his example to be less selfish himself. In one of the film's few quiet moments, the expectant father tells Seok-woo, "I bet you never got to play with your daughter. When she gets older, she'll understand why you worked so hard. Dads get all the shit, and no praise. But it's all about sacrifice, right?" Sang-hwa's words ultimately prove prescient, as first he and then Seok-woo give up their lives to save Seong-kyeong and Soo-an. By the end of the film, the dead-beat dad becomes a desperate (and notably unskilled) hand-to-hand combatant, and he willingly gives up his life so Soo-an and Seong-kyeong can survive.[13]

Cargo (2017) represents another noteworthy international exploration of paternity in zombie films. Developed from a 2013 short film from the same production team, *Cargo*—co-directed by Ben Howling and screenwriter Yolanda Ramke (the only female writer or director of any of the films I am discussing)—represents the zenith of this type of zombie narrative. This Netflix-original feature begins months into a virus-based zombie apocalypse and is set in the unforgiving Outback of Australia. The film's establishing shot drones across the uninhabited desert, revealing untended fires and plumes of rising smoke. Only one figure can be seen, a young aboriginal girl, Thoomi (Simone Landers), running along a faint trail in the sand. After the film's title, the audience is abruptly introduced to Andy (Martin Freeman), Kay (Susie Porter), and their infant daughter Rosie (portrayed by four different babies), a seemingly happy family floating peacefully down a wide river in their houseboat. Yet not all is as it seems: when Andy waves a greeting to a family having a birthday party on the riverbank, he is met by the other father (Andy Rodoreda) sternly flashing a pistol at the boat. Viewers also soon learn that Andy and his family have very little food, they commandeered the dilapidated houseboat, and they don't dare go on the land.

Most audiences would of course know in advance that *Cargo* is a post-apocalyptic zombie movie, but the film nonetheless begins offering subtle clues as to the *type* of zombie movie—and its unique "rules" and themes. In addition to being low on rations, Andy and his family fish "infection response kits" out of the water, kits that include information pamphlets, a mouth guard, zip ties, a 48-hour countdown timer, and a kind of "epi-pen" that shoots out a long spike (for euthanizing an infected person). When the family come across a derelict sailboat, Andy is quick to go aboard to forage for food and supplies—and a bottle of wine for his and Kay's anniversary. Recognizing what her husband has done, Kay sneaks over to the sailboat herself, but she is attacked and bitten severely on her leg. She frantically dons a countdown "watch," demonstrating that this zombic infection takes two days to turn a victim fully—unless they die sooner than that. The film thus becomes a race against the clock, and Andy must take increasingly desperate measures to try to save his wife.

However, *Cargo*, like the other films I'm analyzing here, is about a father's loving relationship with his daughter, not with his spouse. Kay dies before they can find help, and her last human act is to write "Save her" in her own blood—a poignantly formulated dying wish. Unfortunately, her first act as a zombie is to bite and infect Andy, who must now be the one to wear the countdown timer—and his new journey is not about medical help for himself but a safe future for Rosie. At this point, viewers have gotten hints that Rosie doesn't respond as favorably to Andy and she does Kay; he isn't shown to be a bad father at all, but she does most of the childrearing. With her death, though, Andy "steps up" into a desperate paternal role, and while Freeman's Andy lacks physical prowess, violent tendencies, or even survivalist abilities, he taps effectively into his own paternal resolve to see things through to the end. Along the way, Andy rescues and befriends Toomi, becoming a tender kind of father figure to the aboriginal girl, protecting her, calling her "darling," and showing her physical affection.

After several harrowing misadventures and close calls, Andy finally realizes he needs to seek out Thoomie's people for help, and the second important message of *Cargo* becomes clear. Although we don't see the kind of ecological collapse present in the other two films, *Cargo* is nonetheless significant in terms of the anthropocene because of its strong and positive depiction of the aboriginal people, the only ones who seem capable of surviving the apocalypse. In a somber flashback sequence, a group of native children are learning about the "old ways" around a campfire. Daku (David Gulpilil), the old "Cleverman," tells Thoomi and the other children, "They're poisoning this land, you know? This country, changing. It's sick. We all get sick." Although the zombie virus is never named or explained in the film, *Cargo* appears to be linking it to modernization and the "new ways," something that is sickening the land as well as its people. The aborigines have been the ones lighting the fires across the desert; they are burning the infected, attempting to cleanse the land. Furthermore, in an unsettling twist on the zombie creature, the infected often kneel in the sand and bury their heads just before they turn. By preventing themselves from seeing or hearing anything, they hope to prevent their destructive zombic potential.

The boundless efforts of a father to preserve his daughter's (and Thoomi's) life ultimately merge with *Cargo*'s environmentalist and nativist message. According to Chase Pielak and Fanny Ramirez, "in a world in which humanity has already become something other than human, characters must gradually learn to become zombie subjects who nevertheless maintain their essential humanity" (2017, 126), and this fusion of the zombie with the human(e) is exactly what happens to the brave and noble Andy in the end. With Rosie just a baby, Thoomi injured, and Andy about to turn, he makes the ultimate sacrifice in a remarkably pragmatic way. Instead of killing himself or burying his head in the sand, he decides to become a zombie that will continue to help and ultimately save the two girls. He wraps some offal to a stick, tells Thoomi he is "going," and kisses Rosie goodbye. Using supplies from a "zombie kit," Andy puts a bite guard into his mouth and zip ties his own hands. With Rosie strapped to his back, he turns himself into a kind of "zombie rickshaw," and Thoomi uses the entrail stick to lead him forward, riding on his back. Andy thus *does* succeed in bringing Rosie to help and safety, and the aboriginal community, recognizing his sacrifice, solemnly terminates the zombie he has become, entombing him high in a tree, as they do with those of their own clan, instead of burning him.

Although so many of Romero's zombie movies feature female protagonists, the zombie narratives of the twenty-first century primarily focus on male heroes, and, as I have demonstrated, these heroes are increasingly also fathers. So where are the mothers? It seems heroic mothers have little place in zombie narratives, although types of mother-figures *are* out there, such as stepmom Michonne (Danai Gurira) from *The Walking Dead* and teacher Helen (Gemma Arterton) from *The Girl with All the Gifts* (McCarthy: 2016). So why the paternal focus? As stated, most of the films I have discussed here were written by young- or middle-aged men (with the notable exception of Ramke's *Cargo*, arguably the most maternally-minded of all the narratives), and all of them were directed by men who could have young or even teenage children. Furthermore, fans of zombie cinema who discovered the subgenre as teenagers at the start of the Zombie Renaissance (around 2002–2005) would now be in their thirties, and many of them may now be parents. Fathers potentially make up a large portion of contemporary creators and consumers of zombie narratives, and I find it encouraging that the focus on fatherhood we see is one that embraces paternal responsibility, emotional depth, compassion and kindness, and a more feminine perspective, all valuable masculine qualities that can combat the otherwise toxic masculinity against which we as a society continue to struggle, proposing new approaches to familial, biological, and environmental stewardships.

NOTES

1. Some zombie films are more environmentally focused than others, starting, perhaps, with Jean Rollin's *Les raisins de la mort* (*The Grapes of Death*, 1978). More contemporary examples include Carl Bessai's *Severed* (2005), Colm McCarthy's adaptation of *The Girl with All the Gifts* (2016), and even Dominik Hartl's *Attack of the Lederhosen Zombies* (2016).

2. Amanda DiGioia evokes Mary Shelley's Victor Frankenstein to set up her study of the "bad dad" in horror texts (55), he being perhaps the primary progenitor of this character/trope in horror literature/film.

3. See DiGioria for a detailed analysis of the many ways in which Jack Torrence exemplifies the "bad dad" in horror literature, along with his eventual redemption (73–93).

4. The most well-known examples of such psychological fear of the father come, of course, from Sigmund Freud and his theories of both the Oedipal complex and castration anxiety.

5. Many thanks to the prolific horror film podcaster Jason "Jay of the Dead" Pyles for his help brainstorming and workshopping the ideas for this chapter with me, a fellow father with an insatiable desire for zombie movies.

6. See Kyle William Bishop, "Battling Monsters and Becoming Monstrous: Human Devolution in *The Walking Dead*" in *Monster Culture in the 21st Century: A Reader*, edited by Marina Levina and Diem-My T. Bui (London: Bloomsbury, 2013), 73–85, for a more detailed discussion of Rick's devolution into a monstrous protagonist.

7. Granted, players can adjust the difficulty settings of the game to make Joel more "average" and vulnerable, but he still possesses rather superhuman abilities, such as his "Listen Mode" that grants players a kind of echolocation ability.

8. Admittedly, I have been unable to confirm if any of these writers or directors were fathers when they created their respective zombie films, but the possibility is certainly there, and, of course, many of the fans of their films were, are, and will be fathers.

9. The focus on father/daughter relationships in the following three zombie films flies in the face of Harris and Morgan's research—"the lowest level of father involvement occurred in families with all female children" (533)—and hopefully indicates a general societal shift away from masculine-focused paternity.

10. *Maggie* was released in 2015, making the opening radio broadcast eerily prescient: the announcer speaks of hard-hit urban centers, quarantine efforts, weekly

infection reports, and—perhaps most unsettling—how a chief sign of infection is a heightened sense of smell (the opposite of COVID-19).

11. Spoiler: Maggie kills herself, preventing her father from having to shoot her.

12. Furthermore, both narratives have virtually absent mothers—one by death, the other by divorce and distance—forcing action and growth on the part of the fathers, a plot point (seen in both *The Road* and *28 Days Later* as well) that will also come to be key in *Cargo*.

13. The final two survivors of the train are almost killed by a military sniper, but they are recognized as humans rather than zombies because of Soo-an's singing—she sings the song she learned for her father, an appropriate "gift" that confirms Seok-woo's redemption.

WORKS CITED

"About This Group." 2012. *Redefining Fatherhood*. FaceBook group, *FaceBook*, 2012. https://www.facebook.com/groups/338263699550762/about. Accessed July 1, 2021.

"About Us." N.d. *The Fathering Project*, n.d. https://thefatheringproject.org/about-us. Accessed July 1, 2021.

"About Us: National Fatherhood Initiative." N.d. *The National Fatherhood Initiative*, 2021. https://www.fatherhood.org/about-us. Accessed July 1, 2021.

"About Us: Our History." N.d. *The Fathering Project*. https://thefatheringproject.org /about-us/our-history. Accessed July 1, 2021.

Cohen, Sara Simcha. 2013. *Hearth of Darkness: The Familiar, the Familial, and the Zombie*. Electronic dissertation, UCLA Electronic Theses and Dissertations. https://escholarship.org/uc/item/19f833bw. Accessed July 1, 2021

Conlon, Michael. 2007. "Writer Cormac McCarthy confides in Oprah Winfrey." Reuters, 5 June. https://www.reuters.com/article/us-mccarthy-idUSN0526436120 070605. Accessed July 1, 2021.

Dendle, Peter. 2011. "Zombie Movies and the 'Millennial Generation.'" In *Better Off Dead: The Evolution of the Zombies as Post-Human*, edited by Deborah Christie and Sarah Juliet Lauro. New York: Fordham University Press.

DiGioia, Amanda. 2017. *Childbirth and Parenting in Horror Texts: The Marginalized and the Monstrous*. Bingley: Emerald Publishing.

"Everything You Need to Serve Fathers." 2021. *The National Fatherhood Initiative*. https://www.fatherhood.org. Accessed July 1, 2021.

"The Fathering Project." N.d. *The Fathering Project*. https://thefatheringproject.org. Accessed July 1, 2021.

Forster, Marc (dir.). 2013. *World War Z*. Los Angeles: Plan B Entertainment.

Harris, Kathleen Mullan and S. Philip Morgan. 1991. "Fathers, Sons, and Daughters: Differential Paternal Involvement in Parenting." *Journal of Marriage and Family*, volume 53, number 3, 531–544.

Hillcoat, John (dir.). 2009. *The Road*. New York: Dimension Films.

Hobson, Henry (dir.). 2015. *Maggie*. Santa Monica: Lionsgate Films.

Hopkins, David. 2011. "The Hero Wears the Hat: Carl as 1.5-Generation Immigrant and True Protagonist." In *Triumph of the Walking Dead: Robert Kirkman's Zombie Epic on Page and Screen*, edited by James Lowder. Dallas: Banbella Books.

Howling, Ben, and Yolanda Ramke (dirs.). 2017. *Cargo.* Sydney: Causeway.

Jackson, Peter (dir.). 1992. *Braindead.* London: WingNut Films.

Jurgensen, John. 2009. "Hollywood's Favorite Cowboy." *The Wall Street Journal*, 20 November. https://www.wsj.com/articles/SB10001424052748704576204574529 703577274572. Accessed July1, 2021.

Kirkman, Robert. 2003–19. *The Walking Dead.* Portland: Image Comics.

Kirsh, Steven J. 2019. *Parenting in the Zombie Apocalypse: The Psychology of Raising Children in a Time of Horror.* Jefferson: McFarland & Co. Inc.

McCarthy, Cormac. 2006. *The Road.* New York: Alfred A. Knopf.

"Our History." N.d. *The National Center for Fathering.* https://fathers.com/about-ncf /our-history. Accessed July1, 2021.

Pielak, Chase, and Fanny Ramirez. 2017. "Apocalyptic Living." In *Living with Zombies: Society in Apocalypse in Film, Literature and Other Media*, edited by Chase Pielak and Alexander H. Cohen. Jefferson: McFarland & Co. Inc., 124–139.

Romero, George A. (dir.). 1968. *Night of the Living Dead.* Pittsburgh: Imagine Ten.

Schoppe-Sullivan, Sarah, and Jay Fagan. 2020. "The Evolution of Fathering Research in the 21st Century: Persistent Challenges, New Directions." *Journal of Marriage and Family*, Volume 82, February, 175–197.

Straley, Bruce, and Neil Druckmann (dirs.). 2013. *The Last of Us.* Santa Monica: Naughty Dog.

Yeon, Sang-ho (dir). 2016. *Train to Busan.* Seoul: RedPeter Film.

Chapter 2

Undeath, Theatricality, and the Ecogothic in DC Moore's *Common* (2017)

Gheorghe Williams

DC Moore's *Common* is a nebulous play, derided by many upon its premiere at London's National Theatre in May 2017. Kelly Jones neatly summarizes the mixed degree of its success when she describes the play as "wildly entertaining from moment to moment, but difficult to apprehend as a whole" (Jones 2018, 7). Frustrations were likely due to the often-unintelligible dialogue, which was written in "a poetic, earthy, and quasi-archaic register" (Jones, 7),[1] but also a plot that was widely perceived as incoherent, too ambitious in its inclusion of multiple narrative strands. With various nods to environmentalism, queerness, ritual violence, incest, industrialization, class relations and gender politics, the central issue for many, as Fergus Morgan writes in a review for *Exeunt*, was that Moore "never really sinks his teeth into any of it, flirting with issue after issue, constantly telling rather than showing," seeing it as a "classic case of biting off more than one can chew" (Morgan 2017). Thus, even some of the play's most generous commentators were unable to ignore the sheer oddity of its existence: "I kind of admire its total otherness," remarks theatre critic Andrew Lukowski, "though at the same time it's hard to shake the sense that something must have gone wrong for the NT [National Theatre] and co-producers Headlong to allow it to happen" in the first place (Lukowski 2017).

While the intention of this chapter is not to rescue the play from the dismissal engendered by its own obscurity, I do want to suggest that one branch of the narrative is worth consideration through the lens offered by this volume, that of the symmetries between narratives of the undead and the anxieties raised by the "Anthropocene." Set amid the early-nineteenth-century Enclosure Acts in England, *Common* features an enigmatic protagonist, Mary, who is murdered but whose subsequent undeath enables her to seek revenge on her betrayers by participating in a symbolic conflict of ownership over their lands and livelihoods. At the same time, as is often the case for protagonists of Gothic plays, Mary's narrative trajectory is characterized by dubious deeds and questionable moralities, and so our identification with her also leads us to some uncomfortable ecological truths. The primary claim of this chapter is that despite the play's often dizzying incongruity, Mary's narrative offers an insightful meditation on the ecocritical possibilities of staging undeath in our present era of sustained (or *undying*) environmental crises that, put simply, are not going away any time soon. Understanding the play's complex engagement with the uncertainties borne from recognition of the anthropocene will, I hope, lend a greater sense of unity to *Common*'s many narrative arcs, as well as a useful clarity of its political intentions.

The secondary aim of this chapter is to explore, through *Common*, the fruitfulness of the emerging theoretical lens of the "Ecogothic" as a framework for theatre analysis. Where the Gothic is a mode obsessed with "negative aesthetics" (Botting 2013, 1) and the hold of the past upon the present, so is the Ecogothic concerned with the precarity of a present gripped by deleterious ecological legacies, ideologies, and infrastructures from which we desire to escape but, increasingly, fear we cannot—or at least, not without first undergoing a seismic and sublime revolution of the ways we live. As discussed in other entries in this volume, notions of undeath and figures of the undead alike are replete with ecocritical implications that become richly amplified when examined through the "dark glass" (Edney 2020*, 1) of the Ecogothic: from associations with contagion and virality, to re-conceptions of (im)mortality and its role in shaping our identities, ethical frameworks, and relationships to the ecosystems that sustain us. However, while recent years have seen much written about the Ecogothic in relation to literature, cinema, and television (Hillard 2009; Smith and Hughes 2013; Keetley and Sivils 2017; Parker 2020; Edney *2020), the term has, so far, seldom been applied in theatrical performance contexts. For Una Chaudhuri, drama and dramatic modes of representation are particularly well-placed to articulate how we can explore and address the implications of the anthropocene, which, as she puts it, "designates a single species—ours—as a geophysical force" (Chaudhuri 2015, 14). The aptness of drama for these ventures is not only due to its historically "human-centric" disposition (Cless 2012, 159), by its nature offering a suitable set of situated conditions in which to (re-)examine ourselves using alternative, "geophysical" frames. Rather, as Chaudhuri contends, it is also the "certain kind of incommensurability [that] is in fact *constitutive* of theatricality" (13; original emphasis), its oblique methods of representing *in the room* that which is beyond the material limits of the space, that allows drama to engage directly with the "new problems of scale born of emerging ecological realities" (13), referring to "widely-dispersed" geophysical phenomena (such as global warming) that Timothy Morton has called "hyperobjects" (Morton 2013; Chaudhuri 2015).

Common is by no means an exhaustive representation of the ways that the Ecogothic might manifest on the stage. However, I argue that the play exemplifies some of the ways that Ecogothic theatre can dramatize the deeply unsettling effects of recognizing these "new problems of scale" that disturb the ecological present: namely, the use of "chthonic" (Rabey 2018, 22) stage dynamics and aesthetics to lend an anti-realist, recognizably "Ecogothic" framing and significance to the action of the play; and, through this framing, a critical foregrounding of the material and ideological horrors of *anthropocentrism*, a philosophy that privileges the supremacy of the human and human interests above all else, and whose "monstrous anthropocentric gaze" (Del Principe 2014, 1) is the ultimate object of Ecogothic criticism. Prioritizing the anthropocentric may seem a contradictory gesture for a mode dedicated to querying its harmful prominence, yet this contradiction is in fact key to its critical import: if Eco-theatre can be more generally said to advocate the adoption of *ecocentric*, "de-alienated" views of the more-than-human world (Cless 2012, 159), then Ecogothic theatre foregrounds the anthropocentric in order to trouble our capacity to move safely beyond its logics; the Ecogothic stage is not merely a background for action, but becomes itself an active site of anthropic ruin and decay, where the contradictions of human exceptionalism—its unsustainability, but also the question of its seeming inescapability—can be materialized, embodied, and interrogated in performance. Through these strategies, *Common* dramatizes the disconcerting and undeathly persistence of anthropocentrism as a product of its ideological allyship with capitalism, using Ecogothic aesthetics to stage the brutal effects of their shared "logic of domination" (Warren 1994, 129; Garrard 2012, 26). Consequently, Mary's undeath becomes an embodied means of reflecting on how the anthropocentric ideologies exemplified by the Enclosures remain powerfully active in the neoliberal-capitalist landscapes of the twenty-first century.

ENCLOSURE: ECOGOTHIC POLITICS

The events of *Common* unfold around the conniving rogue Mary, as she returns to the countryside village where she once lived after amassing a fortune in London, now hoping to rekindle a relationship with her former lover, Laura. Her return coincides with a political skirmish between the villagers and a local landowner, "named Lord," who is driving efforts to enclose and sell up the common lands surrounding the village. Mary agrees to join the fight in exchange for Laura's promise to elope with her to the United States, but her return whips up the suspicion of the villagers: years prior, her disappearance was enforced by Laura's brother, King, who beat Mary and left her for dead in the river due to his own incestuous desires for Laura. Having convinced the village, and Laura, that Mary simply went mad and drowned, her inexplicable survival causes her to be initially mistaken by Laura as "some walking ghoul" (36) conjured by a nightmare. Her apparent return from the dead quickly becomes the object of their blame for the unusual agricultural hardships that have been plaguing the superstitious community. At the end of Act Two, Mary is betrayed by Laura, who quite literally "*stabs* [her] *in the back,*" and then buried by King and the villagers in an unmarked grave upon the commons (Moore 2017, 73). Act Three opens with a Gothic scene of resurrection, lightning, and Mary's promises of violence and revenge.

The Enclosure Acts are a crucial context for understanding the political tensions that drive the plot of the play. Although practices of enclosure had been informally in use since at least medieval times, the Enclosure Acts formalized in Parliament a legal demarcation of shared or open sections of land into privately owned units of space. These units were bought by wealthy landowners and sold or rented to farmers for high prices in order to maximize the profitability of the available land. While the Acts were justified at the time by claims of economic efficiency and year-round productivity, it was perceived by many that this drive for continuous production became merely "an instrument of oppression" (Chambers and Mingay 1966, 77), as farmers and land-workers were forced either to pay landowners' high prices or move into cities, particularly London, already crowded and poverty-stricken by the Industrial Revolution. John Beckett agrees that the transformation of public lands into private property can only have exacerbated power structures that already exploited those most reliant upon agriculture to maintain an income: "the large and powerful landowners were presented with a means of legally dispossessing their lesser brethren, and they were more than willing to exploit their contacts with Members of Parliament and peers to ensure a smooth passage for their (private) legislation" (1990, 42). By acknowledging their links with philosophies of entitlement and exploitation, it becomes easy to read the Enclosures as both a literal and symbolic expression of the alliance between anthropocentric world-views and capitalist ideologies, a physical implementation of their shared "logic of domination."

This atmosphere of precarious dependency manifests in the prologue of the play, which draws from the aesthetics of folk horror in its depiction of the ritual slaughter of a pig, using puppetry, ribbons of blood and a gathering of villagers "*maskdressed as animaltypes or devilfolk or somepartboth*" (Moore 2017, 5). Later slaughters of other animals confirm this display as the desperate gesture of a superstitious community whose land has not yielded a sufficient harvest, but it is more immediately framed as a political protest. Set in 1809, *Common* falls directly within a period of particularly high anxiety about the availability of food due to the "French Revolutionary and Napoleonic Wars between 1793 and 1815" (Beckett 1990, 37): as "food prices rose rapidly," Beckett explains, so "enclosing activity was designed to take advantage of this change" (37). An early scene in the play depicts a confrontation between some workers from the village and Lord, the owner of the nearby estate who is responsible for the enclosures that are soon to take place. Upon arrival, Lord demands the identity of the man responsible for leaving the corpse of a pig in his library, presuming the deed to be merely another of many recent infractions: "Our plans for Enclosure of the Common which passed through Parliament *itself* have been debased, defiled, ignored, *in toto*. Each attempt to fence the land, agents of unchange messily undo" (Moore 2017, 20–21; emphasis in original). The assumption is not entirely misguided. Laying the pig out on a table at the Inn, the stage directions indicate that the corpse is *"the deceased pig-Lord"* from the prologue, *"Still Lordlydressed"* (20) in ceremonial attire designed to resemble Lord himself. Although the men *"pigbristlesmile"* (20) with recognition of the pig, it is only later revealed that they were not actually involved with the corpse's appearance in Lord's home: it was placed there secretly by Young Hannah, a housemaid introduced in Act Three, for "a little laugh" (117) at the Lord's expense. Regardless, the palpable class tensions produced by the Enclosures are encoded in Lord's assumption of their culpability, betrayed by his arrival in the company of his abrasive *"gamekeeper* Heron & [Heron's] Lads" (20), with clear expectations of a physical altercation; and, likewise, in the men's contentment with supporting the political implications of the act, indicated by their rejection of an opportunity to deny their involvement with it.

Mary's return during this period of unrest, inevitably, disrupts what little harmony remains in the village. Being both native to the village and banished from it, she is precariously, and so radically, situated on both sides of the conflict. It is telling, then, that her loyalty ultimately falls on the side most favored by capital-oriented power structures. Even before her undeath, Mary is marked as an undead harbinger of that which the symbolic order of enclosure and agricultural structures propose to forestall and suppress: death, precarity and social unrest. Rather than comforting and stabilizing, the framing provided by the narrative context of the play instead re-positions this supposed order—and Mary along with it—as a force of monstrous disruption, disturbing the logic of security and necessity by which the Enclosures' inherent violences are "occulted" (Deckard 2019, 174). Mary herself bespeaks this characterization when, in her introductory monologue, she proclaims her arrival from "the darkvapour of that vastchimneycoffin where all evil is born & most goodness dies: London" (Moore 2017, 8), invoking her own polluting effect on the stability of the village community.

Her later conversation with Laura confirms the hellish aspect of this city/
country dichotomy, and of her position within it:

Mary: Two weeks past, I stood on highest hill of Highgate Hill, north of that Devil
   City. Know what I saw, as I looked back behind?
Laura: Hell.
Mary: Hell. A million citychimneys pouring out a giantlung's breath of
   blackrupturingsmoke.
Laura: Well let 'em eat their Londonchoke & burst.
Mary: And what is a factory, yet a greatmetalfurnace citypoor only live & die
   in? And where to find new kindling? Out here 'mong you poorcountrypoor.
   All they talk of in Parliament. How they might take your manycommonacres;
   throw you out to that factoryendingblack. Your Lord now sees same done here.
   (40)

The implications of the comparison are clear: the factories in the city, sickly
and polluted, are a hellscape that intertwines the social oppression and ecological devastation engendered by the excesses of industrial capitalism. The
opposing inference is therefore that the countryside is in danger of infection
from the city and the "blackrupturingsmoke" spilling out into the air, as well
as from the plots of its governing forces. Mary betrays her own allegiances
to capitalistic domains when, contrary to her alleged disgust with the city's
poverty, she reveals that she has, herself, invested her newfound fortunes
(acquired through the extortion of a "Kensington Rich Fuck" (38)) into
"Looms. Mills. Vast new metalbehemoths of Trade" (38), in order to secure
her status as "that mostrarefound thing: a truefree livingwoman" (39).
    The arbitrariness of Mary's care for the village, which she describes as
being as "dead as that drown'd Mary" (41), soon undermines her subsequent
pretense of desire to see it saved, valuing it merely as a means by which she
may reclaim her "Great Undying Love" (41). As Laura suspects, London
has transformed her: "May it not bite you, girl," she remarks of Mary's new
"Magic" freedom, "Unless it already has" (41). Laura's reluctance to trust
Mary here presages the resentment with which she justifies murdering her
at the end of Act Two, when she proclaims that "Nothing of you [Mary] fits
right or free. As you everlive you drag violence, mischief, wrong behind,
allcaged, like growlinghounds of Hell. Brought murder now too & its dar-
kattempts" (72). Accused of marshaling the misfortunes that have recently
plagued the village, Mary is explicitly framed as an "everliv[ing]" omen of
the city's encroachment upon the country. The pointedly undeathly imagery
embedded in these exchanges bespeaks the play's use of undeath as a metaphor for capitalism's social afflictions, articulating the effects of moral decay
it produces in its contagious drive for unending self-preservation. If these

ideas are encoded in Mary's return at the beginning of the play, then their metaphoric connotations are literalized by her actual resurrection in the first scene of Act Three.

MARY RETURNS (AGAIN): ECOGOTHIC SPACE

Mary's resurrection is described in the playtext in a typically Gothic manner:

> *Common.* MARY*'s grave. Night. Thunder begins, distant. A gathering storm.* EGGY ROBERT—*a crow—on a shovel left upright in the ground (where* LAURA *left it). Hand emerges from the ground:* MARY*'s. Piece by piece,* MARY, *bloodied & muddied, her hands mangleruined from their upward dig, crawlemerges from the ground. As if it births her. An orange, Hellish glow rises from the coffin hole.* (77)

Immediately noticeable is Moore's use of, perhaps, the most recognizable icon of the undead in popular culture: a rotting hand reaching up through grave soil, forebodingly announcing the reanimated corpse that will surely follow. Mary's return to the stage in this way exploits a spatial dynamic of intrusion that has been peculiar to Gothic theatre since the late-eighteenth century (Saglia 2013, 362). The Gothic *offstage*, Saglia contends, is "a peculiar locus of transgressions, subversions and the constant return of the abject," a "radically imaginary multiple dimension" (363) of the unstaged/unstageable that infringes upon and threatens the stability of the *onstage*, a space then framed by contrast as the normative (if evidently vulnerable) realm of human understanding. The breaching of the onstage dimensions by a *"Hellish"* underspace imports what David Ian Rabey has called the "chthonic landscape" of Gothic theatre, an "aperture of the uncanny" which presents, "imagistically and thematically, a rooting and/or descent into the ground, soil and earth, an underworld of decomposition which may paradoxically create preconditions for evolution and growth" (Rabey 2018, 22-23). *Common* physicalizes an alignment of the industrial "Devil City" with the more pointedly "chthonic" hellscape of the substage chamber: both are intertwined and embodied by Mary as she crosses back into the onstage world of the play. However, in rupturing and crossing-over these dimensions, the onstage is marked not merely as a space invaded by the chthonic, but also as itself the truly chthonic territory: the stage does not enter a hitherto unknown "underworld of decomposition," but rather her undeath re-signifies as "chthonic" the environment that was already there: in the 2017 production, the floor of the stage consisted of a thick layer of real soil and dirt, through which the actor had to climb in her return to the stage. Here, Moore employs the aesthetic frame of the Ecogothic to signify an ecocritical thematisation of Undeath that is then transmitted through the material environment of the performance space. The symbolic imbrication of the onstage with the off/sub-stage therefore also physicalizes the inherently cannibalistic implications of Mary's undeath, transforming the stage into a chthonic site of abject returns, of earth-in/*as*-Hell: the dead body (and subject) returned upon its former world of living organisms; the banished outsider vengefully returned upon the rural farming community; and the capital-driven forces of industrial production coming back to incorporate and consume (to cannibalize) their pastoral forebears.

The first character that Mary meets after rising from the grave is "a crow" (77), whose strange alterity is made immediately clear when it identifies itself as Eggy Robert, the father of the young crow-scarer Eggy Tom; in the first scene of the play, Tom explains that his father cut his own throat after discovering his wife's affair and subsequently found his soul trapped in the body of a crow. Using his own experience of undeath to clarify the nature and conditions of Mary's, Robert discloses that his migration into a nonhuman form has endowed him the ability to "see all through all time & place":

E. Robert: . . . Since I joined this form I learnt their manyseeingways. What lies
    behind & futurefront.
Mary: What is that glow then in my once-coffin if you know all, bird?
E. Robert: Hell. From which you deep crawl. And do call me Robert do. (77-78)

His perception resembles a recurrent positionality in Ecogothic narratives that is characterized by what Sharae Deckard calls "*telesthesia*—the extension of perception beyond the normal range of the empirical senses to apprehend other situations in time and space" (2019, 175). There are seeds within this expansion of the senses for a more inclusive and ecocentric ethical framework to emerge, the "preconditions for evolution and growth" noted by Rabey (2018). Mary's undeath also leaves her with an expanded sense of reality, although not to the extent of Robert's implied omniscience, a direct result of her remaining in human form, and thus remaining partially constrained by human sensory apparatus. Her perceptual shift, and the audience's own, is indicated by the fact that both are now able to recognize Robert's individual subjectivity where previously they could not. Tom's explanation of the crow's identity in Act One is initially treated as merely an amusing and childish fabrication. Mary's skeptical glance toward the audience invites their participation in a collective acknowledgment the crow's (apparently) contrary animality—that the crow's blank caws are responding to Tom's speech is left in doubt—as well as an illusion-breaking recognition of the obvious fakery of the prop, which is fastened to Tom's arm. Encouraging assumptions of its falseness, the comic framing of the tale implies by extension the intactness of the humanist ontologies that its veracity would violate. The later actualization of Robert as an identifiable "human" subject at the start of Act Three therefore acts as a strange substantiation of Tom's claims. Presaging a broader decomposition of that previously intact ontological framework, the revelation re-implicates the audience's earlier characterization by Tom as uncanny "spiritdemons" (Moore 2017, 9), as they share in her newfound ability to perceive that which was previously beyond perception.

"BREATHE & MOAN & BLEED": ECOGOTHIC OBJECTS

Of further significance to the ecocritical vein of this scene is the theatricality of the crow's presentation, not least because it illuminates one of the means by which the theatre can replicate the uncanniness of the undead as represented in literature and on screen: namely, the liveness/animation of that which is dead/inanimate. In the 2017 production, Robert is made present through a combination of puppetry and live, or pre-recorded, vocal projection. The animation of props and objects to create dramatic narrative is fundamental to numerous cultures and traditions of performance throughout history. In *Performing Objects and Theatrical Things* (2014), for example, Marlis Schweitzer and Joanne Zerdy draw from Jane Bennet's influential study, *Vibrant Matter: A Political Ecology of Things* (2010), to propose a convincing view of "props, costumes, set pieces, and other theatrical objects" not as "background or stage dressing," but as "key players in all performances—as active agents performing alongside rather than behind or in service to human performers" (6). To speak particularly of Gothic performance traditions, these practices of foregrounding the liveness of that which is "unliving" have been particularly useful for its efforts to interrupt habits of dismissal and complacency, rendering supposedly inert—and thus "safe"—objects a suddenly active, unsettling, and even horrifying presence. Such presences may take the form of uncannily animated material objects that are normally designed for human comfort, such as the infamous rocking chair in Stephen Mallatratt's 1988 adaptation of Susan Hill's *The Woman in Black* (1983), which is seen to lurch ferociously back and forth seemingly of its own volition; or they may manifest through the disquieting stillness of human-like forms playing upon the expectation of movement, such as the stage corpse in Howard Barker's *Dead Hands* (2004), a "pivotal stage presence" (Kipp 2018, 43) which, through its protracted and amplified visibility throughout the duration of the play, exerts an uncanny theatrical liveness-of-presence that contravenes its objective deadness. In both cases, the effect of undeathly animation turns around the illusory and ambiguous suggestion of partially-but-not-quite-human subjectivity, mediated through an impression of the object's ominously "active agen[cy]" made visible through strategic theatrical framing.

Robert is similarly dramatized. Although his presence at Mary's grave-side is not necessarily intended to unsettle audiences in the same way as Mallatratt's or Barker's objects, he is nonetheless an uncanny presence that raises the prospect of the destabilization of the humanist rhetoric of Nature-as-object/resource which otherwise drives the events of the play. As a stage prop taking the form of a crow, the material aspect of his presence is doubly linked to paradigms of objecthood: as a theatrical "object," and insofar as anthropocentrism ultimately figures nonhuman bodies as "objects" purposed for human subsistence. The animated theatrical animal-object thus presents an opportunity for Ecogothic subversion: if all the world's a stage, so to speak, and its nonhuman constituents are the props and furnishings by which human actors insist upon (and act out) their claims to the role of eco-systemic protagonist, then the insubordinately "active" agency of theatrical phenomena explored by Schweitzer and Zerdy might speak to the potential for staging acts of Ecogothic revolt against such claims, and indeed against classifications of the nonhuman as being inert, background fodder in the first place. More than a bird who seems to have simply become capable of imitating human speech patterns, Robert verges upon a staging of just such a challenge—even if playfully so—through its embodied fusion of prop objecthood with distinctively human subjectivity, contravening its previous representation in the first scene by asserting and claiming a contrary, "meaningfully alive"-ness (Parker 2020, 71) that is normally reserved for the human. In this regard, Robert stands at a critical intersection between Schweitzer and Zerdy's proposals and Stacy Alaimo's notion of "trans-corporeality," which theorizes that "the substance of the human is ultimately inseparable from the 'environment'" (Alaimo 2010, 2). By "thinking across bodies," Alaimo contends, trans-corporeality "may catalyse the recognition that the environment, which is too often imagined as inert, empty space or as a resource for human use, is, in fact, a world of fleshy beings with their own needs, claims, and actions" (2). In both narrative function (as Mary's undead guide) and dramatic realization, Robert's characterization presents the blueprints for performing an embodied, trans-corporeal infraction of the conventional boundaries of human corporeality, mortality, and perception, exemplifying the potential strategies by which an Ecogothic insurrection against "the monstrous anthropocentric gaze" (Del Principe, 1) might be theatricalized.

"HARVEST BURNS": ECOGOTHIC ENDS

Recognizing the play's pointed consideration of these possibilities is important not simply because they represent the provocative ways that theatre can re-engage with the more-than-human world: perhaps more significantly, the play immediately undercuts the potency of these representations, raising them solely so that they can be denied, and effecting a resurgent inclination toward anthropocentrism that emphasizes its excessive tyranny. Robert's corporeal circumstances may approach a recognition of the nonhuman as "meaningfully alive," but this is made viable only through a dominating, not co-existent, imposition of human subjectivity onto the nonhuman body of the crow, a clear embodiment of the ecologies of imperialism and colonialism. Rather than opening up a new, expanded field of ethical eco-consideration—such as one not predicated on humanist applications of subjective "meaning"—the "manyseeingways" of the crow are instead re-appropriated in service of anthropocentric desire: "What might I do now to see my own future?," Mary asks, to which Robert replies, "As I beak & breathe [you] must take what is Yours by Birth" (Moore 2017, 78). Near instantly, Mary delivers a monologue in which she declares intentions to carry out her deadly revenge upon her betrayers by re-joining the already-in-progress conflict over the Enclosures. The language and politics of her speech are virtually inseparable from Lord's speech at the earlier scene depicting his argument with the villagers, in which he proclaims his own exceptionalism by professing to share a bloodline with his Estate and the grounds contained within, appropriating an ecocentric language to perversely establish a distinctively anthropocentric social hierarchy. Similarly, Mary adopts an anthropomorphic vocabulary to suggest Nature's complicity with her plans and her own unity with Nature: "Now yes She hears me too," Mary exclaims as the "*Lightning begins. Getting closer*," "Nature sings down in her great noisefull thunder. [. . .] Says: I hear you, Lady Katarin. You & I both, we are This Coming Storm. [. . .] This Lady Bastard Oak will bear her acornboy: Vengeance" (79). The speech articulates, once again, an Ecogothic obsession with the incessant durability of anthropocentric frames of representation. By conjuring up, through undeath and the sentient crow, the possibility of a fragmentation of anthropocentric ontologies (and thus, potentially, of ecological revitalization), the play's subsequent reassertion of anthropocentric rule here (and in what follows) seems all the more perverse, as the "monstrous anthropocentric gaze" finds not resistance but renewed purchase through Mary and Robert: in undeath, they have become privy to new temporal and spatial horizons that it may look upon and further consume.

The remainder of the play depicts the carrying out of these politics. Mary, emboldened by Robert's foresight and by her own everliving endurance, effortlessly establishes an alliance with Lord by convincing him to accept her as his new wife in exchange for control of his Estate: "I am a Child of the Land. I seek to Mother it, as she did to I," she professes, although her vision is markedly more industrious than nurturing: "Progress must be seen through. They who resist all-crushed" (84), she argues, persuading him to grant her stewardship of the enclosure program. Laura's suffering becomes central to her revenge plot, though this, too, is linked with the enclosures. A subsequent scene depicts King's discovery of a frantic Laura digging a pit in Mary's now-empty grave, plagued with nightmares of Mary "roam[ing] free from Earth's deepwomb" and pursuing her "in her wild-rabidway"; since I wake all I can do: dig & everdig" (91). A diminished, Lady Macbeth-like figure, Laura is easily coaxed into staging a revolt against Lord by a letter—written by Mary, unbeknownst to her—claiming that none from the village will be hired on Lord's Estate, save for the two Irish workers, Connor and Graham. "As we buried her," Laura declares, "we must bury all" (94). The "body-as-space" correlation that has often been observed in Gothic drama (Saglia 2013; Stratford 2019) is established by the acts of political violence that quickly ensue. Mirroring the earlier death of the *"Pig-Lord,"* Connor is ambushed by the *"maskdressed"* villagers, his throat torn; Lord's hounds are burned in their kennels; Heron's men, under Mary's direction, respond by burning the villagers' harvest fields; the villagers retaliate by confronting them on the commons, though after a bloody battle, Heron's men are able to chase the surviving villagers away from the scene. With the earthen stage a porous spatialization of the "chthonic," so too are bodies rendered a malleable and ruptured terrain of politicized violation. Eventually, a final confrontation occurs between Mary and Laura. Before shooting her, Mary torments Laura by producing a human heart, which she has freshly plucked from King's chest. The act is one of retribution, for Laura's betrayal of her heart and for King's wickedness in depriving her of Laura's, acknowledged in, and forcibly excavated from, the flesh. Laura stabs Mary with her last breath, but Mary is able to turn the blade back onto her, and both collapse into apparent death.

A key observation from Deckard is relevant to the extensive brutality of this sequence: she notes that the matter of whether revolutionary acts in Ecogothic narratives are "a cause for fear or for triumph is a question of the politics of the text" (2019, 174). *Common* seems committed to a politics that is ambivalently placed between both of these poles. As the protagonist, the narrator and our primary interlocutor, audiences are structurally and affectively encouraged to identify with Mary throughout; indeed, many critics, including theatre scholar Dan Rebellato, cited Mary's charismatic portrayal by Anne-Marie Duff as the saving grace of the production as a whole (Rebellato 2017). Yet these final scenes of visceral vengeance undoubtedly challenge this identification, not least because their fruition is tied so directly to another conquest, that of the Enclosure of the commons. This returns us once again to Rabey's conception of the "chthonic" theatre space and its apparent promise of "growth." The promise of industrial progress raised in the final moments of the play is not one of comfort, but instead one which signals only a continued anthropic "decomposition" under the guises of necessity and inevitability that is so often appropriated by neoliberal-capitalist rhetoric. With the villagers slain or forced into labor, the following (and final) scene shows Mary having, somehow, survived—or returned to life—and now living at Lord's manor with "a City to Run. [A] Century to Forge" (118), as the noises of enclosure echo on from the Estate.

In the end, undeath functions as an embodied means of representing these physicalized interconnections between anthropocentric and capitalist modes of violence: emphasizing the longevity of both, Mary is animated by anthropocentrism-as-impulse, an arcane yet eternally latent desire to "write" (Morton 2016, 82) the primacy of the human permanently into the environments that surround us; an impulse then transformed by capitalism into a profoundly animating yet subordinating force. Life itself, for Mary, is a tapped resource. While her undeath is the narrative cause of the play's resurgent humanism, it is also the dramatic device which enables her imbrication of the internal and external dimensions of the performance, putting the symbolic register of the narrative into direct contact with the here-and-now of the theatre space, a quintessentially Gothic "mixing [of] frames" (McEvoy 2007, 217). Exploiting her privileges as narrator and as our conduit-in-chief to the world of the play—a liminality which is internally mirrored by her undeathly transgression of other existential boundaries—Mary's parting words are an explicit nod to the continuation of her world into ours: "And yes I see what World you are in. That which I'll make next. You are Welcome" (Moore 2017, 118).

CONCLUSIONS: UNDEATH AS ESTRANGEMENT

If the world on the stage in *Common* is a profoundly anti-realist reflection of the disturbing ecological legacy of our species, then this seems a logical result of the (Eco)Gothic maxim that realism is insufficient for representing the full extent of our ecological predicament. Partially, this is because we ourselves are constrained by our limited perceptual apparatus: our lived reality can never be commensurate with the "ecological realities" which are now coming into view, realities with which we are deeply involved as a species but over which we can exert no absolute control. *Common* glimpses these other ontologies and brings them into tension with the characters on stage, even materializing them in the form of Eggy Robert and the "radically imaginary" multiplication of the off-/sub-stage—yet they are ultimately irreconcilable with humanist frames of reference, and so remain profoundly strange presences. In doing so, these phenomena fulfill the key Ecogothic imperative of foregrounding the cavernous depths to which anthropocentrism shapes and delimits our relations with the more-than-human world.

Further embodied by these tensions is the simultaneously subordinated-yet-subordinating state of existence that the play explores, through undeath, as a symptom of capitalism. If we cannot die, then death itself will cease to function as a terminus for socio-ecological modes of exploitation: undeath subjects us to an experience of the excesses of capitalism that is unconstrained by conventional ontologies and temporal limits, just as Mary's resurrection ultimately precipitates the violent realization of her financial empire and raises the prospect of its exponential continuation into our future. At the same time, undeath is as much a perversely animated state as it is a force of limitation, and Mary herself is victimized into complicity with its capitalist logic, the sole avenue made available to her for pursuing liberation from the poverty and patriarchal violence into which she was born.

This profoundly strange play's final gesture, Mary's remark that our world is "[t]hat which [she]'ll make next," thus concludes with a provocation to consider undeath as a necessary imaginative framework for estranging ourselves, for thinking beyond our lived realities as we confront, to borrow from Deckard one final time, "those revenants of 'undead' processes in the past that continue to shape contemporary environments" (2019, 184). *Common* exemplifies just some of the ways that Ecogothic aesthetics and sensibilities—and this conceptual frame of undeath in particular—can provide an insightful and productive set of conditions for bringing such deliberately strange and unsettling forms of imagination to the stage.

NOTE

1. Moore creates compound words to form a pseudo-"archaic" language (e.g., "manyseeingways" to connote extra-perceptiveness, "mangleruined" to suggest damage, and so on) that is used both in the characters' dialogue and in the stage directions given in the playtext.

WORKS CITED

Alaimo, Stacy. 2010. *Bodily Natures: Science, Environment, and the Material Self.* Bloomington: Indiana Press.

Beckett, John Vincent. 1990. *The Agricultural Revolution.* Oxford: Wiley-Blackwell.

Botting, Fred. 2013. *Gothic 2nd edition.* London: Routledge.

Chambers, Jonathan David and Gordon Edmund Mingay. 1966. *The Agricultural Revolution, 1750-1880.* London: B. T. Basford.

Chaudhuri, Una. 2015. "Anthropo-Scenes: Theater and Climate Change." *Journal of Contemporary Drama in English* 3, no. 1, 12–27.

Cless, Downing. 2012. "Ecodirecting Canonical Plays." In *Readings in Ecology and Performance*, edited by Theresa J. May and Wendy Arons. New York: Palgrave Macmillan, 159–168.

Deckard, Sharae. 2019. "Ecogothic." In *Twenty-First-Century Gothic: An Edinburgh Companion*, edited by Maisha Wester and Xavier Aldana Reyes. Edinburgh: Edinburgh University Press, 174–188.

Del Principe, David. 2014. "Introduction: The EcoGothic in the Long Nineteenth Century." *Gothic Studies* 16, no. 1 (May), 1–8.

Edney, Sue (ed). *2020. *EcoGothic Gardens in the Long Nineteenth Century: Phantoms, Fantasy and Uncanny Flowers*. Manchester: Manchester University Press.

Garrard, Greg. 2012. *Ecocriticism*. London and New York: Routledge.

Hillard, Tom J. 2009. "'Deep Into That Darkness Peering': An Essay on Gothic Nature." *Interdisciplinary Studies in Literature and Environment* 16, no. 4 (Autumn), 685–695.

Jones, Kelly, Benjamin Poore and Robert Dean (eds). 2018. "Introduction." In *Contemporary Gothic Drama: Attraction, Consummation and Consumption on the Modern British Stage*. London: Palgrave Macmillan, 1–18.

Keetley, Dawn and Matthew Sivils (eds). 2017. *Ecogothic in Nineteenth-Century American Literature*. London: Routledge.

Kipp, Lara M. 2018. "Death, Decay and Domesticity: The Corpse as Pivotal Stage Presence in Howard Barker's *Dead Hands*." In *Contemporary Gothic Drama*, edited by Kelly Jones, Benjamin Poore and Robert Dean. London: Palgrave Macmillan, 43–60.

Lukowski, Andrzej. 2017. "Common." Review of *Common*, by DC Moore. *TimeOut*, 7 June. https://www.timeout.com/london/theatre/common.

McEvoy, Emma. 2007. "Contemporary Gothic Theatre." In *The Routledge Companion to Gothic*, edited by McEvoy and Catherine Spooner. London: Routledge, 214–222.

Moore, DC. 2017. *Common*. London: Nick Hern Books.

Morgan, Fergus. 2017. "Common at the National Theatre." Review of *Common*, by DC Moore. *Exeunt*, 5 August. http://exeuntmagazine.com/reviews/review-common-national-theatre/.

Morton, Timothy. 2013. *Hyperobjects: Philosophy and Ecology after the End of the World*. Minneapolis, MN: University of Minnesota Press.

—. 2016. *Dark Ecology: For a Logic of Future Coexistence*. New York: Columbia University Press.

Parker, Elizabeth. 2020. *The Forest and the EcoGothic: The Deep Dark Woods in the Popular Imagination*. London: Palgrave Macmillan, 11–68.

Rabey, David Ian. 2018. "The Call of the Chthonic: From *Titus Andronicus* to *X*." In *Contemporary Gothic Drama*, edited by Kelly Jones, Benjamin Poore and Robert Dean. London: Palgrave Macmillan, 21–42.

Rebellato, Dan. 2017. "Common." 2 August. http://www.danrebellato.co.uk/spilledink/2017/8/2/common.Accessed September 3, 2021

Saglia, Diego. *2013. "Gothic Theater, 1765-Present." In *The Gothic World*, edited by Glennis Byron and Dale Townshend, 354–365. London: Routledge.

Schweitzer, Marlis and Joanne Zerdy (eds). 2014. *Performing Objects and Theatrical Things*. London: Palgrave Macmillan.

Smith, Andrew and William Hughes (eds). 2013. *Ecogothic*. Manchester: Manchester University Press.

Warren, Karen J. (ed). 1994. *Ecological Feminism*. London: Routledge.

Chapter 3

Maggie in the Necrocene

Johan Höglund

Like all farmers of the Midwest, Wade Wogel must burn his own crops. Smoke rises from the ruined land into a grey sky, blotting out a pale sun. In the city, wrecked and abandoned cars, plundered shops, and dead streetlights greet Wogel as he enters it in search of his daughter Maggie. He finds her in the hospital. She has been bitten and is now infected with the Necroambulist virus, the illness that is destroying the crops and transforming people into the walking dead not just in the Midwest but worldwide. Maggie has a few weeks to go before she loses awareness of who she is and begins to hunger for the flesh of her fellow human beings; a cannibalistic carrier that must be quarantined and euthanized. Against the advice of doctors and police, Wade places his large body between his daughter and the institutions that would take charge of her. He is taking her home. He will protect her. He will fail. He failed long ago.[1]

Written by John Scott 3 and directed by Henry Hobson, *Maggie* (2015) casts Arnold Schwarzenegger in the role of Wade. The vast physical shape and cinematic history of this actor amplify the contours of Wade's heteropatriarchal character immensely. In the poster that wears Maggie's name, he stands between his daughter and the eyes of the viewer, as he stands between her and all people that threaten to take her from him. Even so, this is not a film about the sentimental failure of an (overly) protective father to save his daughter from a terminal illness. It is, this chapter argues, a story about the ruination brought on by heteropatriarchal, capitalist, extractivist settler society to the land, to human and extra-human nature, and to capitalist society itself. Wade may love his daughter and he may be ready to die for her, yet the masculinity that he represents has been literally toxic to her and to the planet. The society Wade grew out of, that he programmatically reproduces, and the (violent) strategies at his disposal, are the root causes of Maggie's illness and abject suffering. In this way, Wade is not his daughter's keeper, but an agent of what Justin McBrien (2016) has termed the Necrocene. This name recognizes that extractive capitalism/colonialism has always generated death in various forms, from the Great Dying of indigenous people that followed the Columbian Exchange, to the slave trade, to the scramble for Africa, the World Wars and on to the present, precipitous moment of mass extinction when dying has become ubiquitous and planetary.

CAPITALISM, PATRIARCHY, AND ECOLOGICAL CRISIS

The most popular denominator of the ongoing and accelerating climate crisis is the Anthropocene. Proposed by geologists Crutzen and Stoermer (2000), it importantly recognizes that human beings are responsible for such profound changes in the Earth's atmospheric chemistry and soil that human agents now constitute the most important environmental factor. Crutzen and Stoermer trace this development back to "the invention of the steam engine" (17–18), but as a number of scholars have noted, the concept blames the Anthropos—humanity as a species—, rather than industrialization, and the capitalist forces that drive this process. In this way, the concept elides the role that extractive and capitalist fossil-fuel dependent societies have played for the climate crisis, and it also directs attention away from the dispersed and uneven nature of this crisis. As Rob Nixon (2011) has influentially observed, what Crutzen and Stoermer call the Anthropocene affects human and nonhuman life in the Global South much more severely than it affects affluent communities in the Global North. These, as Malm and Hornborg (2014) argue, have the means to escape the violence of climate change: "For the foreseeable future [. . .] there *will* be life boats for the rich and privileged" (66, italics in original). In other words, the climate crisis has not been produced by all people equally, and its detrimental effects are experienced far more keenly in vulnerable communities in the Global South than among privileged people in the Global North.

The failure of the term Anthropocene to recognize the material history of climate change and the climate crisis' dispersed and uneven nature has led scholars to suggest alternative denominations. Concepts such as Plasticene (Davis 2015), Chthulucene (Haraway 2015), or Virocene (Fernando 2020) stress different processes, relationships and states that have brought on the current crisis. These are not simply descriptors, but also, as T. J. Demos (2017) notes, "names of resistance" (85) mobilized against the universalizing notion of the Anthropocene. Among these alternative labels, Capitalocene stands out as the concept that most clearly connects the climate crisis to the long material history of the economic system that dominates societies and global relations in the present.

While the concept of the Capitalocene was coined by Andreas Malm in 2009, it has been popularized and explored most readily by Jason W. Moore in a series of publications. The starting point of the concept, as Moore notes in *Capitalism in the Web of Life* (2015), is that the massive carbon emissions that are warming the planet have not been produced by all humans equally. These emissions are the result of a certain way of understanding the world, and of the material processes that this understanding paved the way for. Moore traces the epistemologies and practices in question back to the early beginnings of capitalism and the colonization of the non-European world that made capitalism dominant. It was at this time that nature was reframed by European society into private and extractable resource, enabling the capitalist imperative to literally break new ground, to find new markets, to increase production, and to accumulate. Capitalism thus operated according to a logic of exhaustion where land, seas, animals, and even human beings were rethought as cheap resources and where the waste of extraction (carbon, pollutants) was released out into ecology. The fact that fossil fuels such as coal, oil, and gas became the primary drivers of industry—cheap resources in themselves but also the means by which other resources could be extracted—created the conditions for a warming of the planet so extensive that it is approaching a critical tipping point that, once reached, will cause irrepressible and catastrophic change to the planet (Lenton et al. 2019).

Such change is already well underway, of course. The melting of the polar ice caps, the desertification of parts of Africa and the release of pollutants into the planet's water, atmosphere, and soil are already exerting a violence of such proportions that it is producing a sixth mass extinction of species (Kolbert 2014, Ceballos et al. 2015, Wallace-Wells 2019). This is a dying off of plant and animal life not seen since the Cretaceous-Paleogene extinction event 65 million years ago, when an asteroid destroyed 75 percent of all plant and animal life on the Earth, including the dinosaurs. It is this present crescendo of death, following in the wake of five centuries of deadly capitalist violence that prompts McBrien to name the present moment in ecological time the Necrocene. Arguing that "[c]apital does not just rob the soil and worker [. . .] it necrotizes the entire planet" (116), McBrien thus describes the Necrocene as the extinction stage, or "shadow double" (117) of the Capitalocene. McBrien argues furthermore that capitalism has learned how to manage and embrace the dying that has followed in its wake since the Columbian Exchange, when new invasive plants, animal species and viruses introduced into the American continent caused an estimated 56 million human deaths (Koch et al. 2019). Since then, McBrien writes, capitalism has made environmental risk "the central problem of its survival" (119), from the transformation of biodiverse ecologies into staple crop plantations, to the "catastrophic nihilism" manifested in massive atomic bomb testing and in the "survival economy" of neoliberalism (ibid). The concept of the Necrocene thus "reframes the history of capitalism's expansion through the process of *becoming extinction*" (116, italics in the original). In this way, the concept helps discern even more clearly the stage the planet, under the global management of capitalism, has reached.

The Necrocene/Capitalocene has a material and chemical history that revolves around the global organization of (enslaved) labor, the mining and refining of natural resources, and the release of radiation and hydrocarbons into the atmosphere, but, to return to the question of understanding, it also has an epistemological history. Moore argues that this history revolves around the construction of a binary and anthropocentric dualism that severed the mind from the body and humanity from nature, formulated most influentially by René Descartes. By dividing the human into mind and body, Descartes furnished a binary logic that could be used "not only to interpret the world but control it," and it thus became the "key organizing principle for an emergent capitalist civilization" (Moore 2016, 84). When humanity (imagined as mind) was perceived as fundamentally different from the planet the species inhabits, nature (imagined as body) could be Othered and dissolved into a repository of resources out of which wood, iron, aluminum, coal, oil, grains, and meat could be extracted, refined and sold while little or nothing was done to preserve biodiversity or ecological balance. As capitalism became more widespread, most of global society was organized around the enabling of such extraction.

A crucial point here is that Cartesian thinking about the world was, and remains, deeply informed by notions of class, race, and gender. For extractive capitalism to function well, not all *Homo sapiens* could be recognized as humans. Indigenous people who live on colonized land, slaves and other laborers used in extraction, and women performing unpaid labor, could not be accepted as enlightened interpreters of the world. This would prevent capital from folding them into nature where they could be used as cheap resources, and it would recognize their potentially very different understanding of planetary ecology as valid. Thus, most people during early colonialism were "either excluded from Humanity—indigenous Americans, for example—or where designated as only partly Human, as were virtually all European women" (87). In this way, most people with black and brown bodies and most women were associated with the category of (cheap) nature. This, in turn, made capitalist extraction into an essentially anthropocentric, racist, and sexist endeavor.

This troubled history has been the subject of extensive historical and sociological research. The important work of charting a capitalist colonial program that dehumanized virtually all non-European people, enslaved millions and inserted them into extractive economies in America and other parts of the world has been performed by such as Eric Williams (1944), Achille Mbembe (2017), and Zakiyyah Iman Jackson (2020). Work by Laura Pulido (2015), Rob Nixon (2011), and Kathryn Yusoff (2018) have investigated how racism enabled the extractive practices of the colonial period, and how it continues to structure the relationship between human society, capital, and ecology. The particular role that women were made to play in extractive, capitalist society has been explored in a great number of ecofeminist and ecosocialist texts, including Maria Mies' ground-breaking *Patriarchy and Accumulation On A World Scale: Women in the International Division of Labour* (1986). This study begins with "the recognition that patriarchy and accumulation on a world scale constitute the structural and ideological framework within which women's reality today has to be understood" (3), and investigates "processes and policies by which other countries and women are defined as 'nature', or made into colonies to be exploited by WHITE MAN in the name of capital accumulation or progress and civilization" (4). Thus, Mies' work shows globalized patriarchal capitalism to be an engine of inequality in human society, just as patriarchy is simultaneously revealed to be an instrument of planetary destruction. In other words, white capitalist patriarchy generates not only race and gender-based inequality but also material processes deeply harmful to ecology. The masculinity it represents is literally toxic to the land and to the profoundly entangled species that inhabit the land (of which the human being is one). The ecofeminist and ecosocialist traditions that Mie's work energizes have continued to explore the connection that exists between white heteropatriarchy, extractivist capitalism, ecological erosion, and violence done to marginalized and racialized people. It is with this material and feminist history in mind that I explore the Necrocene moment that *Maggie* takes place in.

BACK TO THE UNCANNY FARM

Wade Vogel is a white farmer; possibly a descendant of the Germans that arrived in the Midwest in the early nineteenth century, following in the footsteps of French fur traders, illegal squatters, Yankee pioneers, and a host of other European migrants from Ireland, Scandinavia, Switzerland, and the Netherlands. These were the first agents of the Capitalocene era in America. Aided by the U.S. government and its military, they eliminated the indigenous nations that lived in these regions via conventional warfare, removal to reservations and the systematic obliteration of the customs, traditions, languages and religions of these nations. Patrick Wolfe has influentially proposed that the motive for this elimination was command of the land itself and what could be extracted from this land. Indeed, land is "necessary for life" (2006, 387) but when land is transformed from multi-species habitat into private property, the life it nurtures is equally that of capitalism.

As a descendant of settler colonizers, as an owner of land, and as a small-time farmer, Wade stands on the shoulders of this material history, stretching back to the arrival of the first Europeans. As Rose Braidotti (2017) observes, noting the dominance of the same Cartesian paradigm that Moore critiques, the constitutive subject of capitalist humanity has always been identified as a "Man of Reason": a being assumed to be not simply male, but "masculine, white, urbanized, speaking a standard language, heterosexually inscribed in a reproductive unit, and a full citizen of a recognized polity" (23). Although Wade is a farmer, this is still a disturbingly precise description of his being. His massive body, the farm, the gigantic blue ford pickup truck that he drives, have all been forged out of settler history and out of the privileges and inequalities inherent in the patriarchal colonial/capitalist project.

However, it is worth noticing that while Wade is an agent of the Capitalocene, he is also an individual existing on the margins of a post-1970s, precarious neoliberal economy. He is likely to be comfortable as long as the economy is doing well and as long as the land does not resist his efforts. This relative comfort is made visible to the viewer through the care his daughter receives from the medical establishment, and through the weary respect he earns from the local police even when he brings his infected daughter back to the community. However, it is also clear that at the moment of global economic and ecological crisis that is the starting point of the movie, his ability to fend for his family has been compromised. It does not matter how much wood he chops, or how hard he clutches his gun, or the steering wheel of his truck. The world he has been brought up to control, the land he has been doctored to "break," and the farm he has built and developed as part of the system, have ceased to do his bidding. The land, diseased and burning, the slowly disintegrating farm, the collapsing nuclear family, and, most importantly, his infected, transforming and dying daughter, have become uncanny. The Capitalocene is collapsing into the Necrocene. When Wade walks through the familiar spaces of his farm and encounters his daughter, she appears before him uncanny; recognizable yet shatteringly and irrevocably different. Like the land, she erodes before his eyes.

The first to leave the farm are the children Wade has with his new wife Caroline. They are too small and vulnerable to keep on the farm now that Maggie has been infected. Wade drives them to an aunt to keep them safe. Back at the farm, Caroline grips the sink powerlessly and prays to God, but she receives no answers. All windows in the house have been papered over with newsprint, to keep the light, dust, and smoke out, to keep the warmth in, to keep them from shattering, leaving the inside of the house in a constant state of semi-darkness.

Wade cannot accept or even constructively contemplate this dissolution. This would be the first step toward recognizing that the epistemic borders and the understanding of life around which his being has been organized are not only delusional, but the very reason why Maggie and the land have become ill. Thus, Wade organizes moments of normality to stave off the overpowering sense of uncanniness that now permeates life on the farm. He speaks to his daughter as if she has a future, and as if the world has a future. They have dinner together, although Maggie is getting worse and eats very little. She sits by him when he works on the ancient Ford pickup—a comforting metonymy for the desired stability of petrocapitalist society. Focused on fixing and lubricating the pickup's engine, Wade can indulge in what Mark Fisher (2009) has termed "capitalist realism": the understanding that capitalism is all there is, and that no other society is thinkable. Within the dimly lit garage, daughter by his side, "there is no alternative" (Fisher 2009, 8) to fixing the car, to keeping its wheels turning, to keeping this crumbling society turning. In other words, when Wade compartmentalizes his life into a set of (extractive) tasks—getting the power back on, getting the car moving—he is able to ignore the joint crumbling of the capitalist social order and planetary ecology that is taking place around his family.

Sitting around the car, Maggie and Wade talk about Maggie's biological mother. Maggie remembers very little of this woman, but we understand that she represents a very different type of motherhood compared to her stepmother. While Caroline comes across as silent, suffering, and devotedly Christian, Maggie's true mother was a bookworm, "smart, beautiful" with "a hell of a green thumb." A lover of daisies, she was also "so strong," someone who fought back when she needed to. In this way, Maggie's mother is furtively written into a resilient ecology. The film does not supply enough information about this lost mother to discern if her subjectivity is that of an essentialized and feminized Gaia, or if she represents a fundamentally different and potentially ecofeminist position. In any case, she is both symbolically and physically dead. Even if she could have offered Maggie and her family another way forward, this road is closed to the living/dying Maggie. Maggie cannot unite with her except in the death that approaches.

During Wade and Maggie's conversation, Wade also tells his daughter that he made her mother a promise: to protect their daughter. But this is, in fact, a promise he broke long ago. As a (patriarchal) agent of capitalist extractivist society, he is part of the reason she is now dying, and the strategies that this society provides him with—masculine violence and denial (of his daughter's impending death and of the fact that capitalist extraction leads to environmental collapse)—are fundamentally futile and pointless. These strategies are in themselves necrotic and cannot be used to piece a broken daughter and a broken planet together.

MAGGIE IN THE WEB OF LIFE/DEATH

The film connects Maggie to an exhausted and diseased ecology from the beginning. The first time the audience sets its eyes on her, she is already infected and rounded up by heavily armed and armored police. By never separating Wade's daughter from the exhausted and diseased land, the film problematizes the imagined separation between humanity and nature. This is visualized in a number of different ways, but primarily through an infected bite mark on Maggie's arm. The viral infection is spreading throughout her body as it is spreading on Wade's fields and across the land. The infected wound joins her to nature, turning her into a liminal entity that hovers on the Cartesian border that divides the world into Nature (imagined as an external entity to be leveraged by humanity) and the Human (imagined as a spirited, intellectual being somehow separate from the nature and the body). When Maggie scratches her wound, Wade barks at her to stop it. Recognizing and exploring the wound is to recognize and explore both the idea that Maggie is infected and dying and the notion that the Cartesian model is a ruse and that humans never have existed outside of what Moore has termed the Web of Life.[2] This rhizomatic, multi-species, entangled Web is a constant challenge to the Cartesian model and thus to the capitalist project itself. As a being folded into this web, Wade is, like his daughter, a victim of this project. However, he is just as prominently a privileged agent of the capitalist project.

This again brings Wade's massive masculinity, his desperate and patriarchal yet utterly futile attempt to save his daughter, his farm, his family, and his land, into focus. Had Maggie not been folded into this dying land, into his uncanny and disintegrating farm and family, this could have been another Schwarzenegger action movie celebrating spectacular masculine violence. It is easy to imagine such a narrative, where Wade/Schwarzenegger's staggering masculinity actually serves to save Maggie and the farm from the virus. Wade constantly locates himself within such a narrative, where he can somehow save a land and a daughter already destroyed, this by *killing* the walking dead that roam the cities and the fields of the Midwest, and by wading through the massacred undead to find his daughter a cure. Wade repeatedly inserts himself into such a narrative. When Wade and Maggie drive back to the farm at the beginning of the film, Wade runs into a zombified human in a gas station restroom. He kills the human but never tells Maggie. Then, shortly after her arrival on the farm, Maggie breaks a finger on her injured arm. Black gore oozes out of the broken appendage, and in desperation, she cuts her finger from her hand with a large kitchen knife. To avoid the terrified gaze of her stepmother, Maggie then runs into a copse of trees close to the farm. There, two zombiefied humans approach her, groaning and possibly hungry. Wade, who has been cutting firewood, finds her staring at this potential threat. He has held on to his axe and he uses it to cut down the first zombie. Wade then turns to the other zombie, but she is not the looming dark presence that we associate with such beings. She is a small girl not yet of school age, in a dirty white dress, blond hair a mess, and her face grey and withered from the illness. She does not look aggressive. She stands forlorn, miserable, lost. We never see Wade kill her, but we understand that he does. He must kill her. This is the only strategy available to him.

This scene is another uncanny sequence in that it locates Wade/Schwarzenegger in a supremely recognizable and potentially utterly comfortable situation. As director Hobson was aware when he cast the role, Schwarzenegger has killed hundreds of people in the cinema.[3] According to a survey from 2013, Schwarzenegger was at that point in time the American actor who has killed the most people (369) on the movie screen (Olson 2013). These killings have been designed to stimulate considerable visual pleasure in the audience. From *Conan the Barbarian* (1982) and *Commando* (1985)—the latter a film where he does indeed save his daughter through the fetishized killing of 87 people (Eoin 2020)—to the *Expendables 2* (2013) and *The Last Stand* (2013), Schwarzenegger's sprees of destruction have been cast as spectacular; moments of extreme, masculine, and frequently eroticized violence intended to provide movie audiences with a profound sense of release. When Schwarzenegger has been cast as the hero, this violence has been depicted as essentially righteous, moral, and, to use Richard Slotkin's (1973) still very apt terminology, "regenerative." The extreme violence wielded by Schwarzenegger thus tends to be portrayed as acts that reshape and bring order to an unruly and chaotic world, ushering in an era of peace and stability in which families, communities and nations can prosper. Out of the many dead, out of the mechanical and militarized cleansing of criminal life, rises the promise of a regenerated and fertile world.

In this way, Schwarzenegger's films have systematically confirmed the patriarchal trope that masculine violence is a necessary preliminary to building functioning human and ecological communities. Once the killing has been done, the world has been made safe for women and for the fertility they represent in these narratives. There is thus a strong relationship between these narratives and the similarly violent extraction of resources from the planet. As Slotkin argues and as I have discussed in *The American Imperial Gothic* (2014), U.S. popular culture has always been involved in a cultural project of displacement and misdirection where the violence of the capitalist settler colonial enterprise has been narrated as masculine adventure. The settlement of the continent and the elimination of indigenous people, and the extension of the American economic and military hegemony beyond the borders of the nation state, have been told by the Western and by American war and action films that stimulate melodramatic pity for white men giving their lives for their nations, and that offer "the vicarious pleasure of satisfying kills" endemic to the mode of adventure, as observed by Agnieszka Soltysik Monnet (2021). In other words, in American popular literature and film, the violent material and epistemic destruction of indigenous people and the similarly violent extraction and destruction of land has typically been cast as a reassuring and spectacular demonstration of white masculine prowess.

But this sense of release, of violence as a catalyst of beauty and regeneration, is constantly absent when violence is practiced in *Maggie*. When Wade walks into the trees to look for his daughter, the audience can see from the set of his jaw and the posture of his shoulders that he will kill something, that he *has* to kill something, but the cutting down of his neighbors triggers no sense of relief or triumph. The killing of the infected, four-year-old girl in her dirty dress and lost expression is too abject and speaks too clearly of what Wade, as a representative of extractivist patriarchy, embodies to even be shown on screen. Wade's hypermasculine body does the work it has been designed to do, but it blatantly fails to regenerate himself, his daughter, or his land. The killing of his neighbors is like the burning of his crops, an ultimately destructive, self-effacing, and hopeless task. This scene is one of the most dramatic in the film's exploration of hypermasculine violence not as regenerative, but as instead a vital component of the destructive material histories, practices and relationships that has brought the land to its current, necrotic state.

That killing does not bring regeneration in this movie is brought out also by the sequence that follows. Before the bodies of Wade's neighbors have been collected, the wife and mother of the dead, a woman named Bonnie, arrives at Wade's doorstep. She is stricken by grief and she holds on to a gun. She wants to see what is left of her family, and maybe she also wants to kill Wade. Wade certainly expects a bullet. After all, Wade/Schwarzenegger has avenged murdered family members in many films before. Revenge is one way in which order is restored in the masculine adventure narratives that he has so frequently starred in. But this is emphatically not an adventure story and Bonnie does not operate according to its masculine logic. Instead, she tells Wade a story of grief and loss, how she took turns with her husband to tend to their infected daughter, and how he one morning locked himself in with the child and would not come out. When Wade brings her to their bodies she collapses to the ground, paralyzed by grief.

Once the police have taken Bonnie and her dead family away, Wade goes to their now empty house. He crosses the yellow police tape and explores a home darker and more dilapidated even than his own. It is a place only of

death now, flies lying in black heaps on the windowsills. The room where
the husband and daughter lived out the last stages of their infection is a
stinking mess of dirty mattresses, torn-down drywall, broken family photographs, and scratched messages: "I love my wife. I love my Daughter. I
love my Family."

Wade also loves his daughter, but the encounter with his infected neighbors and their now empty house reminds him of the killing he has not yet
performed. He must not let things go as far as Bonnie did. He must euthanize
his daughter before she loses her humanity and becomes like a senseless animal, all hunger, all Nature. Killing her will change nothing and it will save
no one, but it is the only thing that remains to him, the only agency left for
him to practice. But rather than to perform this final act of deadly mercy, he
again encourages his daughter to rehearse the rituals of capitalist heteropatriarchal modernity. Maggie is picked up by a friend in her car, and they meet
up with her old friends around a campfire. Maggie is not the only one who is
infected. Her heterosexual love interest Trent is also there, and his illness has
progressed further. He is still Human, but dark veins run up his throat and
across his face and he speaks worriedly about what might happen to him if
he is taken to quarantine. He knows from a relative that this is not a place of
compassionate palliative care, but a site where the infected belonging to different stages are thrown together so that there are "people eating people, and
they don't care." Trent would rather put a gun to his own head, but he does
not get the chance to do so. Only days later, police with automatic rifles and
riot gear appear outside the house where he lives with his father. They are
given the order to "[g]o ahead with the extraction." Trent goes kicking and
screaming, no longer human in the eyes of his father or the authorities. Only
Maggie is capable of grieving when he is driven away in the back of a police
car. Soon she will also cross over into something else, Human no more, dead
yet somehow still life.

The final stage of Maggie's illness arrives suddenly. One morning
Maggie's stepmother smells to Maggie like something she could eat. She
actually does eat a fox caught in a trap in the forest and returns home desperate, frightened, smeared with blood. She looks at her father and the extractivist gaze has been inverted. He is now something to be consumed, but not as
a preliminary to capitalist accumulation. If she eats him it will not be as a
member of settler society or even as a representative of Humanity; she will
eat him as an agent of the necrotic land that surrounds her, as a part of the
damaged planet itself. She is devastated by the thought that this is something
the illness will force her to do, and she pushes her father away when he seeks
to comfort his bloodied and suffering daughter. The family doctor arrives to
outline Wade's options: he can give his daughter up to quarantine, he can
administer the painful shot they give to the undead in quarantine to euthanize

them, or he can make it quick and put her down with his shotgun. Regardless of what option he chooses, Maggie will die and Wade will have participated in the killing.

The film lets Wade off the hook but not by pulling a sudden and surprising victory out of capitalist modernity in the form of a triumphant cure. At the very end of the film, Maggie, now in an advanced stage of zombification, comes down to the living room where Wade is sleeping in an easy chair, exhausted with his gun in hand. She kisses his forehead but does not bite him. She then exits the house and his world. Wade wakes up disoriented and loads his shotgun, finally prepared to take his daughters life, but she has already climbed to the top of the house. We see her standing on the roof, arms outspread, a vogel/bird not just in name. In her final moments, just before she tumbles forward—and as she tumbles forward—she remembers herself as a child on the farm as it used to be, or as a child would remember it, before the ecological collapse had become apparent to her society and her family. Her dead mother is there, a smiling, beautiful, and confident woman. The child Maggie picks a daisy, and they walk hand in hand in pale spring sunshine. The image fades to white and the movie is over. It is a sentimental ending, but not overly melodramatic. We do not see Wade cradling his dead daughter in his arms, grieving his lost child but also thankful that he did not have kill her himself. Indeed, Maggie is the brave one in the end, saving her father both from the ecological violence of which she is now an agent, and from having to perform a nihilistic act of filicide, an act that would force him to confront his own ultimate complicity in her death, and in the death of the land.

CONCLUSION: UNDEAD IN THE NECROCENE

While *Maggie* is not a Schwarzenegger movie, it is a movie that prominently features Schwarzenegger. His face takes precedence on the poster not only because his character tries to stand between his daughter and harm, but because he is the (hypermasculine) star. It is also through his perspective that much of the movie is narrated and it clearly offers the audience the possibility of identifying with Wade and his desperate and ultimately futile attempt to save his daughter even from himself. But this is, ultimately, Maggie's film. It carries her name, it opens with Maggie's voice pleading with her father to not come to the city to save her, and it ends with Maggie falling to her death while remembering her dead mother. What happens if the easy identification with Wade the patriarch is refused in favor of identification with Maggie? What happens if we identify as undead in the Necrocene, rather than as the patriarch whose toxic masculinity has poisoned the world, the farm and the family he thought he was protecting?

To imagine yourself as undead in the Necrocene is not an easy task. To do so is to abandon the material, ontological, and epistemological position Wade/Schwarzenegger inhabits and to refuse the capitalist realist notion that there is no alternative. Wade/Schwarzenegger may think he does not have a choice, that he must go on farming the land, driving his pickup, preventing Nature from invading his house, his family, his daughter, and ultimately kill her. But he can, in fact, refuse to kill his daughter, he can refuse to take the advice his wife, his daughter, and the police present him with. A part of him wants to let his daughter live, even if the life she would enter is an unqualified uncanny, animal, multi-species existence that he finds utterly disturbing and over which he must relinquish control. Maggie, already invaded, already visibly folded into the Web of Life that capitalism refuses to acknowledge, also has a choice. She can refuse the notion that there is no alternative, that Necrocene death is the only option. Even in her infected state, that choice exists. She can refuse the euthanasia that the system her father represents insists is the only alternative. She can go on living the life of the undead. Her father may not respect such a choice, and while Maggie remains connected to capitalist modernity it may not seem a genuine possibility even to her, but it remains a choice even so. McBrien argues that the "logic of accumulation is not capable of outrunning extinction because accumulation and extinction are the same process. They cannot be decoupled. But the human being *can* be decoupled from Capital. Capital is extinction. We are not" (2016, 135). Recognizing that this choice exists, that we can cease to be extinction, is to unthink the very foundation of the binary and death-dealing logic of capitalism. It is a choice that exists for Wade and Maggie, but also for those who are not already undead, already on the brink of destruction, already falling through the air with dreams of a world not burning.

NOTES

1. I want to express my gratitude to the Linnaeus University Centre for Concurrences in Colonial and Postcolonial Studies that funded the research that made this article possible. I also want to thank the members of the Cluster for Aesthetics of Empire at Linnaeus University, and in particular Dr. Rebecca Duncan, for valuable feedback during the writing process.

2. The "Web of Life" is the term Jason W. Moore uses to stress the relations that exist between species on the planet. A proper understanding of ecology must begin, he observes, with the recognition that all living beings are part of an intricate multi-species web. Donna Haraway's concept "Chthulucene" (2016) and Timothy Morton's "Mesh" (2016) also stress this fundamental interconnectedness; an interconnectedness

that makes it impossible to think of the human as in any way or at any time separate from ecology.

3. In an interview with Lesley Coffin, director Hobson observed that whenever "you cast Arnold Schwarzenegger in a movie, he comes with a history of all these other roles and his public personality." The point is that "Because he brings all of that with him, it means I don't have to have scenes of that character beating up men in the bar for joking about his wife or doing something physically heroic. Because I didn't want to have any scenes at the beginning which showed him being this hyper-protective guy" (Coffin 2015).

WORKS CITED

Braidotti, Rosi. 2017. "Four Theses on Posthuman Feminism." In *Anthropocene Feminism*, edited by Richard Grusin. Minneapolis: University of Minnesota Press.

Ceballos, Gerardo, Paul R Ehrlich, Anthony D Barnosky, Andrés García, Robert M Pringle, and Todd M Palmer. 2015. "Accelerated Modern Human–Induced Species Losses: Entering the Sixth Mass Extinction." *Science Advances* 1 (5): e1400253.

Coffin, Lesley. 2015. Interview: Director Henry Hobson on Maggie and Tackling Euthanasia and Fear of Illness Through Zombies. *The Mary Sue*. Accessed March 3, 2021.

Crutzen, Paul and Eugene Stoermer. 2000. "The 'Anthropocene'." *IGBP Newsletter* 41: 17–18.

Davis, Heather. 2015. "Life & Death in the Anthropocene: A Short History of Plastic." In *Art in the Anthropocene: Encounters among Aesthetics, Politics, Environments and Epistemologies*, edited by Heather Davies and Etienne Turpin. London; Open Humanities Press. 347–358.

Demos, Thomas J. 2017. *Against the Anthropocene: Visual Culture and Environment Today*. Berlin: Sternberg Press.

Eoin. 2020. "Kill Count: Commando (1985)." *The Action Elite*, 17 April. http://theactionelite.com/kill-count-commando-1985/. Accessed January 14, 2022.

Fernando, Jude L. 2020. "From the Virocene to the Lovecene Epoch: Multispecies Justice as Critical Praxis for Virocene Disruptions and Vulnerabilities." *Journal of Political Ecology* 27 (1):685–731.

Fisher, Mark. 2009. *Capitalist Realism: Is There No Alternative?* Ropley: John Hunt Publishing.

Haraway, Donna. 2015. "Anthropocene, Capitalocene, Plantationocene, Chthulucene: Making Kin." *Environmental humanities* 6 (1): 159–165.

Haraway, Donna J. 2016. *Staying with the Trouble: Making Kin in the Chthulucene*. North Carolina: North Carolina: Duke University Press.

Höglund, Johan. 2014. *The American Imperial Gothic: Popular Culture, Empire, Violence*. Farnham, Surrey: Farnham: Ashgate.

Jackson, Zakiyyah Iman. 2020. *Becoming Human: Matter and Meaning in an Antiblack World*. Vol. 53. New York: New York University Press.

Koch, Alexander, Chris Brierley, Mark M Maslin, and Simon L Lewis. 2019. "Earth System Impacts of the European Arrival and Great Dying in the Americas after 1492." *Quaternary Science Reviews* 207: 13–36.

Kolbert, Elizabeth. 2014. *The Sixth Extinction: An Unnatural History.* New York: Henry Holt.

Lenton, Timothy M, Johan Rockström, Owen Gaffney, Stefan Rahmstorf, Katherine Richardson, Will Steffen, and Hans Joachim Schellnhuber. 2019. "Climate Tipping Points—Too Risky to Bet Against." *Nature* 575(7784): 592–595. doi: 10.1038/d41586-019-03595-0.

Malm, Andreas, and Alf Hornborg. 2014. "The Geology of Mankind? A Critique of the Anthropocene Narrative." *The Anthropocene Review* 1 (1): 62–69.

Mbembe, Achille. 2017. *Critique of Black Reason.* Durham: Duke University Press.

McBrien, Justin. 2016. "Accumulating Extinction: Planetary Catastrophism in the Necrocene." In *Anthropocene or Capitalocene? Nature, History, and the Crisis of Capitalism*, edited by Jason W. Moore, 116–137. Oakland: PM Press.

Mies, Maria. 1986. *Patriarchy and Accumulation on a World Scale: Women in the International Division of Labour.* London: Zed Books.

Monnet, Agnieszka Soltysik. 2021. *Combat Death in Contemporary American Culture: Popular Cultural Conceptions of War Since World War II.* London: Lexington Books.

Moore, Jason W. 2016. "The Rise of Cheap Nature." In *Anthropocene or Capitalocene?: Nature, History, and the Crisis of Capitalism*, edited by Jason W Moore. Oakland: PM Press.

Moore, Jason W. 2015. *Capitalism in the Web of Life: Ecology and the Accumulation of Capital.* New York: Verso.

Morton, Timothy. 2016. *Dark Ecology: For a Logic of Future Coexistence.* New York: Columbia University Press.

Nixon, Rob. 2011. *Slow Violence and the Environmentalism of the Poor.* Cambridge, MA: Harvard University Press.

Olson, Randy. 2013. "Top 25 Deadliest Actors of all Time by On-screen Kills in Movies." *Randal S. Olson*, 16 April. http://www.randalolson.com/2013/12/31/deadliest-actors-of-all-time-by-on-screen-kills-in-movies/.

Pulido, Laura. 2015. "Geographies of Race and Ethnicity 1: White Supremacy vs White Privilege in Environmental Racism Research." *Progress in Human Geography* 39 (6): 809–817.

Slotkin, Richard. 1973. *Regeneration through Violence: The Mythology of the American Frontier, 1600-1860.* Norman: University of Oklahoma Press.

Wallace-Wells, David. 2019. *The Uninhabitable Earth: A Story of the Future.* London: Penguin UK.

Williams, Eric. 1944. *Capitalism and Slavery.* Chapel Hill: University of North Carolina Press.

Wolfe, Patrick. 2006. "Settler Colonialism and the Elimination of the Native." *Journal of Genocide Research* 8 (4): 387–409.

Yusoff, Kathryn. 2018. *A Billion Black Anthropocenes or None.* Minneapolis: University of Minnesota Press.

Part II

UNDEAD SPACES AND "ZONES" OF THE ANTHROPOCENE

Chapter 4

The Uncanny Valley of the Anthropocene

Short Stories about the Undead under the Brightest of Lights

Nils Bubandt

With Anna Tsing and a group of brilliant and innovative collaborators from anthropology, biology, and science studies, I had the pleasure for some years of being involved in a cross-disciplinary project to study the more-than-human relations and capitalist-colonial histories in which the ecological and political disruptions, often referred to as the Anthropocene, are made. The project *AURA: Aarhus University Research on the Anthropocene* sought to establish a transdisciplinary dialogue between the natural and human sciences to understand the Anthropocene not merely as a temporal epoch but as a particular kind of spatiality, namely a disrupted cospecies and historical landscape (www.anthropocene.au.dk). We defined the landscape of the Anthropocene as patchy (Bubandt, Mathews, and Tsing 2019), an archipelagic space of differences and connections made by the ghosts of multispecies histories and the monsters of co-species entanglement (Tsing et al. 2017), and we proposed that the ghostly and monstrous archipelago of the Anthropocene was amenable to concrete study through a set of critical multispecies methodologies that we suggested calling "rubber boots methods" (Bubandt, Andersen, and Cypher 2022).

My own entry into this project—and my interest in the Anthropocene as a provocative and far from unproblematic concept that nevertheless also seemed like an invitation to a novel and urgent transdisciplinary field of study in a changing world—came from several decades of research into the world of spirits, witches, ghosts, and ancestors in Indonesia. From this angle, living in the Anthropocene reminded me of the particular kind of life with witches and spirits I had experienced and studied for more than two decades in Indonesia. My ethnographic experience and studies of a life with witches has led me to be critical of the conventional idea that spirits, witches, ghosts, and ancestors were objects of belief with symbolic meaning or social functions that somehow grew from political and historical reality. Instead, I suggested that they were better understood as abjects or aporias. Spirits, witches, and ancestors are not fully "there" to the people in Indonesia that I know, neither as objects nor as subjects to be sensed or believed in. Rather, spirits, witches, ghosts, and ancestors are aporias: impossible and intractable problems, the experience of which has no meaningful culmination (Bubandt 2014a).

The impossible reality of witches comes from their many impossible contradictions. Witches on the island of Halmahera cannot be seen, except out of the corners of your eyes. Their screams appear faint when they are in fact close and loud when they are far away. They are spirits that can possess the body of any human, and that human can then assume any form: become a plant, an animal, or an object at will. Such a witch-person is filled with an insatiable hunger for human liver, so it hunts other humans, dislodging its head from its own body to fly out in search of human prey. When it attacks a human victim, it robs that victim of its memory of the event. And yet the witch itself lives without memory of its own actions. Anyone can be a witch, but no one can really know for sure. Witches cannot be truly seen or heard. They cannot be remembered or known. They are a being without a body that can take any bodily form. They can be anyone, even yourself. And you would not even know it.

All of this means that witches on the island of Halmahera do not exist *as such*. Indeed, if they did exist unproblematically, they would not be such a conundrum both to the senses and to the common-sense on this island. Rather, their nature is to haunt corporeal existence and experience in unpredictable yet often undeniable ways that leave imprints on the way social relations are handled, the self is understood, history (un)remembered, and the future anticipated (Bubandt 2009, 2014a, 2014b). Anthropology—and the rest of us moderns—might usefully dispense, so I argued on the basis of my witchcraft studies, with our belief in belief and ontology if we want to study the hauntology and hyper-objectivity of spirits, ghosts and witches. This also means abandoning the barren choice between, on the one hand, a rational, skeptical view of spirits that sees them as either survivals from a superstitious past or epiphenomena to "real" historical dynamics and, on the other hand, an ontological perspective that tries to "take them seriously" but reifies them as "real" in the process and loses an analytical focus on the doubt that attends them from beginning to end (Bubandt 2016).

Thinking of spirits through doubt rather than belief allows for a particular intervention into the Anthropocene as a time-space in which old certainties about the separation of the world of humans from the world of other beings and about modern narratives about progress are collapsing. This intervention is necessary to understand how the end of modern certitude in the Anthropocene is also the reemergence, in a novel and uncanny form, of those animate powers beyond the human that rational modernity denied and romantic modernity sought to cultivate as modernity's "other." The Anthropocene, in short, is the emergence in a new form of the uncanny. When nature is not what it seemed, when nature is no longer thinkable, because modern industrial practices have turned the-phenomenon-formerly-known-as-nature into a myriad of uncontrollable and unpredictable entities that animate our current crisis, then nature has become preternatural—the Renaissance word for miraculous phenomena that escaped the horizons of science. Preternatural phenomena in the Renaissance included all the wonders of the natural world—such the sheep-trees of Persia and the birds-of-paradise from the Far East—as well as spirits, specters, and the undead. The preternatural described the exceptions to the natural order of nature (Daston and Park 2001). It strikes me that the Anthropocene is perhaps best characterized as the unexpected proliferation of preternatural exceptions to the natural order of the world. In the Anthropocene more storms will be freak storms, more endangered species will go extinct, more wildfires will run wild. The only truth about the chaos that is the future that is certain is that it will be more chaotic than we can imagine. The natural order of things is increasingly replaced by an acceleration of the unpredictability, the disorder, and the unthinkability of things. In the Anthropocene, the preternatural proliferates. The space of this proliferation—*as an effect of the way modern industrial practices produce a world increasingly unthinkable through its own categories*—I call the uncanny valley of the Anthropocene.

The concept of the uncanny valley comes from the Japanese robotics engineer, Masahiro Mori. In 1970, Mori coined the term "the uncanny valley" to refer to the experiential space that opens up when technology begins to assume a human likeness in ways that feels uncanny and weird rather than familiar and homely. This space of human-like nonhumans was traditionally the monopoly of the undead: corpses, ghosts, spirits, and zombies. But Mori suggested that technologically engineered objects like prosthetic hands also fall into this uncanny valley (see the dotted line in figure 4.1). A prosthetic hand feels uncanny and discomforting when it has the fleshy look and feel of a human hand and yet has something unfamiliar about it at the same time (Mori 2012). Like the witches I studied in Indonesia, robots with human-like hands are pretend-humans that are not quite human. This makes them uncanny.

I argue, however, that Mori's schematics of the uncanny valley need to be rethought for the Anthropocene. Since 1970 the valley of the uncanny has widened and become crowded at an accelerated pace with new beings and

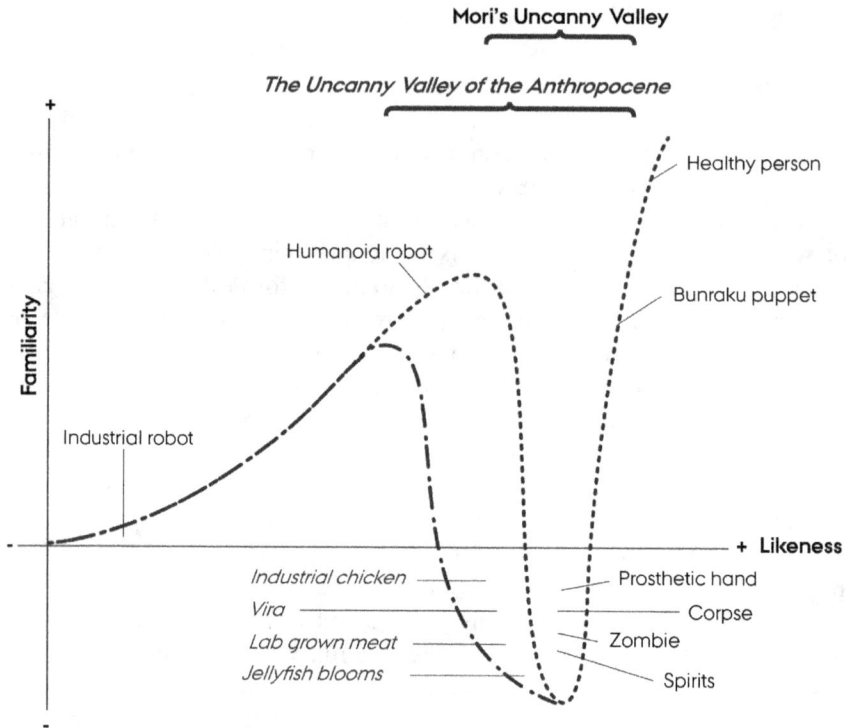

Figure 4.1   Masahiro Mori's Uncanny Valley, modified for the Anthropocene. Image: reproduced with permission by Louise Hilmar.

phenomena far stranger than robotic hands and zombies. Advances in genetic technology and bioengineering have added cloned animals, gene-modified crops, lab-grown meat, and a host of other familiar-yet-strange denizens to the uncanny valley of our time. And the overpopulation of the uncanny valley of our time has arguably exploded after the effects of anthropogenic environmental disturbance have become undeniable. Jelly fish blooms, freak storms, and factory chicken are examples of denaturalized nature that produce a new kind of uncanniness (see the line of dashes and dots in figure 4.1).

In the Anthropocene, the uncanny is no longer merely produced by entities that look human but that in fact are not. Rather, the valley of the uncanny has been widened by the accelerated industrial and scientific production of unnatural nature. We might call this an environmental uncanny. What are we, for instance, to make of the fact that the total biomass of the 20 billion chickens in the world's industrial mega-farms is three times that of all wild birds combined? (Bar-On, Phillips, and Miloa 2018). A chicken is a very familiar bird for sure. But when the industrial chicken is well on its way to becoming the most numerous, and one day soon perhaps the only, bird in the world, its very familiarity takes on a distinctly uncanny hue. If the uncanny may be defined as a "crisis of the natural" (Royle 2003,1), the industrial chicken is but one uncanny facet of a multifaceted uncanniness in the Anthropocene. The uncanny valley of the Anthropocene is that experiential space in the contemporary world where old divisions collapse—not only the divisions between humans and nonhumans or society and nature but also the divisions between fact and belief and between "them" and "us" that hold modern experience and sensibilities in check (Latour 1993). In the uncanny valley of the Anthropocene, robotic hands and vira share space with zombies while fish blooms share space with ghosts in ways that unsettle the dichotomies between nature and culture as well as between science and fiction.

If the kind of undead that seem to belong to the realm of superstition and imagination increasingly cohabit with the undead beings that are the products of natural science and modern industry, how are we to understand this cohabitation? It violates, after all, a central tenet of modernity: that science and modern industry deal in facts, while popular (and primitive) superstitions about ghosts, spirits and the undead are a matter of belief (Latour 2010). This is where my own modest contribution to spirits, witches, and ghosts, not as objects of belief but as aporias of doubt may be useful. It allows a comparative angle on the doubts of witchcraft and the doubts of the Anthropocene that sees them as similar phenomena. In the plausible worlds of the Anthropocene, climate change is as uncanny and truth-like—characterized by the same verisimilitude—as organ-stealing witches and colonial wild men (Bubandt 2017, 2019). This has consequences for the kind of transdisciplinarity required to understand multi-species life and death in the Anthropocene. Anthropocene scholarship needs not merely a natural science and a critical human and social science to understand what is happening at the cusp between humans and nonhumans. It also needs a critical nonsecular approach—that is unafraid of but also not naïvely infatuated with the world of spirits and the undead—in order to understand what happens when the natural world increasingly becomes preternatural and uncanny.

Take climate change. Many people across an ordinarily sun-starved northern Europe welcomed the exceptionally warm May of 2018 as an early start to a great summer. But already by the end of May, it had become clear that it was going to be the hottest month of May on record in the northern parts of Europe and the contiguous US (NOAA 2018). And the heat just continued. The hottest temperature ever in Africa was recorded in Algeria in the summer of 2018, and temperature records were broken in Taiwan, Central Asia, Europe, Canada, and the Western US (Watts 2018a). What was initially experienced as a pleasantly warm weather streak by heat-starved northern Europeans was by July revealed as the hottest El Niña year on record. The hemispheric scale of the heat meant that it began, eerily, to point to more than itself. In early July 2018, a group of leading climate scientists hypothesized that positive feedback loops between changing climate, ocean currents, and other Earth systems could cause cascading effects that would catapult Earth into a "hothouse" state well before existing predictions. The summer of 2018 became an example of this run-away dynamic. This, they suggested, would have massive effects on global environment, societies, and economies (Steffen et al. 2018). Hoping against all hope that they were wrong, one of the authors said that it was urgent to pose this possibility in the context of the unexpected nature of the ongoing summer heatwave of 2018. It was, in fact, "one of the most urgent existential questions in science" (Watts 2018b). In the course of a few months in 2018, weather had gone from being pleasant to existential. It had become uncanny and at once familiar and strange, urgent, and unknowable. In response, science became existential philosophy: a matter not merely of facts but of our experience of the phenomenal world. And this meant something. It meant a shift in how it is possible to experience future weather in the Northern Hemisphere. After 2018, it has arguably become impossible to enjoy a sunny day in the Global North without a certain *frisson*—an emotional shiver that is at once existential and epistemological. Climate change is based on science at every turn, and yet it feels uncannily like an encounter with a spirit.

The Anthropocene, so it seems to me, *is* a time of spirits. In fact, in many ways the Anthropocene is itself a specter. Molten, multiple, and disputed (Swanson, Bubandt, and Tsing 2015), the Anthropocene "is" not in any unproblematic sense. Rather, the Anthropocene presents itself as an undeniable impossibility, an intractable problem, and a future-to-come that unsettles the certainties of a modern common-sense, including history, self, and sociality. As the ontological distinction between "nature" and "culture" dissolves in a world of anthropogenic climate change, human-made extinction cascades, and pandemics driven by industrial ecosystem disruptions, history, self, and sociality assume different shapes, too. History, sociality and the human self, it turns out, were never only human. Other actors—carbon, invasive species, and viruses, for example—have forcefully entered the stage of the modern understanding of the world, a stage that until not so long ago allowed for only humans to be real actors. Nonhuman lives were props in a politics of humans. Now, it seems, the props on stage have come alive.

The Anthropocene is also like a spirit in a second sense: as with spirits, the modern approach to the Anthropocene has frequently taken the form of either disbelief or exhortations to take it all too seriously. The first approach is to disbelieve the Anthropocene. This approach allows us moderns to dream of a climatic regime in which we are able to isolate ourselves and our nations from the effects of the Anthropocene through the dams and fences of our favorite political imaginary (Latour 2017). Alternatively, disbelief allows the Anthropocene—like a spirit—to appear to us as an epiphenomenon of the "real" forces of modern science and capitalism. All we need to do is to tweak those forces of reality to make the Anthropocene disappear. If we only recycle more, create larger natural reserves, scale down consumption, turn capitalism green, nano-engineer the best vaccines and geo-engineer the stratosphere, we imagine that the spirit that is the Anthropocene will disappear under a bright and white new sky (Kolbert 2021). In this scenario, the Anthropocene might even be a Great Anthropocene: a second chance for human ingenuity (Asafu-Adjaye et al. 2015). But even this rational and brightly modern Anthropocene is haunted by a spirit—a Holy Spirit. It entails, after all, a human apotheosis. In the early eighteenth century, the German philosopher Gottfried Wilhelm Leibniz solved the question of why an omnipotent God would allow evil to exist by suggesting that God had the ability to create an infinite number of worlds. The present world might be full of problems, but it was still the best of all these possible worlds. As Clive Hamilton has pointed out, the idea of a Great Anthropocene similarly suggests that humans, if we only are ingenious enough, can be makers—like the God of Leibniz—of the best of all possible worlds (Hamilton 2015).

The Anthropocene, in short, has generated two conventional responses. The first is to deny it. The second and only other approach to the Anthropocene available to us moderns, it would seem, is to take it all too seriously. This option is like the ontological turn that insists on taking spirits seriously but ends up taking them all too literally. Taking the Anthropocene all too seriously is the perspective that has brought us a proliferation of apocalyptic scenarios (Swyngedouw 2010; Weisman 2007). This is the approach from which we are also usually invited to think about the undead in the Anthropocene: as zombies in *The Walking Dead*. I am, however, interested here in another kind of undead, namely the kind that comes not as harbingers of the apocalypse, but as signs of "something else."

For surely, there is a third option available in response to the Anthropocene? An alternative to the impossible choice between "techno-theocratic geoengineering fixes and wallowing in despair" which, as Donna Haraway points out, infects "any possible common imagination" in the current moment (Haraway 2016, 56)? Thinking of the Anthropocene as a spectral moment of doubt and aporia is for me such an alternative. If we think of the Anthropocene as a time (and space) of spirits—and think of spirits not as objects of belief but as ruptures of a common-sense, as those moments of experience that are interminable and cannot find a proper place in language or meaning—it also allows a route into a mode of thinking that Timothy Morton calls "ecological" and which he describes as a shadow of an idea not yet fully thought:

It has to do with amazement, open-mindedness, and wonder. It has to do with doubt, confusion, and skepticism. It has to do with concepts of space and time. It has to do with delight, beauty, ugliness, disgust, irony, and pain. It has to do with consciousness and awareness. It has to do with ideology and critique. It has to do with reading and writing. It has to do with race, class, and gender. It has to do with sexuality. It has to do with ideas of self and the weird paradoxes of subjectivity. It has to do with society. It has to do with coexistence. (Morton 2010, 41–44)

Ecology for Morton is more-than-human, but it is also more than merely about nature and the environment. It is about the forms of connections between humans and other beings that emerge at every turn, and which make the world both an enchanted and uncanny place: "Ecological thought imagines a multitude of entangled strange strangers" (212), beings that seem familiar but nevertheless inhabit the limits of our imagination. That limit is now occupied by many kinds of beings, but it is also archetypically the hiding place of spirits. The Holocene might have taught us moderns to expect spirits only "in the wild": in the dark regions of the popular imagination, urban legends, and backward cultures. In the Anthropocene, however, spirits, ghosts, and a multitude of other forms of the undead well up under the florescent lights of science and industry. I will paint an outline of this uncanny valley through "short stories" of two of the undead denizens of the uncanny valley of the Anthropocene. The first story is about a virus and its destabilization of what life and death—and by implication politics—are. The second story is about a tardigrade and its disruption of time-space and, by implication, being and reality.

SHORT STORY 1: VIRAL CREEP

"The coronavirus isn't alive. That's why it's so hard to kill," read the headline of an article in *The Washington Post* (Kaplan, Wan, and Achenbach 2020). Published only two weeks after the WHO had declared COVID-19 a global pandemic, the article from late March 2020 goes on to spell out the strange scientific status of SARS-CoV-2, a novel type of coronavirus that was the cause of the pandemic. Since then, we have all learned to become amateur virologists. Still, the virus is as strange as ever. According to classical standards of biology, a virus is not alive because it lacks the minimal characteristics of living beings: autopoesis, reproduction, metabolism, and mobility. A virus does nothing until it enters a cell. It is not autopoetic, because it cannot reproduce outside of other living cells. A virus does not convert energy or metabolize. A virus does not move; rather, it is moved. Viruses are therefore not alive, if you ask most biologists. They are "at best chemical zombies," as Lynn Margulis and Dorian Sagan put it (2000, 18).

And yet, viruses are clearly also not just dead. After all, even if viruses are not alive, they are still carriers of the building blocks of life: the genetic information encoded in molecules known as DNA and RNA. And this is not the only viral paradox. Metabolic life conforms to the second law of thermodynamics: it takes in energy, uses it to create an internal order but in doing so increases disorder in the universe around it by producing heat, waste, noise and uncertainty (19). The recent discovery of giant viruses that appear to reproduce semi-autonomously inside of the cells they infect have now challenged the notion that viruses are not metabolic creatures (Claverie and Abergel 2010). And even if a virus has no metabolism, it is still—like a living cell—an internal order that creates entropic chaos in the world around it as an effect of its being. In March 2020, the world was massively disrupted by the SARS-CoV-2 virus and in the first month 15,000 people had been killed by it. A year later WHO put the global number of corona deaths at 2.6 million, but the actual number was likely at least twice as high, and extremely unevenly divided across nations, ethnic, and social groups (Dyer 2021). For a nonliving entity, the SARS-CoV-2 virus generated a massive amount of entropy: chaos, heat, noise, and uncertainty. Faced with the dead-undead paradox of viruses, some scientists have opted in favor of a non-binary solution. *The Washington Post* quotes Gary Whittaker, a Cornell University professor of virology, as suggesting that the SARS-CoV-2 virus switches between being alive and dead (See figure 4.2). It exists "somewhere between chemistry and biology" (Kaplan, Wan, and Achenbach 2020). This confusion is not novel. Already in 1935, after chemist Wendell Stanley succeeded in isolating the tobacco mosaic virus, an RNA-based virus like SARS-CoV-2 and the first virus to be discovered, and then allowed it to crystalize before demonstrating that the virus could still infect tobacco plants even after months in crystalized form, *The New York Times* wrote that the "old distinction between life and death loses some of its validity" (Zimmer 2015:8).

Austrian psychologist Sigmund Freud (1976) famously described how the feeling of dread associated with the uncanny was related to its transgression of the separation between the familiar and the unfamiliar, as when the separation between the living and the dead, between the imaginary and the real, between the virtual and the actual is violated. A dead body can, under certain circumstances, be uncanny, but a zombie is much more uncanny, exactly because it violates familiar conventions of death (by moving and seemingly wanting things). Viruses have been uncanny to science and the popular imagination for almost a century because of their zombie-like nature. But their uncanniness has arguably increased in recent years as the double dead-yet-alive nature of SARS-CoV-2 and other viruses has become more vexing.

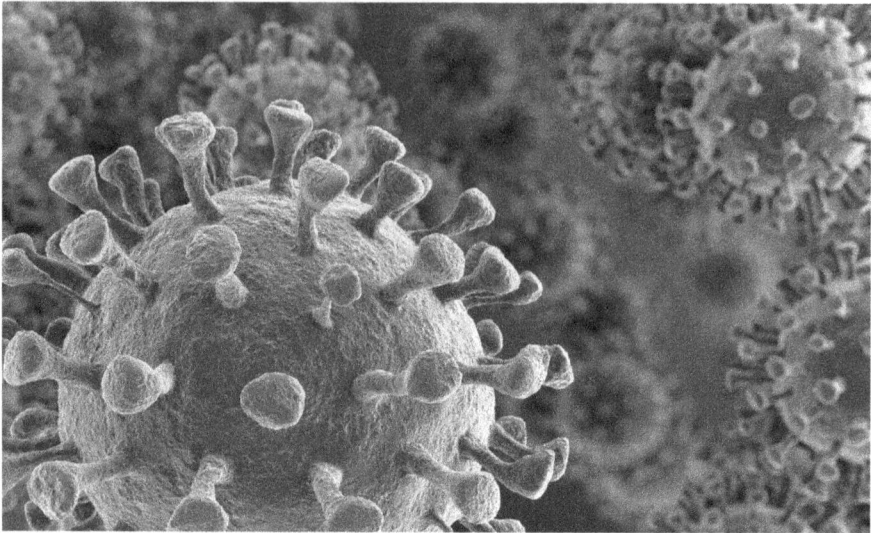

Figure 4.2 Microscope 3D-Rendering of Coronavirus 2019-nCov. Photo: shutterstock/
creativeneko.

On the one hand, the pandemic has taught us all to be DIY-virologists and demonstrated how a virus can remodel everything from the global economy and state governance to the way we interact and even dream. On the other hand, while the global response to the corona pandemic centered on the protection of human life from the effects of viral infection, the definition of "life" itself has been undermined by science. This undermining of the notion of "life" has happened not merely in virology but also in the study of artificial life as well as in "limit biologies" such as synthetic biology, astrobiology, and marine biology, all of which threaten to topple common certainties about the meaning of "life" itself by making the "nature" that is supposed to ground life unstable (Helmreich 2016,16). The idea that "true" life is autopoetic has for instance been challenged by the epigenetic discovery that life always exists and evolves "sympoetically," in association with other life (Gilbert 2014; Sapp 1994). Viruses have emerged as a key player here. Not only are viruses the most abundant biological entity on Earth—with an estimated 10^{31} existing in the ocean alone. Viruses, it turns out, also appear to have been intimately involved in the emergence of life on this planet. This has led to the development of a new field called "astrovirology" which proposes focusing on viruses as the most likely model of life on other planets, too (Berliner, Mochizuki, and Stedman 2018). The irony that a nonliving entity was involved in the emergence of life on Earth and may also be the most apt candidate for life in the universe is not lost on anyone in this field. The prevailing view now is that the problem is not only our understanding of the virus but also our definition of "life." "Life," it is suggested, may not be a useful scientific category at all (Mariscal and Doolittle 2020). But with life out of the frame of the natural order, what uncanny crisis are we left with? What, one might ask, comes after life, if not death? Doubt? What happens, for instance, as Stefan Helmreich asks, to modern (bio)politics—defined as the calculation, administration, and organization of life (Foucault 1980; Rose 2006)—when the idea of life itself "delaminates, escapes itself"? (Helmreich 2016, 3).

The SARS-CoV-2 virus is an example of viral creep, "the ability of a creeping, only partially knowable virus to rearrange relations among people, animals, and objects" in ways that exceeds human attempts at containment, control, and understanding (Lowe and Münster 2016, 118). Like other viruses, such as the elephant endotheliotropic herpesvirus, studied by Lowe and Münster, which poses an existential threat to the Asian elephant, the SARS-CoV-2 virus is "creeping" because it advances unseen—even under the bright lights of scientific scrutiny, the SARS-CoV-2 virus likely existed undetected for decades in populations of horseshoe bats (*Rhinolophus affinis*) before it spilled over to humans (Boni et al. 2020)—and uncontrollably in spite of state lock-downs. Viral creep is therefore also "creepy" because it introduces uncertainty and doubt into the very categories and narratives of control upon which modern politics and self-understanding is built. The irony of the Anthropocene is that the doubts that accompany the uncanny emerge not from the dark corners of backward superstition or the black boxes of popular media but rather from the bright spaces of cutting-edge scientific rationalism and calculation.

SHORT STORY 2: WATER BEAR ON A WIRE

Tardigrades, also known as water bears, are a phylum of micro-animals with over 1,200 species (See figure 4.3). Extremely hardy creatures, tardigrades are found in almost every habitat on earth, on land as well as in water (Schill 2019). Some land-based tardigrades have an ability called cryptobiosis that allows them to lay dormant for decades, entirely desiccated, only to come back to life, when conditions change. Other species of tardigrades are so robust that scientists predict they will be able to survive almost any astronomical (or human-caused) disaster that one can imagine on Earth. Tardigrades can, for instance, withstand radiation energy blasts that would be enough to evaporate the planet's oceans. Tardigrades might literally survive the end of the world (Temming 2017), a hardiness that has made them model animals in space research and astrobiology (Weronika and Łukasz 2017). Like viruses, tardigrades teeter at the limit of life. Like viruses, this has ironically made tardigrades the ideal model for alien life forms and the possibility that life might seed itself throughout the cosmos. And like viruses, tardigrades are among the candidates to be the first travelers into another kind space as well, namely quantum reality (Romero-Isart et al. 2010).

In 1935, the same year as chemist Wendel Stanley conducted his experiments on tobacco mosaic viruses to show they were both alive and dead; the Austrian-Irish physicist Erwin Schrödinger described a thought experiment involving a cat. The cat is experimentally put into a quantum superposition of the same kind in which atoms exist. According to the quantum theory of Niels Bohr and Werner Heisenberg, an atom in superposition is indeterminate—it is in multiple positions at the same, simultaneously existing and not-existing in any given place—until it is observed by the scientist. Meant to expose the "ridiculous" logic of Bohr and Heisenberg's theory, Schrödinger claimed the cat would be both alive and not alive until observed (Trimmer 1980). But as has happened in biology, life has become stranger in quantum physics since the 1930s. No longer a ridiculous thought experiment, life in a superposition of being both dead and live is now a matter of serious experimental research (Clegg 2019). Today, experimental quantum physics, keen to test where the mind-bending laws of quantum mechanics end and the physical laws of "classical reality" begin, are proposing to test Schrödinger's thought experiment on tardigrades. After successfully creating superpositions in individual and collections of atoms and photons, there are now plans to take the next

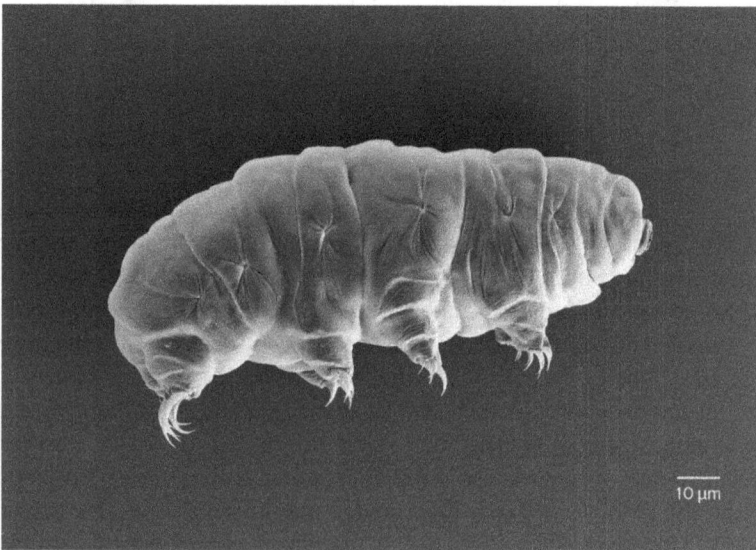

Figure 4.3   Tardigrade (Water Bear). 3D-Rendered Illustration. Photo: Shutterstock/3Dstock.

logical steps into the animal kingdom. Dutch scientists propose to place a tardigrade on a millimeter-size silicon nitride membrane. Using a laser beam, the researchers hope to bring the membrane into an oscillation pattern that is so fast that it, and the tardigrade on it, will be pushed into a quantum superposition—a condition of being where the tardigrade would be nowhere and everywhere on the oscillation curve at the same time (Folger 2018). The tardigrade in a quantum superposition would cease to "be there" in any classical physical or common-sensical way. It would be the first biological entity to be scientifically induced into a ghostly state of pure potentiality. Like the witches I have studied in Indonesia, the tardigrade would be unavailable to a common-sense understanding of being. Uncannily, it would be alive and not-alive, be-there and not-there at the same time. Only hardy creatures can endure such radical indeterminacy. Tardigrades in quantum reality are like the witches I studied in Indonesia: impossible beings that are there and not-there at the same time.

CONCLUSION: THE NEW UNCANNY

The modern understanding of the world is held in place, Bruno Latour (1993) argues, by a belief in two oppositions or distinctions. The first distinction separates things that are natural from those that belong to the world of humans. This distinction sorts the world of natural phenomena and facts from the world of culture, fiction, and politics. This distinction also separates beings that are alive and have agency from objects that are dead. The second distinction separates "us moderns"—who live in the conviction that we are able to tell fact from fiction and animals from monsters—from those that are not modern (the primitive or exotic people who live in the tropics, the countryside and other places of uneducated superstition) and who habitually mix up fact and belief, animals and spirits all the time.

The strange strangers discussed in this chapter—industrial chickens, pandemic viruses, excessively warm summer days and quantum mechanical tardigrades—unsettle the first distinction by introducing the undead as a scientific fact beyond the limits of life itself. When the undead move from backward superstition to scientific superposition, they rattle not only the first distinction between the facts of life and human fiction, they also throw the second distinction—the one that guarantees the ability of "us moderns" (unlike our superstitious cousins) to tell animals from monsters—into radical doubt. In the Anthropocene, zombies and viruses, climate change and ghosts, tardigrades and witches are indexes of the same uncanniness. The Anthropocene is an increasingly crowded uncanny valley where the modern distinctions between fact and fiction, between reason and superstition are crumbling. This crumbling of a modern world order is itself an element in the uncanniness of the Anthropocene.

The Anthropocene requires in that sense also a reappraisal of Sigmund Freud's notion of the uncanny to dislodge it from its modern roots. There is no doubt that for his time, Freud's early twentieth-century analysis of the uncanny was both transgressive and novel. Still, Freud's notion of the uncanny is very much a product of a modern fantasy of the world that was convinced it could separate fact from fiction and the modern rational world from the world of superstition. Rejecting the idea that the feeling of unease, eeriness and discomfort inherent in the uncanny or *das Unheimliche* is evoked merely by that which is novel or unfamiliar, Freud began instead in the observation that in the German language the adjective *heimlich* denoted not just the homely, familiar and intimate but also referred to the tameness of domesticated animals as well as to that which was secret, magic or hidden from view (Freud 1976, 620). The equation of the uncanny with the unfamiliar, Freud observed, was therefore incomplete and even misleading. The uncanny was not so much a feeling of unease generated by the unknown or unfamiliar. Rather, the uncanny was generated by the eruption of a wild and secret unfamiliarity that haunts the familiar itself. The uncanniness of *das Unheimliche* referred to the wild, hidden secret that attended the known world, in particular the intimate and apparently tamed world of familiar things. Still, Freud's notion of the uncanny was a very modern concept. After all, Freud's interest in the uncanny stemmed from his theory of psychological repression. The uncanny, he suggested, "proceeds from something familiar which has been repressed" (638). A severed hand, for instance, was uncanny because it was a return of the repressed fear of castration, or the fear of being buried alive emerged as the return of a repressed desire for intra-uterine existence. As befitted his nineteenth century, middle-class viewpoint, Freud made a direct link between castration anxieties and other "infantile" psychological fantasies and so-called primitive beliefs. In the same way that being buried alive was uncanny to a person with infantile fantasies of returning to the womb, ghosts were for Freud uncanny to the secular mind when they appeared as a return of repressed primitive beliefs about the dead.

> We—or our primitive forefathers—once believed that these possibilities [of sorcerous power, the return of the dead or other uncanny phenomena that Freud associated with "primitive" animism] were realities, and were convinced that they actually happened. Nowadays we no longer believe in them, we have surmounted these modes of thought; but we do not feel quite sure of our new beliefs, and the old ones still exist within us ready to seize upon any confirmation. (639)

The uncanny for Freud was a feeling that assaults a failed ideal of modern subjectivity. It erupts either from the return of irrational beliefs that Western modernity thought to have surmounted or from repressed psychological complexes that similarly have no proper place in the rational mind. Just as a psychologically aware person will feel nothing uncanny about severed hands or being buried alive because they have effectively dealt with their psychological repressions, the truly secular and modern mind "who has completely and finally rid himself [sic] of animistic beliefs will be insensible" to an uncanny reaction to ghosts, sorcery or the living dead. For Freud, the uncanny signaled a failure of an ideal modern subjectivity. The well-balanced—distinctly Western, secular, and male—subject would find nothing uncanny, because he was able to securely distinguish fiction, animism and neurosis from fact. As Freud put it: "The whole thing is purely an affair of 'reality-testing,' a question of the material reality of the phenomena" (639).

However, Freud's conviction that for the rational and psycho-analyzed mind the uncanny was a merely matter of fact is no longer tenable, because the uncanny in the Anthropocene infects the realm of scientific reality-testing itself. In the uncanny valley of the Anthropocene, the scientific and material reality of phenomena—from climate chemistry to virology—is now the site in which the uncanny is produced, not the site of its eradication. The truly uncanny nature of the Anthropocene therefore is that the proliferation of the undead and other strange strangers in its rapidly overpopulated uncanny valley happens not at the margins of the real—in the shadows of superstition or the black boxes of the popular imagination—but rather in the most authoritative modern centers of the real and under the brightest of scientific lights.

WORKS CITED

Asafu-Adjaye, John, Linus Blomqvist, Stewart Brand, Barry Brook, et al. 2015. *An Ecomodernist Manifesto.* Available at http://www.ecomodernism.org/manifesto. Accessed October 8, 2016.

Bar-On, Yinon M., Rob Phillips, and Ron Miloa. 2018. The Biomass Distribution on Earth. *PNAS* 115 (25), 6506–5611.

Berliner, Aaron, Tomohiro Mochizuki, and Kenneth Stedman. 2018. Astrovirology: Viruses at Large in the Universe. *Astrobiology* 18 (2), 207–223.

Boni, Maciej F., Philippe Lemey, Xiaowei Jiang, Tommy Tsan-Yuk Lam et al. 2020. Evolutionary Origins of the SARS-CoV-2 Sarbecovirus Lineage Responsible for the COVID-19 Pandemic. *Nature Microbiology* 5 (11), 1408–1417.

Bubandt, Nils. 2009. Interview with an Ancestor: Spirits as Informants and the Politics of Possession in North Maluku *Ethnography* 10 (3), 291–316.

———. 2014a. *The Empty Seashell. Witchcraft and Doubt on an Indonesian Island.* Ithaca: Cornell University Press.

——. 2014b. *Democracy, Corruption and the Politics of Spirits in Contemporary Indonesia, Modern Anthropology of Southeast Asia*. London: Routledge.

——. 2016. Book Symposium. When in Doubt . . .? A Reply. *HAU: Journal of Ethnographic Theory* 6 (1), 519–530.

——. 2017. From Head-hunter to Organ-thief: Verisimilitude, Doubt, and Plausible Worlds in Indonesia and Beyond. *Oceania* 87 (1), 38–57.

——. 2019. Of Wildmen and White Men: Cryptozoology and Inappropriate/d Monsters at the Cusp of the Anthropocene. *Journal of the Royal Anthropological Institute* 25 (2), 223–240.

Bubandt, Nils, Astrid Oberbeck Andersen, and Rachel Antoinette Cypher, eds. 2022. *Rubber Boots Methods for the Anthropocene. Curiosity, Collaboration and Critical Observation in Multispecies Fieldwork*. Minneapolis: Minnesota University Press.

Bubandt, Nils, Andrew Mathews, and Anna Tsing. 2019. Patchy Anthropocene. The Frenzies and Afterlives of Violent Simplifications. Special issue of *Current Anthropology*. Wenner-Gren Symposium Supplement 20.

Claverie, Jean-Michel, and Chantal Abergel. 2010. Mimivirus: The Emerging Paradox of Quasi-Autonomous Viruses. *Trends in Genetics* 26 (10), 431–437.

Clegg, Brian. 2019. Quantum Theory: The Weird World of Teleportation, Tardigrades and Entanglement. *ScienceFocus*, 23 January 2019.

Daston, Lorraine, and Katharine Park. 2001. *Wonders and the Order of Nature, 1150-1750*. New York: Zone Books.

Dyer, Owen. 2021. Covid-19: Study Claims Real Global Deaths Are Twice Official Figures. *BMJ* 373: n1088. DOI: https://doi.org/10.1136/bmj.n1188.

Folger, Tim. 2018. Crossing the Quantum Divide. *Scientific American* 319 (1), 20–27.

Foucault, Michel. 1980. *The History of Sexuality. Volume 1: An Introduction*. New York: Vintage Books.

Freud, Sigmund. 1976. The "Uncanny" (trans. James Strachey, original 1919). *New Literary History* 7 (3), 619–645.

Gilbert, Scott F. 2014. Symbiosis as the Way of Eukaryotic Life: The Dependent Co-Origination of the Body. *Journal of Bioscience* 39 (2), 201–209.

Hamilton, Clive. 2015. The Theodicy of the "Good Anthropocene." *Environmental Humanities* 7, 233–238.

Haraway, Donna. 2016. *Staying with the Trouble. Making Kin in the Chthulucene*. Durham: Duke University Press.

Helmreich, Stefan. 2016. *Sounding the Limits of Life. Essays in the Anthropology of Biology and Beyond*. Princeton: Princeton University Press.

Kaplan, Sarah, William Wan, and Joel Achenbach. 2020. The Coronavirus Isn't Alive. That's Why It's So Hard to Kill. *Washington Post*, March 23, 2020.

Kolbert, Elizabeth. 2021. *Under a White Sky. The Nature of the Future*. New York: Crown.

Latour, Bruno. 1993. *We Have Never Been Modern*. New York: Harvester/ Wheatsheaf.

——. 2010. *On the Modern Cult of the Factish Gods*. Durham: Duke University Press.

——. 2017. *Facing Gaia: Eight Lectures on the New Climatic Regime*. London: Polity Press.

Lowe, Celia, and Ursula Münster. 2016. The Viral Creep: Elephants and Herpes in Times of Extinction. *Environmental Humanities* 8 (1), 118–142.

Margulis, Lynn, and Dorian Sagan. 2000. *What is Life? The Eternal Enigma*. Berkeley: University of California Press.

Mariscal, Carlos, and W. Ford Doolittle. 2020. Life and Life Only: A Radical Alternative to Life Definitionism. *Synthese (Dordrecht)* 197 (7), 2975–2989.

Mori, Masahiro. 2012. The Uncanny Valley [original 1970, trans. by K. F. MacDorman and N. Kageki]. *IEEE Robotics & Automation Magazine* 19 (2), 98–100.

Morton, Timothy. 2010. *The Ecological Thought*. Cambridge, MA: Harvard University Press.

NOAA. 2018. Contiguous U.S. Had Its Warmest May on Record. *National Oceanic and Atmospheric Administration. News and Features*, 6 June.

Romero-Isart, Oriol, Mathieu L. Juan, Romain Quidant, and J. Ignacio Cirac. 2010. Toward Quantum Superposition of Living Organisms. *New Journal of Physics* 12 (3), 033015.

Rose, Nikolas. 2006. *The Politics of Life Itself: Biomedicine, Power, and Subjectivity in the Twenty-First Century*. Princeton: Princeton University Press.

Royle, Nicolas. 2003. *Jacques Derrida, Routledge Critical Thinkers*. London: Routledge.

Sapp, Jan. 1994. *Evolution by Association. A History of Symbiosis*. New York: Oxford University Press.

Schill, Ralph. 2019. *Water Bears: The Biology of Tardigrades, Zoological Monographs*. Dordrecht: Springer International Publishing.

Steffen, Will, Johan Rockström, Katherine Richardson, Timothy M. Lenton et al. 2018. Trajectories of the Earth System in the Anthropocene. *Proceedings of the National Academy of Sciences of the United States of America* 115 (33), 8252–8259.

Swanson, Heather, Nils Bubandt, and Anna Tsing. 2015. Less than One but More than Many: Anthropocene as Science Fiction and Scholarship-in-the-making. *Environment and Society: Advances in Research* 6, 149–166.

Swyngedouw, Erik. 2010. Apocalypse Forever? *Theory, Culture & Society* 27 (2–3), 213–232.

Temming, Maria. 2017. Water Bears Will Survive the End of the World As We Know It. *ScienceNews*, https://www.sciencenews.org/article/water-bears-will-survive-end-world-we-know-it. Accessed October 1, 2021.

Trimmer, John. 1980. The Present Situation in Quantum Mechanics: A Translation of Schrödinger's "Cat Paradox" Paper. *Proceedings of the American Philosophical Society* 124 (5), 323–338.

Tsing, Anna, Heather Anne Swanson, Elaine Gan, and Nils Bubandt, eds. 2017. *Arts of Living on a Damaged Planet. Ghosts and Monsters of the Anthropocene*. Minnesota: University of Minnesota Press.

Watts, Jonathan. 2018a. Heatwave Sees Record High Temperatures Around World This Week. *The Guardian*, 13 July.

84   *Nils Bubandt*

——. 2018b. Domino-effect of Climate Events Could Move Earth into a 'Hothouse' State. *The Guardian*, 7 August.

Weisman, Alan. 2007. *The World Without Us*. New York: St. Martin's Press.

Weronika, Erdmann, and Kaczmarek Łukasz. 2017. Tardigrades in Space Research—Past and Future. *Origins of Life and Evolution of Biospheres* 47 (4), 545–553.

Zimmer, Carl. 2015. *A Planet of Virus (Second edition)*. Chicago: The University of Chicago Press.

Chapter 5

Mutants and Tourists

Horror Film, Sacrifice Zones, and Chernobyl Diaries *(2012)*

Steffen Hantke

When HBO's *Chernobyl* was nominated for six Emmys in 2919, winning a total of three awards, the success of the miniseries demonstrated the lasting interest in what to date remains one of the most serious accidents involving the peaceful use of nuclear power.[1] More than any accident of comparable gravity, including the one at the Fukushima Daiichi plant in 2011, the Chernobyl disaster in the spring of 1986 has enjoyed an afterlife within popular culture as a key moment in formation of what one might call the global nuclear imaginary. At earlier moments, popular cinema has worked through the implications of the event in a rather oblique manner; *Star Trek VI: The Undiscovered Country* (1999), for example, re-imagined a catastrophe much like the one in Chernobyl as the cause for the imminent collapse of the Klingon Empire, while Kathryn Bigelow's *K-19: The Widowmaker* (2002) took the malfunction of a nuclear reactor on board a Soviet submarine in 1961, superimposing this smaller event on the large-scale disaster at Chernobyl and merging small secret history with grand world historical events. But as HBO's 2019 version of the historical events at Chernobyl shows, a contemporary audience, ready for a more direct and literal approach to history, followed the miniseries' painstaking autopsy of the disaster, its meticulous tracing of cascades of human and systemic errors and miscalculations, and its assigning of blame to the lumbering bureaucracy of the Soviet system as it placed ideological orthodoxy over pragmatic problem-solving, and heroic recognition to the singular individuals trying to reorient that system from orthodox blindness to a recognition of the facts. Bigelow's film, in its search for a historical explanation for the collapse of the Soviet Union and to reorient its American audience in regard to the former ideological enemy in the post–Cold War world, and HBO's recent miniseries, in its critique of political partisanship and propagandistic erosion of cognitive authority, demonstrate that, historical distance notwithstanding, the Chernobyl disaster seems to demand an explanation and to invite an ideological narrative that might have little to do with the history of the Soviet Union but explain much about American history at the present moment.

Among the texts that have constructed a compelling ideological narrative around the Chernobyl disaster—and are likely to end up permanently overshadowed by the success of texts like the HBO's miniseries—is Bradley Parker's film *Chernobyl Diaries* (2012), which has enjoyed none of the critical accolades lavished upon Bigelow's *K-19* or HBO's *Chernobyl*. Dismissed by most reviewers as an uninspired piece of hack work—not so much for "the sick novelty of referencing an actual catastrophe" (Scott Tobias 2012) and more for its lackluster execution and lack of originality—the film has never received much critical attention. On purely cinematic terms, the reviewers are correct; *Chernobyl Diaries* does not merit in-depth critical attention.[2] And yet as a contribution to popular culture's attempt at grafting an ideological narrative onto the Chernobyl disaster, regardless of its cinematic qualities, or lack thereof, the film occupies a serendipitous position in the development of the horror film and the progressive mapping of various sources of anxiety that drive and animate the genre. It will be the goal of this discussion to map this position: as a horror film at the intersection of the torture porn cycle (in its later stages) and the zombie film cycle (back then still in its early stages), and harking back to 1970s "hillbilly horror" films; as a cultural response to anxieties that had emerged in the wake of the 9/11 attacks in 2001, and, respectively, the global financial crisis in 2008, which the film then uses to think about "sacrifice zones" within global capitalism under a surprisingly resilient neoliberal regime. In merging all of these ideas, it is exactly the film's lack of originality, its sheer derivativeness, that makes it function like a thermometer taking the general temperature of the global sphere. While critics bemoan the film's tendency to gesture at issues rather than naming them, to sketch in ideas rather than developing them, and to leave loose ends dangling, depending on viewers to fill in the blanks allows the film to develop an unexpected predictive intelligence; claiming that it is "prophetic" would go too far, but seeing it as attuned to emergent cultural trends is not far off the mark. In its raw assemblage of the rudimentary, it does provide an inventory of issues that marks the transformation of horror film as a popular genre in dialogue with an ongoing discussion of the Chernobyl disaster as an inexhaustible resource for thinking through the transformations of the local within the global.

CHERNOBYL DIARIES: HORROR FILM GENEALOGY

Chernobyl Diaries revolves around a group of American twenty-somethings, arranged in two romantic couples, who decide as part of their Grand Tour through Europe to forego a trip to Moscow in favor of an excursion to the site of the Chernobyl nuclear accident in Ukraine. Putting a local tour guide named Uri in charge, the four get under way in a rickety van, picking up one more couple of backpackers along the way. After being denied access to the exclusion zone through Uri's conventional channels, the group enters via back roads, making its way into the town of Pripyat.[3] At the end of the day, the group discovers that their van has been sabotaged, stranding them in the exclusion zone over night. After Uri walks away from the van and disappears in the dark, the van is attacked by feral dogs, in concert with barely glimpsed human figures, and one of the tourists, Chris, is injured. His inability to walk out of the zone and back to safety motivates members of the group to venture out and discover along the way Uri's body which shows signs of having been cannibalized post-mortem. As the group gets attacked and its members picked off by groups of the humanoid assailants, the last two survivors stumble through what is ultimately revealed as the Chernobyl reactor building itself. Radioactively contaminated, they are discovered by Ukrainian military, who shoot the last male survivor of the group and drag the film's final girl, Amanda, to a facility where she is not treated and released, as she and we might have expected, but shoved into a room where a group of the radioactive mutants grabs her, and her body is submerged by the zombie-like crowd in the film's final shot.

For an audience at the time of the film's initial release in 2012, *Chernobyl Diaries* comes across as an inventory of familiar torture porn tropes. Much like Eli Roth's *Hostel* (2005), the film that single-handedly initiated the torture porn cycle, *Chernobyl Diaries* subjects its characters to the mandatory punishment that follows the trespass of American tourists onto unfamiliar (post–Cold War Easter European) ground. Like its canonical predecessor, the film begins with a brief moment in which Europe is framed as a paradise of narcissistic self-fulfillment; for *Hostel*'s male characters, this was still coded primarily as sexual license. But *Chernobyl Diaries* conceptualizes Eastern Europe more broadly as a space of adventure. For one of the two romantic couples, it serves as a space for bourgeois self-realization, as Chris plans to propose to his girlfriend Natalie during the trip. For his brother Paul, who lives temporarily in Ukraine, the trip provides the potential to follow suit, as he hopes for a romantic chance with Amanda. Like its canonical predecessor, *Chernobyl Diaries* marks the disappearance of such normalizing prospects with the re-gendering of the space of the other. Just as women conspicuously vanish from *Hostel* the moment the film's mood turns sinister, the two male

Americans in *Chernobyl Diaries* run into a group of Ukrainian men hitting on the two women, resulting in a conflict barely avoided by Paul interceding, before encountering the vaguely hostile soldiers guarding the exclusion zone (coded as dauntingly masculine in a shot that has Chris cringe and crouch down under their suspicious gaze inside the van). While *Hostel* allows one of its male characters the opportunity for "regeneration through violence" as a form of remasculinization, *Chernobyl Diaries* ends with a final girl, albeit one who, having been granted what looks like a final escape as a form of personal triumph, ultimately suffers the fate of being absorbed—as a member or as dinner—of those who have been chasing her all along.

The film's final twist—not allowing Amanda to escape but forcing her into complicity with the radioactive mutants who have been killing and cannibalizing her friends—harks back to the "hillbilly horror" cycle of the 1970s. As reviewers like Berardinelli (2012) and Tobias (2012), who explicitly cite *The Hills Have Eyes* and *The Texas Chainsaw Massacre*, as inspirations for *Chernobyl Diaries*, have noticed, the film's ending plays on the idea that survival does not redeem a character so much as to demonstrate the fluid boundary between self and other. Having tried to escape from the mutants throughout the film, Amanda, covered in the wounds and physical marks of radiation poisoning herself, ends up being one of them by the end. This ending would have pleased Robin Wood, the most vocal of defenders of the 1970s horror film and its ability to blur the line between self and other, bourgeois normality and demonic outsider, in order to allow for a critical engagement with the inherent violence and brutality of bourgeois insiders rather than the xenophobic rejection of a demonized other.[4]

This final image of the film—Amanda submerged in a mass of writhing mutant bodies—also links *Chernobyl Diaries* to the cycle of zombie films initiated by Zack Snyder's 2004 remake of George Romero's *Dawn of the Dead*, anticipated two years earlier by Danny Boyle's *28 Days Later* (2002). By virtue of its very vagueness, *Chernobyl Diaries* allows viewers to imagine its radioactive mutants as zombies, whatever the specific pathology might be that defines them as monsters. Throughout the film, Parker takes care to keep those mutants off camera, providing brief glimpses that barely go beyond shadowy outlines and aggressively curtailed hard edits. A warm campfire site, casually concealed by tour guide Uri so as not to alarm his customers, shows the mutants' rudimentary civilisatory accomplishments. Except for a brief stand-alone moment featuring a medium long shot of an eerie little girl standing with her back to the camera, the mutants mostly appear as a dehumanized primitive horde, a devolved form of humanity, a pack analogous to the feral dogs wandering the exclusion zone, hunting together but barely socially organized above and beyond this one shared activity. Their cannibalism is what ultimately identifies them as close relatives of the post-2004 zombie.

In the merging of the two genre-specific iconographies—that of the torture porn cycle, and that of the post-2004 zombie film cycle—*Chernobyl Diaries* also seems to accept the specific historical forces that have, respectively, animated each cycle and given it urgency and topical relevance in its own moment. With the torture porn cycle, American culture responded to the hyperbolic suspicion that Americans were truly "innocents abroad," not warmly welcomed outside the security of their "homeland" or would, at best be prized as prestigious hostages or outright prey. The films also responded to revelations about human rights abuses in the wake of the US invasion of Afghanistan and Iraq and the abuse of prisoners in the Abu Ghraib prison revealed in the 2004 release of photographs.

Meanwhile, the origins of the zombie film cycle are somewhat more complex as that cycle would begin to diversify more quickly and radically (thereby ensuring its impressive longevity).[5] Still, one of the central concerns of the zombie film expressed in images of suburban and urban spaces, spaces of leisure and consumption, and other spaces of bourgeois normality—all reframed as abandoned, devastated, or otherwise rendered uncanny, and its original "normal" inhabitants reduced to primitive subsistence or nomadic precariousness—is clearly the global financial crisis starting in 2008 and its devastating effects on middle class economic stability. If negative criticism of *Chernobyl Diaries* is to be believed, then the film never develops a topical agenda of its own, assembling instead imagery from two interweaving cycles of its chosen genre in a late-cycle attempt at recycling or bricolage (squeezing a last few dollars at the box office out of the material before the genre would move on). Without the aesthetic emphasis on originality, or the film's lack thereof, however, *Chernobyl Diaries* might mark a moment in which the hybridity of its two constituent cycles is more than an exercise in recombination of genre-specific tropes. Instead, it might be possible to read the convergence of post-9/11 xenophobia and post-2008 economic anxiety as a configuration typical of an emergent ideological structure—one that goes beyond the binary of self/other in the national imaginary of the post-9/11 horror film and the binary of middle-/lower-class in the social imaginary of the post-2008 film cycle. In order to find a way into this emergent configuration, one might start by looking at the fantasies surrounding the "exclusion zone," the radioactively contaminated no-go area around the Chernobyl reactor.

WELCOME TO THE ZONE: WEALTH EXTRACTION FROM PAST DISASTER

For director Brad Parker, the historical fact of the so-called exclusion zone surrounding the contaminated Ground Zero of the Chernobyl reactor must have offered a serendipitous alignment with the rich tradition of "zones" in literature and film—from Boris and Arkady Strugatzki's novel *Roadside Picnic* (1972), loosely adapted by Andrei Tarkovsky in *Stalker* (1979), to Thomas Pynchon's concept of "the Zone" in *Gravity's Rainbow* (1973), and on to the eponymous space of the Southern Reach in Jeff Vandermeer's trilogy of novels (2011), the first adapted by Alex Garland in *Annihilation* (2018). Within this tradition, the film situates itself by having first Uri, the tour guide, and then some of the tourists interpret the exclusion zone as a space where history has been suspended, time has been reversed, and Nature has made a return. Some shots early on seem to underscore this bucolic aspect of the zone, but the sentiment is quickly rebuked when what looks like natural serenity is revealed as simply the absence of human beings, and the even that sentiment is revealed as being false. The silence that one character poignantly remarks upon is, in fact, not a natural phenomenon; it is the manifestation of Nature after the erasure of some species—humans among them—and the subsequent rewriting of the species that have failed to relocate in the course of the emergency evacuation and have made a permanent home in the zone. The group's encounter with a bear may look like Nature returning but turns out to be animal behavior having been altered by the changed conditions within the zone. The bear, though physically unaltered, is not supposed to be on an upper floor of an abandoned apartment building. Similarly, the hunting behavior of the feral dogs might, to some degree, still be part of the animals' natural social behavior; and yet the fact that the dogs are hunting humans pushes this behavior past the natural and into the realm of altered ontological ground rules that apply only within the zone. Yet more explicitly, the film shows fish that, as a result of radioactive contamination, have mutated into Piranha-like predators, eyeless and gruesome and indiscriminately aggressive. Eventually, the film has refuted the erroneous assessment of Nature reclaiming the zone and substituted the recognition that the reactor accident has not evacuated technology from the zone but, on the contrary, has permanently overwritten what used to be natural and turned it into technology. From bears and dogs and horrid fish to mutant humans, there is no Nature left within the zone.

This ghostly afterlife of "Nature as Other" within the exclusion zone appeals to the audience's recognition that this used to be the site of one of the Soviet Union's most highly advanced and proficient technological accomplishments—an accomplishment rendered obsolete by its spectacular failure. The obsolescence is that of the economic system of the now defunct Soviet Union, a system associated with the Fordist industrial production that had, all ideological declarations about the unique historical formation of Soviet Communism aside, always been the ideal of the enforced Stalinist industrialization of the nation. During what were to be the few remaining years of the

Soviet Union, the former global super power would be in economic decline, riding roughshod over citizens in the transition from communism to capitalism with a few plutocrats emerging as the winners. In the post–Cold War world, the Global East would be the new Global South. And within this distressed region, the exclusion zone around the Chernobyl disaster site would be an economic black hole, absorbing and destroying industrial output from the national economy. The effort to contain its pernicious influence would sap the economic strength of the Soviet Union to a degree that it might have been the final push toward collapse for an already strained industrial system. The massive investment in the exclusion zone, by absorbing industrial strength and prosperity elsewhere, would demanding a national sacrifice disproportionate to its brief life as a generator of value.

With its innocent American tourists abroad, Chernobyl Diaries demonstrates that the industrial destruction, its aftermath preserved in a state of suspended animation, now functions within the context of a different economic framework, while historical progress marches on in the world around it. International tourism has discovered the exclusion zone as an emergent economic space with increasing viability, having identified a niche clientele for what Francesca Street has referred to as "dark tourism" or other might call disaster tourism.[6] For these tourists, the attraction is to gaze upon sites where industrial production or resource extraction have wreaked such environmental and social havoc that indigenous landscapes and communities are rendered useless for further production of economic or social value, and are thus excised from the circulation of value through the global sphere, its remaining inhabitants marginalized and disenfranchised. The term popularized for such spaces is that of "sacrifice zones" (by, for example, Steve Lerner's 2012 book *Sacrifice Zones: The Front Lines of Toxic Chemical Exposure in the United States*, or, more recently, by Chris Hedges' and Joe Sacco's *Days of Destruction, Days of Revolt* from 2014), and though no one in Parker's film uses this term, it takes little imagination to recognize behind the official terminology of the Chernobyl exclusion zone the "sacrifice zone" of Lerner, Hedges, and Sacco.

Like the tourists marveling at the postindustrial ruins of Detroit, taking selfies in front of the earthquake damage in Kathmandu, or diving down to the wreck of the Titanic, various national governments have started to see the economic potential in travelers recording the ruins of technological failure or the sad spectacle of urban decay in video after video, photograph after photograph, posting the results on personal pages, blogs, and public sites online. As *Chernobyl Diaries* tracks the progress of its American tourists across the exclusion zone, it frames this informational rendering of the disaster site as an activity with economic implications, and, in the process, plots this new economy against the one it appropriates, commodifies, and commercializes—that of the former Soviet Union, its failure a matter of historical obsolescence, and that of the US, its success demonstrated by the economic capital spent promiscuously and conspicuously on leisure activities.

The film spends some time differentiating carefully between these two economic models. As a brief anecdote told by tour guide Uri to the hapless tourist tells us, the exclusion zone does not provide the material benefits of direct material plunder or recycling. The removal of actual objects from the zone as souvenirs or mementoes has caused bodily harm to those trafficking in and consuming those objects because of radioactive contamination. Resource extraction in that conventional sense of the term thus belongs to that failed old world of industrial production. In contrast, the digital images taken incessantly by the American tourists are free of such destructive potential. As artifacts, they speak of the space of their origin at best as a transitory space: as a space to be traversed, crossed, passed through, rather than one to be permanently inhabited (a "space" rather than a "place," in the parlance of one critic). They transform, in other words, the material space into "experience" in order to make it consumable. The imperative of the impermanence of human physical presence in the exclusion zone is made up for, however, by the permanence of the record created by humans during their brief stay: the photographs, the digital accounts in blogs, travelogues, and other forms of communications (the internet, for better or worse, never forgets). Unlike those ill-fated material objects removed from the exclusion zone, they constitute considerable economic capital within the larger economy of information, data, and images that now circulates in the global sphere within which the Chernobyl exclusion zone is embedded. Though none of the tourists are professional photographers, making money directly out of the pictures they have taken, their picture-taking for ostensibly personal reason links with the more subtle and highly differentiated processes that translate symbolic social capital into economic payoff (number of followers or "likes" online). There is a hint here of an emergent economy that will accommodate companies like Uber and Airbnb that have written on their banner the slogan, slightly adapted to the liberation chant of an earlier generation: the personal is professional![7]

At first glance, the process of translating the exclusion zone, or one's subjective experience of it as a tourist, into images, data, and discourse appears to redeem and recuperate the exclusion zone from its damnation as a "black hole" in the fabric of the global economic system. In a slightly more peripheral way, someone like Uri already makes a living taking tourists to, and through, the dangerous terrain. By contrast, the military personnel guarding and policing the boundaries of the space and containing whatever inside is of it seems to represent the cost, the sacrifice imposed upon the Ukrainian economy; but then even here, the film suggests that an illegal economy of bribery and graft has taken hold, and that we might just be small step away from government officials being replaced by private contractors. Not much good for anything else, and actively hostile to repopulation and reindustrialization, the exclusion zone is reinjected with new economic life once it has been refashioned as a proper tourist destination. This is the vision fostered by the likes of Uri and embraced by his affluent international clientele—a vision that, in its benevolence and optimism, is undercut by the film's reminder that there are still native inhabitants of the zone and that their interest in the tourists is far more literally one of exploitation. Not only is the zone not "Nature," it's also not empty. These two ideas are, to be sure, essential elements in the narrative "consumed" by the tourists as part of their visit: presented to them by others (like Uri, who knows what his customers like to hear) and anticipated by them in advance of their actual experience (part and parcel of the status of contemporary tourist experiences as simulacra). It is exactly in this reframing of the exclusion zone—from the old Soviet-style manufacturing economy to the new postindustrial information economy—that the exclusion zone is transformed into a "sacrifice zone"—a space with far more sinister connotations than those projected upon it by global disaster tourism—and reoriented toward a new paradigm. Here, in other words, is where Chernobyl Diaries is attuned to a peculiar economic configuration that usually gets little attention in popular political discourse.

CONCLUSION: HOW NEOLIBERALISM REIMAGINES SACRIFICE ZONES

Though *Chernobyl Diaries* ends with stalemate of sorts—these tourists have suffered a grisly fate, but by the logic of disaster tourism, that fate might very well attract others—the film does raise a larger question about its setting. Currently the discourse on sacrifice zones—what to do to redeem, revitalize, and fix them—comes in two major variants, each offering a unique view incompatible with that of the other. On the conservative spectrum of political opinion—call it perhaps the current Republican view—there is a return (regressive and nostalgic rather than conservative) to the earlier forms of industrial manufacturing which had often been the cause of environmental degradation and economic exploitation and disenfranchisement. From strip-mining and mountaintop removal in the Appalachian region, to deindustrialization in the US rust belt, the conservative political position of recent years imagines a return to traditional resource extraction and heavy industrial manufacturing, stripped conveniently of its complicated cost in human health and environmental integrity. The Trump administration's odd fascination with the coalminer as an icon of this economic model, demographically outnumbered by an army of Walmart greeters, adjunct professors, and other low-income players in the "gig economy," provides a striking example of this attitude. There is little of a solution to the problems raised by sacrifice zones contained within this model, unless one were to accept that the twisted logic by which the spread of environmental degradation and economic exploitation from precisely circumscribed geographic spaces to the national economy at large as a way of "dissolving" sacrifice zones.

On the other end of the political spectrum—what one might call progressive, part of the political brand of the Democratic party in the United States—is the recognition of human and environmental toll extracted by sacrifice zones. The declared intention of "dissolving" sacrifice zones by re-integrating them into the larger economy is, however, not based upon a nostalgic longing to return to industrial manufacturing but recognizes and embraces the postindustrial information economy. The replacement of geriatric industries like coalmining with sustainable economic alternatives, and the retraining of the work force to adapt to these new formations, would then allow capital flow and investment to reverse environmental degradation and, in turn, re-integrate geographic space itself into the logic of the (real estate) market. The remarks made by then-presidential candidate Hillary Clinton about the prospect of retraining a work force left behind by deindustrialization in the American rust belt, abandoning in the process all pretensions that coal mines might ever re-open, laid out the progressive counterproposal to Republican nostalgia for the golden days of American industrial manufacturing and resource extraction.

In between these two positions is the third option, laid out in *Chernobyl Diaries* with a clarity derived from engaging with the actual economic practices emerging from and surrounding sacrifice zones rather than the ideologically encoded idealizations for a recuperative future. In this third option—a model with increasing economic viability given the rise and spread of global mobility of both bodies and information—sacrifice zones are being colonized by a new form of global tourism. At first glance, this new "disaster tourism" translates older forms of leisure travel onto a new global map; tourists from rich countries have traveled to poor countries for the past two centuries, returning with stories about the picturesque natives and their quaint customs, some of them perhaps with a delicious shudder at the poverty, squalidness, and degradation of poor living conditions witnessed alongside historical landmarks and fabulous landscapes. To some extent, contemporary forms of disaster tourism replicate this pattern. And yet they are unique in the fact that disaster tourists actively seek out dangerous locations and degraded spaces while traditional tourists tended to accept them as an inevitable side effect to be endured in pursuit of natural and cultural beauty, serenity, and enlightenment. The references to accepting and enduring residual radioactive contamination within the exclusion zone in *Chernobyl Diaries*, characters having to plan and alter their routes through the territory to avoid more heavily contaminated hot spots, and the remaining characters' final progress into the radioactive hear of darkness, the Chernobyl reactor building itself, all illustrate the management of risk as a factor to be courted and cultivated as a defining feature of disaster tourism.

This third option—the neoliberal colonization and exploitation of sacrifice zones—constitutes a troublesome specter haunting the conservative and progressive bookends on each side of the political spectrum alike. For a progressive vision, the generation and extraction of economic value from a sacrifice zone via tourism appears to be, for lack of a better term, "distasteful." Expressions of this distaste can be found in the rhetoric of reviewers passing moral judgment on the film, like Scott Tobias, when he suggests an analogy between disaster tourists and filmmakers: "Directly evoking an ongoing human tragedy—like, say, the 1986 Chernobyl disaster—for a few ghoulish scares might be in questionable taste. And yet here's *Chernobyl Diaries . . .*" (2012). A sideline to this dubious transformation of historical suffering into commercial entertainment might also be Parker's own access to the exclusion zone where the director shot coverage of the actual disaster site to be included in the film before moving on to other Eastern European sites for shooting; the look of such sites might have helped to evoke post-evacuation Pripyat, but lower production cost and a non-unionized workforce are likely to have been part of the calculation as well.[8] To the extent some sacrifice zones are still inhabited (though the inhabitants of Detroit, Michigan, or Bhopal, India, are very much real, the mutant cannibals of Chernobyl are not), the vision of an economy based on tourists consuming the spectacle of the natives' disenfranchisement might be hard to extricate from the more obvious connotations of base economic exploitation. No wonder *Chernobyl Diaries*, like many of hillbilly horror films of the 1970s, torture porn films of the early 2000s, and zombie films after 2004 have to imagine inhabitants of sacrifice zones in utterly dehumanized form, lest they expose their main characters to moral condemnation. And even with these demonized natives, as *Chernobyl Diaries* demonstrates, there is residual unease with the narcissistic self-absorption of the tourists, their lack of genuine interest in and curiosity about the deep history of the space they are consuming.

Similarly, the conservative view of sacrifice zones, unless one were to dismiss its nostalgia as inauthentic and hypocritical, is haunted by the implications of disaster tourism. At face value, this view should have fewer problems with the sheer fact of economic exploitation, at least to the degree that some of the economic value produced would flow back into the space itself (even if the lion's share goes elsewhere, toward some national or global center of capital accumulation and management). But the full acknowledgment of the postindustrial appropriation of the failed industrial space moves a domestic sacrifice zone dangerously close to the status of one in the global south, the third world, or whatever other term we have to describe spatial patterns of global inequality. Apart from delivering an insult to the national imaginary, which would be hard pressed to acknowledge such devastation within the confines of its constituent geographic space, the embrace of disaster tourism would also permanently foreclose all avenues to nostalgia. So much of conservative ideology depends on this nostalgia to conceptualize postindustrial labor, eliminating the precariousness of economic lives in the new economy by reimagining them within the framework of economic crises from which Americans, by virtue of thrift and hard work, have extricated themselves successfully in the past. Once you have turned into one of the mutants who inhabit the exclusion zone in *Chernobyl Diaries*, there is no way back—this is why Amanda, the film's final girl, being swallowed by the writhing bodies of the mutant pack in the film's final shot is an image of pure economic and social horror.

There is a more obvious and superficial way in which Amanda's final absorption into the other registers as horrific, and this way has something to do with the term "cannibalism" that has been used throughout the discussion so far. Since the mutants are seen only to attack and consume outsiders—from Uri, the tour guide, to members of the group of tourists—they qualify as cannibals in the sense that they eat human flesh, but not in the sense that they eat their own kind. The distinction is not purely technical since they function within an economic allegory. They themselves are being consumed, that is, as objects of interest that have been radically othered by the tourist gaze. As a perverse but predictable outcome of the film's strategy of keeping the mutants largely off camera, the tourist gaze, mediated by the cinematic gaze, is attached to this image held perpetually in abeyance. Not surprisingly, the film's final jump cut is to the horde of mutants with Amanda in their midst. Already recruited into the film's ongoing engagement with matters of economy, it is not far-fetched to consider for a moment the economic implications of these two possible meanings of the concept of cannibalism. The mutants' consumption of intruders actually constitutes a sustainable economic model, as incoming tourists will continue to replenish their vital resource, thereby increasing the risk and danger associated with entering the exclusion zone, which, in turn, increases its attractiveness to disaster tourists from around the world. Actually cannibalism, meanwhile, would not be sustainable since eating their own kind would mean decimating and eventually eradicating the group. On this level of the film's discourse, horror derives from the realization that sacrifice zones might very well remain connected to the larger sphere of economic exchange after they have been exploited, voided of value, and abandoned; and, what is worse, that the processes of resource extraction are now, more than ever, reciprocal.

In the final instance, this realization the film steers toward is politically ambiguous. On the one hand, it might register as a gleeful turning of tables between exploiters and exploited—as one group enacts its economic privileges, it is, in fact, acted upon in much the same manner. The rich, self-absorbed, historically clueless American teenagers are getting their comeuppance after all: a conclusion that resonates with the flattest affect of the previous cycle of torture porn films. On the other hand, what *Chernobyl Diaries* illustrates might just be business as usual, the enactment of a capitalist logic which, in its neoliberal manifestation of disaster tourists experiencing a sacrifice zone with even their own victimization integrated in the production of value, steers clear of progressive and conservative visions of recovering and redeeming such sacrifice zones. *Chernobyl Diaries*, meanwhile, suggests that sacrifice zones need no redemption, at least not in the sense that something dead must (heroically) be brought back to life. They have never been dead to begin with; economically speaking, neoliberalism does not allow for anything in its sphere ever to die. Limping along, covered in sores from radioactive contamination, there is life in these places yet. Undead ain't dead.

NOTES

1. Journalistic work that may have prepared the ground for this commercial success may have included Svetlana Alexievich's oral history *Voices from Chernobyl: The Oral History of a Nuclear Disaster*, already written and published in 1997, but attracting a new readership, especially outside Russia, because of Alexievitch's receiving the Nobel Prize for Literature in 2015. More directly related is Adam Higginbotham's *Midnight in Chernobyl: The Untold Story of the World's Greatest Nuclear Disaster*, published in February of 2019 to great critical success.

2. See, for instance, James Berardinelli's review of the film: "*Chernobyl Diaries* is so derivative that hardly a moment goes by without triggering a strong sense of déjà vu. This, in and of itself, is not necessarily a bad thing, but the movie fails to do much that's interesting with all the material it pilfers. Even lazy horror fans will notice similarities in style and/or story to *The Hills Have Eyes*, *The Blair Witch Project*, and *The Ruins*. Die-hard aficionados will be able to add at least another dozen titles to that list . . ." (Berardinelli 2012)

3. This is where director Brad Parker had opportunity to shoot some of the coverage before retiring to locations in other Eastern European nations for the rest of the shoot. Shooting locations for the film, which include various places in Hungary and Serbia, are themselves implicated in the global logic of zones of exclusion and/or sacrifice, marking an area where film production, regardless of the specificity of diegetic locations, comes at a significantly lower price than in areas where salaries and wages are higher, labor is unionized or otherwise organized in its own self-interest, and production is regulated by legal protections for all those involved.

4. For the sake of completion, it is necessary to acknowledge the influence on the film by producer and co-writer Oren Peli, bringing some of the found-footage aesthetic to the film (in an attenuated form throughout, and in its full display in a scene that has two characters watch the digital recording made by two of their friends who have vanished under suspicious circumstances) that had been his trademark since *Paranormal Activity* (2007) and a central feature in a horror film cycle of its own from that point on.

5. In his review of the film in the *New York Times*, Andy Webster makes the link to post–9/11 xenophobia explicit when he point out that you "could conceivably consider it a warning about nuclear power, but it's really about the dangers of seeking adventure in a foreign country and trusting former Soviets," before, like many other reviewers, going on to dismiss the film altogether: "But please, don't give it that much thought" (Webster 2012).

6. See, for example, Francesca Street's article from 2019 "Chernobyl and the dangerous ground of 'dark tourism'" (https://edition.cnn.com/travel/article/dark-tourism-chernobyl/index.html), or Katie Mettler's article from 2019 "Ukraine wants Chernobyl to be a tourist trap. But scientists warn: Don't kick up dust." (https://www.washingtonpost.com/travel/2019/07/12/ukraine-wants-chernobyl-be-tourist-trap-scientists-warn-dont-kick-up-dust/).

7. Among the characters, the most outstanding example of this is Amanda, who carries the biggest camera and takes the most photographs. In fact, the film goes so far as to translate this semi- or proto-economic activity into the conventional horror film trope of vigilance, as Amanda is the first to discover evidence of the mutants' presence in one of the pictures she has taken. Entrenching her the most deeply in this new economic structure, the film then saves her degradation for its climactic final moment.

8. Apart from shooting in Pripyat, Parker used locations in various places in Hungary and Serbia. For a list of shooting locations, see IMDb.com (https://www.imdb.com/title/tt1991245/locations?ref_=tt_dt_dt).

WORKS CITED

Berardinelli, James. 2012. "*Chernobyl Diaries* (United States, 2012)." *ReelViews*. http://www.reelviews.net/reelviews/chernobyl-diaries>. Accessed October 1, 2021.

Hedges, Chris, and Joe Sacco. 2014. *Days of Destruction, Days of Revolt*. New York: Bold Type Books.

Lerner, Steve. 2012. *Sacrifice Zones: The Front Lines of Toxic Chemical Exposure in the United States*. Boston: MIT Press.

Mettler, Katie. 2019. "Ukraine Wants Chernobyl to be a Tourist Trap. But Scientists Warn: Don't Kick Up Dust." *Washington Post*. https://www.washingtonpost.com/travel/2019/07/12/ukraine-wants-chernobyl-be-tourist-trap-scientists-warn-dont-kick-up-dust/. Accessed October 1, 2021.

Street, Francesca. 2019. "Chernobyl and the Dangerous Ground of 'Dark Tourism.'" *CNN*. https://edition.cnn.com/travel/article/dark-tourism-chernobyl/index.html. Accessed October 1, 2021.

Tobias, Scott. 2012. "*Chernobyl Diaries*. A.V. Club. https://film.avclub.com/cher-nobyldiaries-1798172925>. Accessed October 1, 2021.

Webster, Andy. 2012. "Jaunt Through Fallout Zone Goes (Shock!) Awry." *New York Times*. https://www.nytimes.com/2012/05/26/movies/chernobyl-diaries-co -produced-by-oren-peli.html?ref=movies. Accessed October 1, 2021.

Chapter 6

A Panic on the 4th of July

Municipal Malfeasance, Mutation, and Monstrosity in Barry Levinson's The Bay (2012)

Rebecca Stone Gordon

Barry Levinson's eco-horror film *The Bay* (2012) is an effective brew of science and speculative fiction. Stylistically, the mockumentary/found footage sensibility may seem like a departure for the writer/director/producer of Hollywood fare such as *Rain Man* (1988), but *The Bay* echoes the realism in Levinson's more politically charged work such as the television series *Homicide: Life on the Streets* (1993–1999). The setting, a (fictional) Maryland town on the Chesapeake Bay, and protagonist, an American University Communications student, are also thematically coherent within his body of work.[1] *The Bay* uses the 4th of July as a touchstone. American Gothic motifs and depiction of the ideologically dark waters beneath the surface of the American Way of Life pay homage to 4th of July eco-horror kin *Frogs* (1972) and *Jaws* (1975). The influence of folk horror is also visible in the emphasis on local community rituals and totemic references to blue crabs, Maryland's cultural and economic symbol. While *The Bay's* provocative disaster scenario is fictional, it is situated in the reality of the impending ecological collapse of North America's largest estuary and can be viewed as a conversation with *Frontline Poisoned Waters* (2009), a PBS documentary about the growing anthropogenic dead zone in the Chesapeake Bay and Puget Sound. Levinson is quoted in interviews estimating that *The Bay* is "about 80% factual," built on research his production company conducted for a potential documentary (Wheeler 2012).

Ultimately, Levinson and co-writer Michael Wallach used this material as the basis for a chillingly effective mockumentary horror film. Critical reviews of the film, no matter how positive, tended to foreground the found footage aspects, effectively damning it with faint praise. Distinguishing between found footage and mockumentary is more than a matter of categorization. As Richard Wallace (2021) explains, the central conceit of the mockumentary takes advantage of our familiarity with documentary conventions such as voice and authenticity. While it may incorporate found footage, Wallace defines mockumentary as a separate genre. Cecilia Sayad (2016) argues that mockumentary horror is effective because it enables filmmakers to present familiar horror tropes in the visual style of non-fiction storytelling, which collapses boundaries and reframes how the viewer processes information. Sayad concludes that this opens up opportunities for nonallegorical explorations of the horrific. This doesn't foreclose allegorical readings of mockumentaries, but that is a topic far beyond the narrow approach in this article. I bring an ecocritical anthropological perspective to my close reading of *The Bay*, informed by the cultural history of American Cold War era monster and eco-horror movies. In the 1970s, eco-horror films multiplied at the multiplex like radioactive rabbits. However, atomic tropes didn't disappear, they merged with rising concerns about the environment and falling confidence in the Federal government, a trio of existential terrors which articulated neatly together. I pay particular attention here to the historical trajectory of these films' depictions of institutional responses to and resolution of crises, particularly the privileging of economic protections over environmental concerns, which is far from a modern development. In her work on what she terms the Rural Gothic, Bernice Murphy connects the themes in modern eco-horror back to early American attitudes toward the wilderness. She writes that these films operate by "combining an urgent sense of present-day crisis with a much older awareness of the fraught relationship between the white colonist and the unfamiliar landscape inhabited by potentially hostile plants, animals, and humans" (Murphy 2015, 182). Throughout *The Bay*, this tension is explored through the town's relationship to the desalination plant, which at first seems a source of salvation but instead delivers destruction.

THE RETURN OF THE REPRESSED: *THE BAY'S* MOCKUMENTARY FORM

The Bay opens with a montage of "ecological mysteries." These news clips of fish kills and mass bird die-offs, located first in Maryland but including ecological disasters around the world by the end of the sequence. The language of incredulity the commentators employ reflects corporate media hesitance to acknowledge anthropogenic climate change despite overwhelming evidence of ecological collapse. The opening montage fades to black before white text appears on screen: "Those events were covered by the media. The following story was never made public." Donna Thompson (Kether Donohue), a weary-looking young white woman, appears onscreen in a medium close-up shot. She sits in front of empty beige walls and looks directly into the camera, addressing an unseen and unidentified interviewer over a skype connection as she prepares to narrate her film. She was an intern at a Claridge television station three years prior, documenting the town's traditional 4th of July festivities when an outbreak killed over 700 people, including her camera operator.[2] The use of a skype interview is an organic device for incorporating present-day footage around and into Donna's film, as well as emphasizing her sense of isolation. If this framing device felt contrived to viewers in 2012, after the COVID pandemic in which broadcast interviews over Zoom, Skype, and other videoconferencing platforms became common, it now seems logical and natural. I refer to the assembled film being presented by the character of Donna as "Donna's film" and the feature film itself as *The Bay*. Framing Donna's film with the "present-day" Skype interview gives *The Bay* an epistolary quality.

Donna's film is an amalgamation of her own recovered footage, and leaked sources which include squad-car dashcam and 911 recordings, video communications between the local hospital and the CDC, hospital security footage, an oceanography team's video-diary, an undercover environmental investigation website and home videos. Juxtaposition of audio elements such as recovered voicemails over recovered footage eliminates the found footage contrivance in which a video documentarian stays at the center of the action. These segments also heighten our understanding of the chaos and personalize the tragedy, destabilizing the sense of security we might otherwise derive from our experience with mystery reconstruction narratives. One example is the playback of a series of voicemails left for Stephanie (Kristen Connolly) and Alex (Will Rogers), a young couple who spend 7 hours of The *Bay's* story-time sailing to Claridge with their infant to spend the day with Stephanie's parents. Cellular communications break down as soon as the crisis begins so Stephanie is unable to contact her parents during the trip. Stephanie's mother relates that Stephanie's father is sick, that his leg has been amputated in a failed attempt to save his life, and that she, herself, is now infected. The images of Stephanie and Alex sailing blissfully towards doom with an American flag majestically waving behind the yacht are intercut with images of the overwhelmed hospital where medical staff frantically amputate limbs as terrified patients out in the crowded lobby plead for help.

The Bay provides an unflinching, clinical view of a fast-spreading pandemic's bodily horrors, but it is the actions of humans which are the most monstrous elements on display. Crustaceans known as isopods erupt from the viscera of the townsfolk as a sunny, carefree day of celebration in Claridge devolves into a nightmare. The isopods are not the true villains, they are not invaders who march in from the unknowable sea seeking revenge. It will become clear over the course of the film that the toxic brew of pollutants and powerful steroids in poultry waste drive the isopods to frenzied hunger in an area where the fish are dying out, leaving them with neither food nor home/ hosts for their offspring. Humans and fish have similar endocrine systems but jumping from a host in their aquatic environment to a terrestrial one seems disadvantageous and perhaps even stressful for the isopods. In a brief scene, a group of recreational boaters catch a fish. An isopod leaps from the fish mouth and bites the fisherman. It is a classic jump scare, but it is also a misdirect, a red herring invoking the classic creature feature trope of a single marauder which the audience understands to be a signal of an overwhelming swarm to follow. Instead, the scene ends quickly with the isopod frantically scrambling away from the humans, off the boat and back into the water. The dead zone is creating a crisis point for the isopods which parallels the human crisis in Claridge.

THE (UN)DEAD ZONE

The term "dead zone" is neither hyperbolic nor fictional. Under pressure from climate change and pollution, bodies of water can become hypoxic, devoid of oxygen and unable to support life. High concentrations of nutrients in industrial, agricultural, and livestock run-off spur rampant algae growth which leads to the depletion of the available oxygen in the water. The resulting mass die-off of suffocated fish, shellfish, and aquatic plants creates ripples through the eco-system, as birds and other foragers starve and rotting sea life becomes a breeding ground for bacteria. There is no starker, more appropriate term for such a devastated place than dead zone. Gulf of Mexico historian Jack E. Davis describes the seafloor as "an eerie oceanic version of nuclear fallout" (Davis 2017, 445). It would seem perverse to anthropomorphize an anthropogenically created disaster by using the term "zombie." However, literary scholar T. May Stone's observation on the characteristics of the undead human figure of the zombie resonates through my reading of *The Bay*. Stone writes:

> The zombie's core characteristic is absence, an intrinsic lack, which is concretized by death; what had once been a complete subject when alive has suffered a vital loss. The magic of the zombie—whatever the actual zombification mechanism—is that the absence continues to be present, signified in the literal form of the zombie. A zombie is a present absence. (Stone 2018, 421)

The margins around the zones expand and contract as areas of water are re-oxygenated, but the entire region is conceptually undead as long as it contains a hypoxic center, a reframing I argue disrupts the socio-cultural implication of normality inherent in the dead/recovering dichotomy. The specter of death haunts these fragile places. The water's appearance gives no indication where oxygen ceases to be present and suffocation begins.

The Bay is an indictment of our collective inability to respond to anthropogenic environmental destruction and climate change, but Levinson acknowledges the complexity of these struggles at the community level in a scene in which a resident yells at the mayor about the "chicken shit" which is running into and killing the Bay. In the scene, which is file footage of a past encounter, the mayor deflects this statement with the assertion that it is the EPA's responsibility to monitor the water, obscuring that this is not, in fact, true. *The Bay* and the documentary *Frontline Poisoned Waters* reveal the evidence of poultry industry pollution quite differently. In *The Bay,* an activist's night vision footage exposes what we are led to believe is a hidden practice. It is dramatic, but it blunts the banal reality that agricultural waste is unregulated, and the EPA doesn't monitor the water for the chemical steroids used to rapidly accelerate chicken growth. In *Frontline Polluted Waters*, Rick Dove takes the PBS crew out in broad daylight to see mountains of chicken waste readily visible from public roads and waterways. He explains that Perdue's 570 million chickens produced 1.5 billion pounds of waste in Maryland in 2008 alone, a significant source of the nutrients driving algae blooms. Levinson does not belabor the source of the damage, instead using the work of the oceanographers to explain how the waste products seem to vanish in the Bay, but their constituent chemical compounds are no less dangerous. They make the connection between the growth hormones and the unnaturally enlarged isopods, but all of their warnings go unheeded. After all, the freshwater supply is crystal clear and Mayor Stockman (Frank Deal) has assured the townspeople that they have the purist, cleanest drinking water he's ever tasted. Even though things are going wrong in the Bay, the town believes they are safe. The terror at the heart of *The Bay* is not, in fact, *out there* in the water, it is *of* the water. The danger enters the town of Claridge in the drinking water, which turns out to be swarming with microscopic larva.

THE MAYOR OF SHARK CITY

The desalination plant was built to benefit the poultry industry which needs the water to expand, but Mayor Stockman has convinced the town it is for their benefit, supplying them with green lawns and crystal-clear swimming pools. The town's illusion of power and control over their environment represent what Simon Estok refers to as "ecophobia," an inherent loathing for the natural world that manifests not only in overtly destructive practices but also in the development of artificial replacements for ruined natural places (Estok 2009). The Bay is dirty, and, arguably, made dirtier by the poultry industry's renewed growth, but the plant also cleans the water so that they can create a new, safer place to swim. Two types of location recur throughout Donna's film: Claridge's Main Street and unspecified locations in and around water. These water-centric images contrast the murky brown of the Bay with the sparkling water in the carnival dunk tank, pools, and lawn sprinklers. On Main Street, a young woman (Keyla Childs) in a sparkling sequin crab tiara and pageant sash looks into the camera in the early hours of the day. Donna features her interview at the beginning of her film, as she sweetly looks into the camera and says that she thinks it's every girl's dream to be Miss Crustacean. She is an echo of Tina, Amity Island's teenage beauty queen in *Jaws 2*, but our expectation that sweet, innocent Miss Crustacean will survive the outbreak is upended at the end of the film when we see her lifeless body sprawled on Main Street, her reign as their titular queen undone by the parasitic crustaceans which have burst from her abdomen.

The outbreak itself seems, initially, to be food-borne, as participants at the lunchtime crab-eating contest suddenly become ill. The ironic image of well-nourished white Americans gorging on the imperiled species around which they form their identity and then violently vomiting on the patriotic red, white and blue decorations reads as a meta-commentary on the entire film. The events unfolding on the 4th of July form the backbone of the film, but the video diary of a pair of oceanography Fellows (Nanski Aluka and Christopher Denham) is used to introduce a longer narrative arc into the film. The oceanographers contextualize dead zones as a process rather than an event. Likewise, their footage shows Claridge's crisis as both long-term process and event. Through Donna's reconstruction of their footage, we see the oceanographers' piece together the mystery, at each turn sending reports to the Mayor and the Chesapeake Environmental Council which are ignored. On May 18 they capture footage of fish whose stomachs contain a form of unknown larva. Specialists in the Chesapeake watershed, they do not recognize the larval form of the Pacific isopod. On May 28, they report on exceptionally high levels of toxins in the water current flowing directly towards Claridge. On June 2, they document bizarre injuries to fish they find floating in the bay. Laid out on a lab table, the injured mouths and torn bellies reads as an homage to the scene in *Jaws 2* (1978) when the Mayor dismisses the first tangible evidence of danger: a dead killer whale on the beach with a bleeding gash on the side of its mouth and a large wound to its belly. Collecting samples around Claridge, the oceanographers are attacked by ravenous isopods, an attack which is officially attributed to sharks, evoking what is perhaps the most iconic 4th of July horror film of all time, *Jaws* (1975).

Jaws and *Jaws 2* have an important intertextual relationship to *The Bay*. While Amity's Mayor Vaughn is infamous for his refusal to close the beaches on the 4th of July and the phrase "Jaws Mayor" has entered the lexicon as reference to an elected leader who puts the economy ahead of safety, it's instructive to remember that Mayor Vaughn is still the mayor of Amity in *Jaws 2*, which takes place four years later. Not only has he been re-elected, but the town council is overtly controlled by developers who will again decide to put tourism dollars and development ahead of public safety when a threat emerges in the water. When the threat becomes undeniable in the first film, shark hunter Quint asks the assembled townsfolk if they want to be on welfare all winter if they forego tourist dollars, as much a commentary on the inadequacy of the American social safety net as it is a critique on the American equation between moral failure and economic crisis. The 4th of July is the start of New England's beach season, but here it is also symbolic of the paradoxical relationship between this projected image of freedom and rugged individualism and the manipulated artificiality of the idealized ocean resort town. *The Bay's* Mayor receives a report about the deaths of the oceanographers 16 days before the 4th of July which conclusively states that they were not killed by a shark, but he conceals this information. Later, we will learn that Federal agencies were also aware of the developing situation but unwilling to act, which is in keeping with the historical trajectory of the American disaster film formula.

Throughout the 1950s, Hollywood depictions of atomic experiments suggested that a little fallout in the air was the price of freedom. "Nuclearism," Robert Jay Lifton's (1982) term for the process of infusing nuclear ideology into the ideology of everyday life, enabled Americans to learn to at least live with the bomb, and normalized the environmental consequences of nuclear technology. As the narrator informs viewers at the beginning of the classic giant ant thriller, *Them!* (1954): "When man entered the Atomic Age he opened a door to a new world. What we'll eventually find in that new world nobody can predict!" For decades, the predominant narrative is one in which heroic scientists and the military save the day with solid organizational skills, cutting-edge technology, and just a dash of authoritarianism. In her analysis of the political economy of Hollywood, Cultural historian Joyce Evans (1988) discusses how Vietnam changed public opinion about the capability of the U.S. Military and emboldened Hollywood filmmakers working in the 1960s and 1970s to subvert the political logic of those earlier films. For example, in director Joe Dante and screenwriter John Sayles Jaws parody/politically conscious eco-thriller, *Piranha* (1978), the military response is laughably inept. The Colonel in charge of the operation turns out to be an investor in the new resort in the desert, an "ecological miracle" named Aquarena Springs, which is in the path of the marauding fish.

The publication of Rachel Carson's *The Silent Spring* (1962) pushed the dangers of pesticides into the public sphere just as the 1963 Limited Test Ban Treaty, an acknowledgment that nuclear tests posed real risks to the Biosphere, pushed testing underground and out of site, but not entirely out of mind. Barrels of nuclear waste increasingly appeared in movies such as *Empire of the Ants* (1977) as a visual shorthand for the violence of pollution.[3] The radioactive waste barrel was a potent image, but it often reinforces themes of individual responsibility, with reckless workers rather than corporate or governmental agencies shown polluting a location. Efforts to radicalize citizens against corporate polluters were largely undermined by corporate-financed efforts such as the Keep America Beautiful campaign, which pivoted in 1971 to exploit counter cultural fetishization of Indigenous culture and reframe responsibility for pollution away from corporations and onto individuals, a subject explored in depth by *Finis Dunaway* (2015). One year after Iron Eyes Cody (an Italian American actor born Espera Oscar de Corti) became omnipresent in American media, shedding a tear over litter, *Frogs* (1972) opened with a scene in which photographer Pickett Smith (Sam Elliot) canoes through the Florida swamp documenting floating litter and inadvertently landing at the wealthy Crockett family's 4th of July celebration. Patriarch Jason Crocket (Ray Milland) hates nature and boasts of his right to poison and kill as much of it as he can to make a new world and further enrich his family. The local frogs, who have developed psychic powers in response to toxic pollution, soon marshal the assistance of the swamp's inhabitants to enact revenge and, it is implied, wage war on all of humanity. Jennifer Schell points out that films such as *Frogs* are themselves problematic in the ways in which they advance the idea of "natural ecosystems as possessing innate self-correcting mechanisms" (Schell 2015, 60).

While the isopods in *The Bay* are neither legendary eating machines nor explicitly vengeful, the intertextual references to animal attack and eco-horror films are an unsettling counterpoint to the realism implied in the mockumentary form. A brief scene involving a pair of Claridge teenagers serves as more than an homage to the countless teens in films such as *Jaws* and *Piranha* who venture into troubled waters. The young woman jumps in the water off of a dock and beckons to her boyfriend, a more chaste re-enactment of the opening scene in *Jaws* when doomed, naked Chrissie takes her own fateful midnight swim. It's notable that the boyfriend in *The Bay* laughingly assumes his girlfriend is being stung by jellyfish when she screams for help. That he chooses not to swim at first because he assumes the presence of jellyfish is an indication that negotiating the consequences of the dead zone are a way of life for the youth of Claridge. Jellyfish, which need little oxygen to survive, arrive and reproduce in astonishing numbers around dead zones, posing new health hazards to humans and marine mammals, complicating the recovery of native species, and damaging the intakes of water filtration systems, nuclear plants, and other industrial plants (Gershwin 2014).

NEW CONTAMINANTS IN OLD CONTAINERS

Prior to the isopod crisis, one of the Mayor's supporters is shown acknowledging the declining health of the Bay, saying "I know it looks a little different" before going on to unironically suggest they continue on the same path to "develop the hell out of the Bay, and then we can pay to clean it up!" Donna shows that the mayor has been complicit in advancing technological solutions which can't adapt to emerging threats while promoting the purity of the town's new water supply. That faith will complicate the early medical response to the outbreak, biasing how the emergency medical staff at the Claridge hospital diagnose the first patients they treat and leading the U.S. Centers for Disease Control (CDC) to attribute the first wave of the outbreak to the bacterium *Vibrio vulnificus*. This bacterium infects humans through contact with ocean water or ingestion of infected seafood and can be fatal within 48 hours without rapid treatment. Discussion of *Vibrio* is realistic in the film, describing it as an increasing threat in warming waters, and one which is often not recognized early enough in regions where it has only recently arrived due to climate change. The sudden, rapid onset of boils on the townspeople and tourists on Main Street is at first consistent with *Vibrio*, but as the day progresses the viewer learns that deaths across town are occurring which are not yet connected being connected to the apparent disease outbreak.

As the crisis accelerates, recordings from a local radio call-in show offer a glimpse of the fear taking hold in as hundreds of people descend on the overwhelmed hospital and communications systems break down. Paranoid conspiracy theories circulate through the community, with fears about terrorism, vaccines, satanic cults, and pesticides at the forefront. Although many of the conspiracies offered by the townspeople involve nefarious action or experimentation by the government, the danger all along has been, of course, inaction or obfuscation by political leaders and law enforcement. In addition to the environmental issues it foregrounds, *The Bay* raises urgent questions about the ability of agencies such as the U.S. Centers for Disease Control (CDC) to diagnose and react to both emerging and unexpected pathogens due to climate change. Additionally, the film critiques the (in)ability of the CDC and the Environmental Protection Agency (EPA) to function in a political system which prioritizes Capitalism over the common good and militarizes public health decision-making. The CDC is hampered by lack of information-sharing from other agencies who are aware of the developing situation, notably the EPA and Homeland Security. Dr. Williams (Robert Treveiler), the CDC communicable disease specialist, is a mild-mannered diagnostician. He is depicted as caring and competent but hampered by lack of information sharing and lack of data on the emerging threats climate change facilitates. He and his cohort of sensibly dressed colleagues gather to work the problem from a bland, utilitarian call-center in their Atlanta headquarters, a sharp contrast to dashing, globe-trotting epidemiologists in outbreak films such as *World War Z* (2013).

More than 350 patients have died at the hospital and hundreds more lie dead on Main Street when Alex and Stephanie finally dock in Claridge and walk into the lifeless town. Their arrival in the early evening and their stunned walk past the carnage on Main Street evokes the imagery of zombie apocalypse films, raising questions about the as-yet unknown potential of the isopods. Will the dead be reanimated by this pathogen? This question adds to the tension over whether any of the three are infected, particularly Alex, who Stephanie pushed into the water earlier in their trip. *The Bay* also draws on the legacy of the mind-control/alien invasion genre which flourished in Hollywood in the 1950s and has enjoyed periodic resurgence during times of political or social instability. In a scene in which deputies come upon a household which is in the early stages of infection, we lose sight of the deputy when he enters the house, and we only hear the events taking place in the house via the squad car radio. We can hear the infected pleading with the deputy to kill them, we have no way of knowing if they are begging to be relieved of their pain and terror, or if they also fear loss of identity and control to the parasite inside them. The film effectively uses our expectations around both of these horror tropes to heighten tension before subverting our expectation. The dead stay dead, while the adult isopods seem to flee the scene whenever they exit a body. The unresolved uncertainty about where the erupted isopods go or whether they will swarm, however, will create some ambiguity at the end of the film.

THE NIGHTMARE BELOW THE SURFACE

Homeland Security's apathetic response to the Claridge disaster is more frightening than the bumbling military response in *Piranha* (1978), but it also draws power from that film's conclusion, in which officials are confident they have neutralized the threat while viewers are offered evidence some of the piranhas have instead escaped into the open ocean. At the end of Donna's film within *The Bay*, we hear a recording of a call in which the military declined to intervene when they first became aware of the potential threat because a quarantine would be unpopular and could hurt the tourism economy. Instead, when the outbreak erupts, they close the bridge and trap everyone in the town. They wait until the next morning to quarantine the survivors, who apparently did not drink the tap water in town, and then use chlorine to kill the isopods. Over 700 people are dead, the survivors are paid for their silence, and the outbreak is officially attributed to *Vibrio vulnificus*. We are left to assume that Claridge's tourism industry evades social contamination, as outbreaks of bacteria such as *Vibrio* are spoken of as a sort of "new normal" in a world with warming seas. Mayor Stockman dies in a car crash as he tries to leave town. Claridge, like the water, had grown dangerously imbalanced due to the cascading disasters on the 4th. Donna explains that his injuries probably weren't fatal, but he died because there were no available first responders. We are left with the realization that the identity of the offscreen interviewer remains unknown to us, and, potentially, to Donna. Is Donna being manipulated by either the government or the poultry industry? Have we viewed Donna's film at all, or some mediated version of the Skype recording session? Was Donna's film ever made public at all? Does the real-life box-office failure in 2012 of *The Bay* now work in the film's favor to amplify our sense of unease over this inconclusive ending of the film within the film?[4] That we do not know if Donna's fears about her safety are valid, what her fate is, or what the interviewer does with the film after their session does, in the end, seem to co-locate The Bay as perhaps both mockumentary and found footage.

As she stated at the beginning of the film, Donna is compelled to complete this work for both personal reasons and because of her fervent belief that social and environmental injustice and criminal behavior have gone unpunished. She mourns the diminishment of the town not merely because of her presence as a reporter during the crisis but because of her long-term relationship to the town. Levinson chooses to give her relationship to Claridge the illusion of depth, but her nostalgia is not based on long-term residency. She grew up spending summers in Claridge with her family, which gives her a somewhat childish impression of the town as a place of leisure. Her work to uncover the roots of the 4th of July crisis parallels her growing understanding of the precarious ecological state of both the region and the world. Raymond Williams (1980) describes how the rise of industrial Capitalism entrenched the idea of a pristine and natural world in the cultural imaginary by reframing it as an idealized place of leisure and retreat far from the bustling urban centers and belching factories of the Western Industrial World. In the twenty-first century, it is increasingly difficult to ignore the reality that the by-products of those belching factories are inescapable. Donna has internalized the region's sense of self in the way she speaks of her own rites of passage, identifying Claridge as the place she ate her first crab and the place she had her first kiss. Her privileged perspective makes her an outsider, nevertheless, and she echoes the perspective of *Poisoned Waters* in her view of the Chesapeake as a place of recreation, a source of seafood, and tourism, rather than a complicated ecosystem that has been subjected to the unsustainable exploitation of settler colonialism in little over 100 years since the town was established. Although the film was released prior to widespread public engagement with the concept of the Anthropocene, *The Bay* is an unflinching acknowledgement that anthropogenic environmental damage has profound consequences for all life on the planet. In a scene in which the oceanographers are out in their research vessel on a glorious, cinematic spring day, one of the scientists addresses the camera. He cautions that the Bay is beautiful but that at least 40% of the total area is dead. He concludes with the ominous statement: "You have no idea of the nightmare underneath here." Strategically, this is the only scene in *The Bay* in which the water of the Bay appears healthy, blue, and alive.

NOTES

1. His directorial debut, *Diner* (1982), was the first in a cycle of films set in Levinson's hometown of Baltimore, Maryland. Levinson, an AU Communications alumni, also directed *Good Morning Vietnam* (1987), an acclaimed film about AU Communications alumni Adrian Cronauer's experiences as a DJ during the Vietnam War.

2. Locating the story in a fictional town adds to the viewer's sense of realism and unease. No town wishes to experience the fate of Burkettsville, Maryland, location of the found footage film *The Blair Witch Project* (1999), which invented and imposed folklore on the unsuspecting town.

3. Although *The Bay* is not a nuclear-themed movie, there is mention of potential groundwater contamination from an earlier accident, followed by the (accurate) explanation that the EPA does not monitor radiation levels, so they are not reflected in water safety reports

4. The producers of the film are unlikely to see it this way.

WORKS CITED

Carson, Rachel. 1962. *The Silent Spring*. New York: Penguin.
Dante, Joe (dir.). 1978. *Piranha*. Los Angeles: Shout! Factory.
Davis, Jack E. 2017. *The Gulf: The Making of an American Sea*. New York: W.W. Norton.
Douglas, Gordon (dir.). 1954. *Them!* Burbank: Warner Brothers.

Dunaway, Finis. 2015. *Seeing Green: The Use and Abuse of American Environmental Images*. Chicago: University of Chicago Press.

Estok, Simon. 2009. "Theorising in a Space of Ambivalent Openness: Ecocriticism and Ecophobia." *Interdisciplinary Studies in Literature and the Environment* 16 (2), 203–225.

Evans, Joyce. 1988. *Celluloid Mushroom Clouds: Hollywood and the Atomic Bomb*. Boulder: Westview Press.

Gershwin, Lisa-ann. 2014. *Stung! On Jellyfish Blooms and the Future of the Oceans*. Chicago: University of Chicago Press.

Gordon, Bert I. (dir.). 1977. *Empire of the Ants*. Beverley Hills: MGM Home Entertainment.

Levinson, Barry (dir.). 2012. *The Bay*. Santa Monica: Lionsgate.

Lifton, Robert Jay and Richard Falk. 1982. *Indefensible Weapons: The Political and Psychological Case Against Nuclearism*. New York: Basic Books.

McCowan, George (dir.). 1972. *Frogs*. Los Angeles: American International Pictures.

Murphy, Bernice. 2015. *The Rural Gothic in American Popular Culture: Backwoods Horror and Terror in the Wilderness*. London: Palgrave/Macmillan.

Sayad, Cecilia. 2016. "Found-Footage Horror and the Frame's Undoing." *Cinema Journal* 55 (2), 43–66.

Schell, Jennifer. 2015. "Polluting and Perverting Nature: The Vengeful Animals of *Frogs*." In *Animal Horror Cinema: Genre, History and Criticism*, edited by Katarina Gregersdotter, Johan Högland, and Nicklas Hallén. London: Palgrave/Macmillan, 58–75.

Spielberg, Stephen (dir.). 1975. *Jaws*. Universal City: Universal Pictures Home Entertainment.

Stone, T. May. 2018. "The Literary Zombie in Robin Becker's Brains: 'How Pop Culture Illuminates and Comments on the Current Zombie Crisis'." *The Popular Culture Studies Journal* 6 (3), 420–440.

Szwarc, Jeannot (dir.). *Jaws 2*. Universal City: Universal Pictures Home Entertainment.

Wallace, Richard. 2021. "Documentary Style as Post-Truth Monstrosity in the Mockumentary Horror Film." *Quarterly Review of Film and Video* 38 (6), 519–540.

Wheeler, Timothy. 2012. "Scientists find a little to like in 'Bay' film." *The Baltimore Sun*, 2 November.

Williams, Raymond. 1980. "Ideas of Nature." In *Materialsm and Culture*, edited by Raymond Williams. London: Verso. 67–85.

Young, Rick (dir.). 2009. *Frontline Poisoned Waters*. Available at https://www.pbs.org/wgbh/frontline/film/poisonedwaters/. Accessed October 1, 2021.

Part III

THE ANTHROPOCENE AND
THE END OF "TIME"

Chapter 7

"Dying All the Time"

The Future as the Extended Present and the Zombification of History in the Anthropocene

Elana Gomel

Since the beginning of the COVID-19 pandemic, we have been living in the extended present, in which the past and the future seem to have disappeared. Our sense of time has been scrambled; our ability to tell a coherent story of ourselves compromised.

> Just about everyone agrees that time is passing very strangely since COVID-19 took hold in early 2020. Some days take forever, while months are flying by, partly because there is so much "sameness" in being stuck at home every day. A survey conducted in the UK revealed more than 80% of participants felt like their perception of time had shifted during the past few months of lockdown restrictions compared to pre-quarantine times.(Lindberg 2020)

The situation described here is not limited to individuals. Collective narratives of history have become equally problematic. We have entered a phase of "presentism," in which history-writing struggles with the possibility of imagining the future different from the present or remembering the past in its essential alterity.

But this "strangeness" of time, the sense that the linear arrow of past-present-future has somehow been bent and broken, is not a simple effect of repeated lockdowns. We had been living in the extended present long before COVID struck. Indeed, the pandemic has simply exposed what was already happening with our collective sense of time. Plagued by the premonition of some final catastrophe, which never quite arrives, we are stuck in the "Limbotopia" of gradual deterioration (Gomel and Shemtov 2018). As with every socio-cultural pathology, there is a monster to represent it. The rotting time of the Anthropocene is incarnated in the rotting flesh of our era's most popular monster: the zombie. Zombies are monsters of duration and repetition; of collapsed narratives and broken histories; not of death but of dying. Repetitive, boring, and mindless, the zombie encapsulates our historical anomie. And while the popularity of zombie movies and novels per se has waned somewhat in the last couple of years, it is arguable that we no longer need the walking dead because we are already living in their world, the world of the Anthropocene. I do not claim that climate change is the only cause of the zombification of history Indeed, in my previous work with Vered Shemtov on this topic, we argued that the death of utopian ideologies, whether communism or Zionism, is a primary factor in the emergence of Limbotopia. Here, however, I want to explore the relationship between the eternal present and the Anthropocene and to do it specifically through the lens of speculative narratives that link zombies with climate change.

As Paul Ricoeur famously argued, "temporality [is] that structure of existence that reaches language in narrativity, and narrativity [is] that language structure that has temporality as its ultimate reference" (2002, 35). In other words, narrative temporalities closely track the cultural and psychological perceptions of time. Narrative time, as per Gerard Genette, has three different aspects: chronology, duration, and frequency (1980). Any widespread shift in the relationship among these three aspects has to correspond to a cultural change in temporality and therefore historicity. And while ecological zombie fictions, seem at first glance to be a rather niche genre, I will argue that their structural and thematic features reflect the widespread historical malaise of the Anthropocene.

THE PRESENT SHOCK (AND OTHER CHRONIC CONDITIONS)

In his 2014 book, Hans Gumbrecht described our current perception of history as the "chronotope of the broad present":

> Different from the ever shrinking and therefore "imperceptibly short" present of the historicist chronotope, the new present (that continues to be our present in the early twenty-first century) is one in which all paradigms and phenomena from the past are juxtaposed as being available and ready-to-hand. For this present, instead of leaving the past behind, is inundated with pastness, and at the same time it is facing a future which, instead of being an open horizon of possibilities, seems occupied by threats that are inevitably moving towards us (think of "global warming," as an example). (15)

The concept of chronotope is central to narratology. Derived from Mikhail Bakhtin's work, it describes the artistic unity of representation of space and time in a literary text. Chronotope is the spacetime of a fictional world. But Gumbrecht applies the notion to culture as a whole, following in the footsteps of such historians as Karl Schloegel who wrote a "synchronous narrative" of Stalinism not as a series of dates and events but as an "experiential space" with a particular emphasis on how this cultural chronotope is reflected in, and refracted by, narrative texts (2012, 4).

The chronotope of the Anthropocene is shaped by the disjunction between two timescales: that of climate change and that of individual human lives. As Timothy Morton points out: "The worry is not whether the world will end, as in the old model of dis-astron, but whether the end of the world is already happening, or whether perhaps it might already have taken place. A deep shuddering of temporality occurs" (2014, 352). This "shuddering of temporality" started with the discovery of deep geological time in the Victorian era. Lyell and Darwin already realized that the incommensurability between the millions (later billions) years of evolution and the short span of an individual human life delivered a profound psychic wound to humanity's self-importance. And this wound had narrative consequences as well, since as opposed to the Bible and other sacred texts that synchronized human and geological history, Darwinism drastically disconnected the two. Fictional narratives of evolution, such as H. G. Wells' pioneering *The Time Machine* (1896), used the device of time travel to bring them back together. Though the Time Traveler covers hundreds of thousands of years of geological time, his own subjective experience of it is neatly folded into a week of adventure. Later, SF employed the format of "future history" to enable a panoramic view of geological time while retaining an individual-centered perspective. Olaf Stapledon's *Last and First Men* (1930) and *Star Maker* (1937) experimented with a collective and/or superhuman point of view with intermittent success.

But the Anthropocene differs from geological time in general because its scale, while exceeding individual perception, is not measured in millions or billions of years but in decades or perhaps centuries. While not arriving with the bang of a mushroom cloud, climate change is not as slow as plate tectonics. It is both here and somewhere in the future; both arriving and having arrived; both avertable and inevitable. Morton describes this quality of Anthropocene time as "viscosity": the gooey sense of duration and slowdown that the pandemic made into everyday reality. We are forced to coexist with geological temporalities on daily basis. A point made as he further observes "All humans . . . are now aware that they have entered a new phase of history in which nonhumans are no longer excluded or merely decorative features of their social, psychic, and philosophical space" (2014, 467).

The end of the world, according to Morton, has a beginning, which is the Industrial Revolution. But it does not have an end. Or rather, "the end of the world has already occurred" (201). It is instructive to compare the sense of doom today with the fear of the nuclear war in the twentieth century. Then, speculative fictions describing the nuclear catastrophe were invariably cast in the modality of the traditional apocalypse that descended from the Christian Book of Revelation to contemporary dystopias. The apocalyptic plot, described in such classics as Norman Cohn's *Pursuit of the Millennium* (1970) and Lee Quinby's *Millennial Seductions* (1999), has a clear and rigid chronology: from signs and portents to the Tribulations, and then the Millennium. Whether in its religious or secular modality, the traditional apocalypse is the ultimate in what Frank Kermode called "the sense of an ending": the human desire to have a clear-cut beginning, middle, and end; to give a narrative shape to the shapelessness of experience (Kermode 1967). The last century articulated its fears and hopes through what Quinby called "techno-millennialism": the premonition of the ultimate end of history (18). Whether this end arrived in the form of the nuclear war, the technological transcendence, the Thousand-year Reich, or the classless communist society, it signified an absolute break between the present and the future. The twentieth century lived in the constant state of future shock.

Today, however, we are reeling from what Douglas Rushkoff describes as the "present shock," in which everything is happening now, and the interval between beginning and ending has been stretched out to encompass the entirety of history, scrambling chronology, and undercutting the "grand narratives" of the past: ". . . prophecy no longer feels like a description of the future but rather, as a guide to the present. . . . The messianic age is no longer something to prepare for; it is a current event" (2013, 1).

If prophecy has become "a guide to the present," what, then, becomes of the apocalypse? So-called zombie apocalypse is a trending category on Amazon. But I will argue that it is a misnomer. Zombie narratives, while accurately reflecting the temporality of the Anthropocene, are in no way apocalyptic. Rather, they demonstrate a narrative mutation of the genre which indicates precisely how history has fallen victim to the chronic disease of climate change.

BORED TO/OF DEATH

Despite the stunning popularity of the zombie and literally entire libraries written to explain this phenomenon, there is still something mysterious about it. The zombie is not only ugly and revolting but also irredeemably boring. It does nothing but literally recycles itself: the dead rise, eat the living, rise again—rinse and repeat. The vampire is sexy and alluring; Frankenstein's monster is both terrible and pitiful; even the werewolf offers some moments of genuine dread as it navigates the borderland between human and animal. But the zombie is monotony made flesh. I do not mean that zombie movies, games, and novels cannot frighten or gross out their consumer but rather that the thrills they offer is peculiarly static, defying the Aristotelian arc of beginning, middle, and end. The trajectory of a zombie narrative, in whatever medium, is that of repetition.

In his entertaining cultural history of zombies, Roger Luckhurst asks the question of "why this particular figure of the undead has become so all-pervasive?" (2016, 10). He gives a long list of reasons, from the economy of global capitalism to the legacy of colonialism. But one particular strand in zombie history is the medicalization of death and the emergence of dying as a distinct and prolonged state of being.

Death is the ultimate ending. Kermode argues that the traditional shape of narrative—beginning, middle, end—is natural and universal precisely because it is so tied to the biology of human existence. But this is not the only possible narrative form:

> Traditional stories, with traditional linear arcs, have been around for a long time because they work. They seem to imitate the shape of real life, from birth to death. . . . While it seems natural to us today, this familiar shape did not become the default structure of stories until pretty late in human history. . . . (Rushkoff 2013, 18)

Rushkoff points to the emergence of seriality as a counterbalance to the "linear arc." Serial narratives, whether online, on the TV, or in streaming, undercut the traditional dependence of narrative on chronology and emphasize duration or repletion instead: "the timelessness, even the purposelessness, of living in the present" (2013, 30). Seriality is ubiquitous in popular culture today, and nowhere more so than in zombie narratives. Indeed, they positively require seriality. As opposed to ghosts and vampires who are always embedded in a unique story-arc, zombies are monsters of repetition. The ghost story is rooted in a particular location, a particular transgression, and a particular chain of supernatural consequences. Not so zombie narratives: they can—and do—take place anywhere. Zombies are globalized monsters, indifferent to their origin and careless of their consequences. Zombification erases narrative identity. Even vampires who undergo a wrenching ontological metamorphosis retain traces of their pre-mortem identity; in fact, the metamorphosis itself is often the result of their individual actions, as in Dracula's necromancy or Lucy's sexual transgression in Bram Stoker's *Dracula*. But zombies have no names, no memories, and no histories. Theirs is the horror of endlessly replicating simulacra. And while a zombie narrative must, by necessity, end somewhere, the cut-off point is arbitrary.

The fortunes of *The Walking Dead* show epitomize the strange chronotope of zombie history. The show, having broken all records of popularity, is slated to end next year (2022) after an eleven-year run. By now, it is no longer a show or even a franchise but a "universe," expanding horizontally and gobbling up more and more timelines, characters, stories, and places. And yet, despite Norman Reedus promising a "mindblowing" twist in the last season, nobody really expects a cure, a final defeat of the zombies, or even an explanation of where they came from (Bone 2021). The words "apocalypse" means unveiling or revelation, but no revelation is forthcoming at the end of the series that has, meanwhile, spawned a whole ecosystem of sequels, prequels, and sidequels. The show is no longer about zombies but about ordinary people trudging through their zombie-fighting routines. It is not about the dead but the dying.

In the popular Netflix series *Russian Doll,* the time-loop-caught heroine Nadia quips: "Doesn't matter. I die all the time." This line can be read in two ways: as repetition and as duration. Nadia dies repeatedly; but she is also dying all time, never ending quite dead. It seems that today, she shares her predicament with all of humanity. In his book *Learning to Die in the Anthropocene* (2015), Roy Scranton argues that our failure at the face of climate change is inevitable, and that the only freedom we have left is the choice of how to fail. We are living in the in-between time of interminable dying. We are already zombies, but we behave as if we are not.

But while TV shows and video games are uniquely adapted to the durational temporality of zombiehood, allowing for multiple seasons or (in the case of video games) multiple timelines, traditional literary narratives do not have this luxury. Of course, trilogies, sequels, and series have become ubiquitous in the world of publishing, but they are still limited by the exigencies of book trade and the very real possibility of reader fatigue. And so, literary zombies have to struggle harder to reconcile the anti-narrative temporality of zombiehood with the demands of traditional fictional genres. Precisely for that reason, they are particularly illuminating.

In this essay, I take a somewhat counter-intuitive approach by focusing on literary narratives exclusively. It is not because movies, shows, and games cannot be used for analyzing cultural chronotopes. Rather, the form of the literary narrative works against the zombie temporality and thus lays bare its structural and thematic underpinnings. I will look at the use of generic hybridity and other literary techniques, such as pastiche and intertextuality, as a counterweight to the "presentism" of the zombie. And I will argue that the failure of these techniques to provide an adequate closure signifies the failure of the collective imagination to come to terms with dying in the Anthropocene.

CRUSADES OF THE UNDEAD

In Tim Lebbon's *Coldbrook* (2012), zombies (called "furies" in the novel) escape from a lab and conquer Earth. The lab, however, is not some virus-breeding secret installation. It is, in fact, a physics facility, engaged in exploring the multiverse through constructing "quantum bridges" to parallel worlds. A fury crosses over, and the epidemic of the living dead ensues. The novel was positively reviewed but some readers expressed bewilderment at its unusual combination of alternative-history science fiction and zombie horror. Indeed, Lebbon, better known for his horror and dark fantasy novels, has several stories of the more traditional zombie-invasion kind. But *Coldbrook* is striking not only in its generic hybridity but also in the way this hybridity is used to explore the fissure between "zombie" and "apocalypse."

The idea of the multiverse is predicated on the so-called Many Worlds solution to the quantum uncertainty principle and basically states that anything that can happen does happen—in one of the infinity of parallel universes. Alternative history is a popular subgenre of SF, in which a single "what if" unfolds into a new historical timeline. Alternative history is the opposite of zombie history because it undercuts the very idea of repetition. No road can be taken twice; no action can be replayed; every alteration in the past generates a unique future. Moreover, as opposed to the void of subjectivity represented by zombies, alternative history places individual agency at the center of historical process. No matter how seemingly insignificant, every choice creates a whole new universe.

Lebbon's attempt to fuse these two genres in a single text fractures its chronotope. The repetitive downbeat of furies killing and infecting first individual characters and then entire communities is juxtaposed with the narrative arc of adventure and discovery as Jonas, the scientist who created Coldbrook, uses the quantum bridge to explore new worlds. Moreover, this exploration brings about the traditional closure of an apocalyptic plot: the millennium. The new world is literally new, as the survivors of Coldbrook move onto a pastoral version of Earth. Causality, conspicuously absent in most zombie narratives, is also restored. Luckhurst points out that the cultural evolution of the zombie got rid of most explanations for its existence, from black magic to viral infections. The walking dead simply *are*. But in *Coldbrook*, the reason for the furies is strikingly metafictional: they are literally the death of history.

It turns out that the furies epidemic, raging across the infinite "what might have been" of the multiverse, is not a random disease but a religious crusade. It is engineered by an alternative version of the Catholic Church which regards the open-ended tree of possibilities as a blasphemy. Their goal is to prune this tree back to its main trunk, to reduce the infinite number of possible worlds to "God's only world" (Lebbon 2012, 631). The furies are a weapon in the war against time. At the end of the novel, Jonas releases the furies virus in the alternative Vatican whence the disease originated by infecting himself. His deliberate self-sacrifice repudiates the void of subjectivity represented by the zombie. Indeed, his zombification is paradoxically a restoration of humanity, as in his last moments, he sees the furies as "a very human tragedy" of misguided faith (630). Choices have consequences. Holly, another scientist who takes her last stand against the furies, feels that her actions matter on a universal scale: "Even here, she felt realities hinging on one act or one object. If this screw failed, realities might change. If this capacitor was faulty, stars might crumble" (605).

A common response to the Anthropocene is apathy or despair, and most zombie narratives reflect this in their characters' attitudes. Struggle for survival is the only possible reaction to the zombie plague. *Coldbrook* explicitly reframes both zombification and resistance to it in terms of collective and individual choices. Zombies are a deliberate human creation predicated on a toxic ideology that longs for an end to historical contingency. Escape from zombiehood requires restarting history in a new—and better—world. While narratively far more satisfying than most zombie novels, *Coldbrook* does not (so far) have a sequel. Lebbon's most recent novel, however, addresses the same issue of zombie history versus human history, but this time explicitly engaging climate change.

GAIA OR LILITH?

Lebbon's novel *Eden* (2020) takes place in the ecologically depleted future, devastated by climate change. To enable nature to regenerate, "pure" preservation zones have been set aside, cleansed of all human presence. A group of extreme-sports adventurers illegally venture into one such zone nicknamed Eden. But instead of paradise, they encounter—zombies. Reanimated by a mutated orchid, walking dead attack the group, helped along by creepily sentient wildlife.

The novel is remarkable in its refusal to adapt to the current eco-discourse, in which nature is anthropomorphically represented as an innocent victim of human predation, Gaia under attack. Instead, *Eden* goes back to the Darwinian poetics of H. G. Wells and other twentieth-century SF British writers, such as John Wyndham, who represented nature as the ultimate Other: indifferent, overwhelming, and sublime in its disdain for humanity. As they flounder through Eden, one of Lebbon's characters describes her experience:

> I can't call it unnatural, 'cause I think it was purely natural. Maybe it was inhuman. . . . There's this Jewish legend. Says that God left a corner of creation

unfinished and challenged anyone who thought themselves greater than Him to
finish it for themselves. . . . And 'if there's any place on Earth similar to what
they were talking all that time ago, it's Eden. (Lebbon 2020, 40)

Eden is what is "left over" from the human narrative of creation; in which
nature is brought into the sphere of culture as either a mother or a virgin (the
preservation zones are dubbed Virgin Zones). Eden is a personification of one
of Morton's "hyperobjects": an intrusion of the inhuman into the sphere of
humanity, a locale where "nonhumans make decisive contact with humans"
(Morton 2014, 172). I use "personification" and "locale" interchangeably
because Eden is both: an entity and a place; an actant (in the narratological
sense of a character who does not have to be a human being) and a setting.
The personified aspect of Eden is called Lilith: an "elemental," borrowing
her name from the Jewish legend of Adam's first wife who did not eat of the
fruit of Knowledge of Good and Evil and who therefore remained outside
both morality and mortality. Excluded from the Biblical narrative of human
history, Lilith exists in the infinite duration of geological time.

The landscape of Eden is sublime in its commingling of beauty and terror. The zone is "beautiful and disturbing"; "there would be dangers here,
but there were wonders as well" Lebbon 2020, 84). The zombies, nature's
ultimate weapon against humanity, are monsters created by lovely flowers.
Dylan, the head of the expedition, is killed by the zombie of his ex-wife
whom he has come to Eden to find. But this undead Kat is not a mindless,
rotting flesh-eater of *The Walking Dead* variety. Instead, she has become
something else, something strange, alluring, and most of all, inhuman. As
Dylan embraces her in his last moment, he embraces Eden itself.

The chronotopes of *Coldbrook* and *Eden* are an attempt to reconcile zombie history and human history through generic hybridization, bringing in elements of other speculative genres to offset the monotony of zombiehood. In
Coldbrook, it is alternative history that mitigates the fury of time-devouring
zombie plague. In *Eden*, the text uses the chronotope of the Zone: a science-
fictional device of the inclusion of a heterotopic space, in Foucault's sense of
the word, within the larger spacetime matrix of the text. This device is familiar from such classics as the Strugatsky brothers' *Roadside Picnic* (1978)
where it is used to offer an alternative to the writers' humdrum sociopolitical
reality. But in *Eden*, the Virgin Zone is not a refuge but a trap. Its flower-
zombies are embodiments of the slow catastrophe of the Anthropocene, the
"broad present" of evolution in which time is always "now." The escape from
Eden hinges on the incongruity of the two temporalities: that of humanity and
that of Lilith, the zombie goddess of nature. As the last surviving expedition
member, Kat's daughter, crosses the border of Eden, she still has the ghost
orchid that can return humanity to the paradise of the undead. The choice is

the same as in *Coldbrook*: time or timelessness, history or forgetting, death or dying. Jenn chooses history:

"For a long while she simply held it, two uncertain futures resting in her muddy hand. Then she trailed her hand in the water and let the petal float away" (2020, 268). Rather than offering a utopian alternative to civilization, the Virgin Zones are places of horror because of the incongruity between human time and nature time.

Warnings about climate change often ignore the fact that the danger is to humanity rather than the planet. Earth has undergone a number of major extinction events in its geological past, including several caused by high levels of CO2. And yet evolution went on, generating new species. It is not that the biosphere is dead. It is humanity who is dying:

"Thing no one gets is, no matter how much we've fucked ourselves, the planet's gonna be just fine."

"Eventually," Lucy said.

"Eventually's too long for us, but the blink of an eye for nature," Selina said. (Lebbon 2020, 40)

THE WORLD WITHOUT HISTORY

In his book *Black Earth*, historian Timothy Snyder describes Hitler's bio-politics as a "world without history" (2015, 7). Since Hitler saw everything through the prism of eternal biological struggle, specific conflicts between nations and ethnicities only masked the underlying ineluctable law of nature: racial survival at all costs. Repetition was Hitler's master narrative, explaining, for example, why Nazi propaganda could easily equate capitalism and communism as identical expressions of the underlying spirit of the Jewish "anti-race." Since nothing new could possibly occur in the struggle (at least until the final millennial cleansing of humanity from the Jewish menace), the "broad present" was merely a series of repetitive clashes between races understood as species. Biology subsumed history. But Snyder's own interpretation of the contemporary world bears an uncanny similarity to Hitler's: not, of course, in the sense of giving any credence to the latter's racial theories but rather by emphasizing the ecological factors that shape politics, specifically the climate change: "the planet is changing in ways that might make Hitlerian description of life, space, and time more plausible" (326). Just like during World War II, the past and the future are subsumed by the never-ending present. For the Nazis, if "past and future contained nothing but struggle and scarcity, all attention fell upon the present" (322). But this is the same "broad present" that characterizes the contemporary post-utopian zeitgeist: "In much of the world, the dominant sense of time is coming to resemble, in some respects, the catastrophism of Hitler's era" (325). Perhaps the makers of the Zombie Army Trilogy video game, in which Hitler unleashes an army of the walking dead upon the West, should be credited with more historical sense than most people would be willing to admit![1]

Two famous zombie novels explicitly address mid-twentieth-century wars. Max Brooks' *World War Z* (2006), subtitled "an oral history of the Zombie War," is modeled on Stud Terkel's celebrated compilation of personal narratives *The Good War: An Oral History of World War Two* (1984). It is clearly an attempt to revive the patriotic "we-are-in-it-together" spirit of *The Good War* in a fictional setting. And in Manel Loureiro's entertaining trilogy *Apocalypse Z* (2007–2012), a zombie invasion revives the Spanish Civil War. As the protagonist and his girlfriend travel through zombie-overrun Europe, they eventually shelter on the Canary Islands which is torn by a political and military struggle between the "Royalists . . .[who] would control Gran Canaria under the protection of the military junta" and the Republicans who declare Tenerife "the Third Spanish Republic" and elect a "National Emergency Democratic Government" (Loureiro, 114). Much mayhem ensues, with the survivors furiously debating the pros and cons of "a democratic monarchy" versus the republic and tossing the moth-eaten insults of "royalist scum" and "communist" at each other, while the zombies are the gate (2; 199–200). The two novels are not so much histories of the undead, as they are undead history.

However, while ordinary zombies merely rewind history, Anthropocene zombies often erase it altogether. In Joshua David Bellini's YA *Ecosystem* cycle (2018–2020), attempts to fight off the sixth extinction of the Anthropocene lead to the inadvertent creation of a sentient Ecosystem: nature purposefully rebelling and targeting humanity. This malevolent Gaia kills off most of humanity, reducing the rest to a hunter-gatherer lifestyle. But the eusocial bee genes that have been spread through the ecosphere to bind it all together also generate a caste of human "queens" who can command the living and the dead. Zombies are human beings infested with the "black vines" of the corrupted Ecosystem, doing the bidding of their undead queen.

The hunter-gatherer society of *Ecosystem* is far from ideal—its small villages are repressive; its queen-ruled townships caught in dynastic battles; and the sentient nature itself is predatory and dangerous, even more so than in *Eden*. But for some historians today, it seems that the only way out of the coming catastrophe of climate change is to go back not just to the preindustrial age but even earlier. The invention of agriculture and the rise of larger settlements, known today as the Neolithic revolution, are blamed for the Anthropocene. David Wallace-Wells argues in *The Uninhabitable Earth: Life After Warming* that agriculture was the first step in the wrong direction.

Stating (without much evidence) that our Paleolithic ancestors were happier and healthier than we are, he argues that the entire concept of history is misguided:

> And already in this age of nascent ecological crisis, you can read a whole new literature of deep skepticism—proposing not only that history can move in reverse, but that the entire project of human settlement and civilization, which we know as "history" and which has given us climate change, has been, in fact, a jet stream backward. (2019, 218)

But since agriculture is not likely to be abolished, Wallace-Wells' argument is not so much about history as a process as about historiography as a narrative. What would the master narrative of history be if progress, even qualified and limited, is rejected? It would not be the cyclical temporality of some Eastern cultures because climate change is a genuinely new phenomenon. But nor would it be linear and teleological. Instead, we would be confronted with a horde of refurbished and reanimated stories, shambling around and ready to eat our brains:

> But climate change isn't likely to deliver a neat or complete return to a cyclical view of history, at least in the premodern sense—in part because there will be nothing neat, at all, about the era ushered in by warming. The likelier outcome is a much messier perspective, with teleology demoted from its position as an organizing, unifying theory, and, in its place, contradictory narratives running uncorralled, like animals unleashed from a cage and moving in all directions at once. (Wallace-Wells 2019, 221)

The Anthropocene zombie becomes a figure not so much of the end of history as of its purposeless and mindless recycling. Not quite buried, not completely rotten, neither dead nor alive, the zombie's unchecked proliferation undercuts the very idea of meaningful agency: "The problem of the zombie, in these terms, is a problem of incomplete exorcism or unsuccessful burial, and the zombie becomes the incarnation of some deep unease about history" (Berger 2013, 18). The evolutionary adaptation that has become increasingly popular in zombie narratives today is parasitism, epitomized by the so-called zombie fungus, *Ophiocordyceps unilateralis*, which takes over the brains of ants and some other insect species to modify their behavior to suit its reproductive needs. This kind of parasitism crops up in the *Ecosystem* series, in Joseph Wallace's *Invasive Species* (2013), in which parasitic wasps reduce humanity to their slaves, and in M. R. Carey's popular *The Girl with All the Gifts* (2014), to name but a few. In all of them, the outbreak of parasitic infections is explicitly linked to climate change.

Parasitism acts to erase the distinction between nature and culture, as humans become enslaved by the mindless biological processes instigated by "lower" organisms: insects, fungi or viruses. But at the same time, parasitism functions as a covert alibi for what has been called "climate apathy": refusal to confront the reality of the Anthropocene, as we "proceed, zombie-like ourselves, down a path to ruin" (Wallace-Wells 2019, 161). If history is merely evolution by other means, humanity is absolved of all responsibility. Our interactions with the hyperobjects of climate change, geological time, speciation, and extinction shatters the human capacity for telling a coherent story of where we came from and where we are going, and therefore render impossible any kind of meaningful change. While zombie slaves of wasps, fungi, or the Ecosystem seem to be a warning against ecological degradations, in fact they offer an easy way out for climate change pessimists and skeptics alike. In a world without history, there is nothing to be done to atone for the past or change the future.

The chronotopes of the novels mentioned above exhibit the same kind of hybridity as *Coldbrook* and *Eden*, incorporating elements of pastiche and intertextuality in Brooks and Loreido, romance in Bellini, pastoral in Wallace, and even utopia in Carey. These elements sit uneasily with the durational temporality of zombiehood, creating strange rifts and contradictions in the fabric of the plot. But they are the only way to rescue the narrative from monotony, repetitiveness, or simple incoherence. Since zombiehood alone cannot provide a closure, it has to come from somewhere else. The problem is that by recycling generic templates, Anthropocene zombie narratives simply replicate their monsters' recycling of human bodies. No matter how much we try to reach into the future, we are locked in the world without history.

The chronotope of the broad present, the Limbotopia, the present shock. All of them describe a world in which narrative itself is in crisis—not a particular genre, form, or topic but storytelling as a fundamental (perhaps *the* fundamental) human tool for coming to terms with passage of time, change, and mortality. While the explosion of narratives online and in various forms of electronic media seems to push against this grim prognosis, the figure of the zombie functions as a metaphor for, and a warning against, reproduction as the only metric of success. There are many more stories told today than in any other period in human history. But do they function in the way Ricouer envisioned narrative to function: as a way to apprehend time itself? It seems that what they offer instead is a mere repetition of the Anthropocene malaise: "the triumph of an undead species, a mindless shuffle toward extinction" (Wallace-Wells 2019, 236). Despite the alarmist projections of the planet becoming uninhabitable soon, we are not dead yet. We are just dying all the time.

NOTE

1. See http://www.zombiearmy.com/. Between 2001 and 2013, at least eleven films featuring Nazi zombies were made, mostly in Europe. The previous five decades had only four.

WORKS CITED

Gomel, Elana and Vered Karti Shemtov. 2018. "Utopia, Dystopia, Limbotopia: A Case for Expanding the Genres of the Future." *Comparative Literature*, Vol. 70, Issue 1, 60–71.

Bakhtin, Mikhail. 2002. "Forms of Time and of Chronotope in the Novel." In *Narrative Dynamics: Essays on Time, Plot, Closure, and Frames*, by Brian Richardson. Columbus OH: Ohio University Press, 15–25.

Bellinie, Joshua David. 2018. *Ecosystem.* Kindle Editions.

Berger, James. 2013. "Zombies and the End of Society." http://www.e-ir.info/. 2 15. Accessed September 23, 2015.

Bone, Christian. 2021. "The Walking Dead's Norman Reedus Teases A Mind-Blowing Final Season." *We Got This Covered.* 2 August. https://wegotthiscovered.com/tv/the-walking-deads-norman-reedus-teases-a-mind-blowing-final-season/. Accessed October 1, 2021.

Brooks, Max. 2006. *World War Z: An Oral History of the Zombie War.* New York: Crown Books.

Carey, M. R. 2014. *The Girl with All the Gifts.* New York: Orbit Books.

Genette, Gerard. 1980. *Narrative Discourse.* Ithaca NY: Cornell University Press.

Gumbrecht, Hans Ulrich. 2014. *Our Broad Present: Time and Contemporary Culture.* New York: Columbia University Press.

Kermode, Frank. 1967. *The Sense of an Ending.* Oxford: Oxford University Press.

Lebbon, Tim. 2012. *Coldbrook.* London: Hammer.

———. 2020. *Eden.* New York: Titan Books.

Lindberg, Sara. 2020. "Perception of Time Has Shifted During COVID-19, New Survey Reports." *Very Well Mind.* 24 August. < https://www.verywellmind.com/why-time-is-passing-so-strangely-during-covid-5075438>. Accessed October 1, 2021.

Loureiro, Manel. 2007. *Apocalypse Z: The Beginning of the End* [2012], trans. by Pamela Carmell. Las Vegas: Amazon Crossing.

Luckhurst, Roger. 2016. *Zombies: A Cultural History.* London: Reaktion Books.

Morton, Timothy. 2013. *Hyperobjects: Philosophy and Ecology after the End of the World.* Minneapolis: University of Minnesota Press.

Quinby, Lee. 1999. *Millennial Seduction: A Skeptic Confronts Apocalyptic Culture.* Ithaca NY: Cornell University Press.

Ricoeur, Paul. 2002. "Narrative Time." In *Narrative Dynamics: Essays on Time, Plot, Closure, and Frames*, by ed. Brian Richardson, 35–46. Columbus: OSU Press.

Rushkoff, Douglas. 2013. *Present Shock: When Everything Is Happening Now.* New York: Current.

Schloegel, Karl. 2012. *Moscow, 1957.* Cambridge: Polity Press.

Scranton, Roy. 2015. *Learning to Die in the Anthropocene.* City Lights Open Media.

Snyder, Timothy. 2015. *Black Earth: Holocaust as History and Warning.* New York: Random House.

Wallace-Wells, David. 2019. *The Uninhabtable Earth: Life After Warming.* New York: The Duggan Books.

Chapter 8

Avenging the Anthropocene

Returning the Dead to Life while Destroying the Planet in **The Avengers** *Films*

Kevin J. Wetmore Jr.

"No more resurrections this time," asserts Thanos (Josh Brolin) in the opening scene of *Avengers: Infinity War,* calling attention to the idea that superheroes and villains come back from the dead all the time. Indeed, in *Avengers: Age of Ultron,* Captain America (Chris Evans) tells the members of the team as they fight Ultron's robots, "You get hurt, hurt 'em back. You get killed—walk it off." But with Thanos, death is inevitable and permanent. He proceeds to kill Loki (Tom Hiddleston), a god from Asgard and trickster figure known for escaping impossible situations. Instead, Loki is permanently dead in the first few minutes of the film. It is as much a signal as one can have that one of the larger themes of the film is the new-found permanence of death in a genre known for bringing back the dead all the time. One need not think of superhero cinema as gothic, but there are the occasional overlaps of genre elements.

AVENGERS INTRODUCES DEATH INTO THE MCU

The Marvel Cinematic Universe (MCU) is an ever-expanding group of films and television series loosely tied together by taking place within the same shared universe of superheroes. These films include series based on the characters Iron Man (Robert Downey, Jr.), Thor (Chris Hemsworth), Hulk (Mark Ruffalo), Spider Man (Tom Holland), Captain America, Black Widow (Scarlett Johansson), the Guardians of the Galaxy, Black Panther (Chadwick Boseman), Ant Man (Paul Rudd), Doctor Strange (Benedict Cumberbatch), and Captain Marvel (Brie Larson), all of which ultimately coincide in the four-film Avengers series: *The Avengers* (2012), *Avengers: Age of Ultron* (2015), *Avengers: Infinity War* (2018), and *Avengers: Endgame* (2019). Previous and intermittent films include significant parts of the larger narrative of the MCU, telling of the rise of superheroes, the conflicts with villains and between heroes with conflicting agendas, and the slowly expanding awareness of those on Earth of a galaxy full of similar beings, facing many of the same issues on their respective planets. The four films in the *Avengers* cycle chronicle first the development by Nick Fury (Samuel L. Jackson), director of S.H.I.E.L.D., of the "Avengers Initiative," a loose organization of a half-dozen superheroes (initially), that expands to include a few dozen members, tasked with protecting the Earth from existential threats. The irony is twofold in that the heroes themselves often represent the existential threat and the greatest battle they have is with a galactic being concerned with the dangers of overpopulation and overconsumption, which requires them to defend a lifestyle that is ultimately destructive of the environment.

The two films *Avengers: Infinity War* and *Avengers: Endgame* form a dyad that first sees the eponymous group of superheroes fighting to prevent the deaths of trillions across the galaxy, then fighting to bring back the dead without transforming or losing any person or event that has occurred in the five years since half the population disintegrated into nothingness due to Thanos's plan. The *Avengers* dyad introduces a gothic element into superhero cinema: much of the two films take place on devastated and ruined worlds, such as Titan and a post-Thanos Earth. Thanos, after ending half the life in the galaxy, returns to Titan and lives in the ruins. The films also focus on fear and madness, grief and loss. Captain America, called "The First Avenger" in the title of the first *Captain America* film, is reduced to the role of grief support group leader at the opening of *Endgame*. The dyad is gothic in that the films center on death, loss, madness, fear, and life among the ruins once the great catastrophe has come to pass. The two key aspects of this film dyad is that it presents twin existential threats to humanity: the ability of humanity and superheroes to affect the globe to the point of mass destruction and the end of civilization as well as the threat of Thanos to solve that issue through unbelievable mass murder, and that the dyad itself is a rumination on death, mortality, and returning from the dead—the un-dead superheroes and regular humans killed in the first film (billions!) who are brought back to life in the second. Vampire, zombies, and ghosts wish they had this level of returning from the dead available to them. The *Avengers* series, at heart, concerns uncanny bodies and uncanny beings fighting to preserve the Anthropocene as it is, fighting against the embodiment of death.

Thanos is a shorting of the Greek name Athanasios, meaning "immortal." I am also assuming Jim Starlin, the creator of the character, conceived echoes of "thanatos," Greek for death. Indeed the two words are related, with "Athanasios" being seemingly closer to "deathless" than the English "immortal," which is actually an Anglicization of the Latin word "deathless." Thus, the character's name means both "death" and "deathless." Thanos is the embodiment of death and the embodiment of deathlessness. He seeks to end half the universe, but he seeks to do so for sustainability. He brings death on a massive scale; but he does so to ensure that life itself will continue and not end. He seeks sustainability, the deathlessness of both environment and population, through death. His plan is not merely to end half the life on Earth—the point is made many times in both films that Thanos plans to end half the life in the entire universe. Sight unseen, he will solve imagined challenges of overpopulation and resources stretched beyond nature's capacity amongst every intelligent species in the known universe by ending half the life everywhere. Captain Marvel tells the other Avengers her absence from Earth can be explained by the fact that "There are a lot of other planets in this galaxy, and unfortunately they didn't have you guys," thus implying Thanos's solution to the dangers posed by the Anthropocene (or equivalent on each planet) generated far more problems than he imagined it solved (*Endgame*).

The plot of the entire metanarrative of the MCU and the Avengers films in particular concerns Thanos's quest for the infinity stones, six stones created at the beginning of the universe that allow one to control aspects of the universe: time, mind, space, soul, power, and reality. Gathering the six together allows one absolute control over the fabric of reality and Thanos seeks them as a shortcut for his plan. Up until this point, Thanos had practiced his goals by going from planet to planet and slaughtering half of the inhabitants. This is what had happened to the Kylosians, represented in the MCU by Drax the Destroyer (Dave Bautista), one of the Guardians of the Galaxy, and to the Zehobereians, represented by Thanos's adopted daughter Gamora (Zoe Saldana). Both individuals witnessed Thanos slaughter their families as part of his campaign. However, Thanos realized that this approach was slow and inefficient, and thus began looking for a way in which to achieve his goal on every planet simultaneously. *Infinity War* shows the gathering by Thanos and his allies and servants of the Infinity Stones and his use of them to snap his fingers and achieve his aim. *Endgame* shows the effort of the surviving Avengers to bring the dead back to life and defeat Thanos without the loss of any of those born after the snap.

Clive Hamilton, François Gemenne, and Christophe Bonneuil remind us that, "humans have become a telluric force, changing the functioning of the Earth as much as volcanism, tectonics, the cyclic fluctuations of solar activity or changes in the Earth's orbital movements around the Sun" (2015, 3). Metahumans, the "enhanced" in Marvel's parlance, are an even more telluric force, capable of shifting planets, moving through time, and even reshaping reality. There are entities such as Groot, a living, sentient tree who can immediately grow his limbs to any length and use them as weapons, Thor, the Hulk, and even Iron Man who, though just a man, is capable of radical change to the environment locally and globally through technology (and what is that if not a metaphor for what the Anthropocene is—mere humans changing the planet through technology?). If, in the words of Timothy Morton, humanity is "an entity that is a geophysical force on a planetary scale" (2019, 9) then superheroes are a geophysical force on a galactic scale.

They see it as their job to protect the earth and its inhabitants. This is a concept repeated often in all four films: the job of the Avengers is to protect the Earth in all senses of the world. Iron Man tells Thanos, "If we cannot protect the Earth you can be damn sure we'll avenge it" (*Infinity War* 2018). Included in that protection should be protection against the forces of climate change and devastation. If the enhanced have an extended effect on the planet, they can use their powers to also protect and save it. Anthropogenic change thus requires a solution generated primarily by the nonhuman, the metahuman, and the enhanced human. However, the solution is not presented.

To be sure, the first film begins with an attempt to provide a simple, safe, waste-free source of power. Tony Stark, after decades of making weapons, uses the same technology that powers his heart to make a clean, nondangerous, limitless energy that powers Stark Tower. The film then demonstrates that the power source is what attracts Loki, as he can use that power source to open a portal above New York to allow the Chitauri, an alien species in the service of Thanos, to enter our world and begin to destroy it. The sole attempt to be responsible towards the environment is responsible for an invasion that does tremendous damage to New York City and the environment. At the end of the first film, the carnage in New York is unimaginable, thousands of dead bodies in the buildings, ruins, and streets.

WHO CARES ABOUT THE PLANET; IS SPIDER MAN OKAY?

Metahumans, the enhanced, superheroes, aliens and otherworldly entities are themselves indicative of a human body made uncanny—the Incredible Hulk is both Bruce Banner and the "enormous green rage monster" (as Tony Stark terms it in *The Avengers*), a changing and transforming body which changes from human to utterly uncanny and inhuman. Captain America, Frankenstein's monster-like, as a result of scientific experimentation on the human body, finds himself unnaturally strong and capable of taking more damage than a human body should be able to. Spider Man is a teenage boy bitten by a radioactive spider and transformed into something more than human. Technology allows Iron Man and Falcon to recreate superhuman acts.

Doctor Strange and Wanda Maximov use actual magic to warp reality. Vision is an artificial intelligence in a simulated post-human body. Thor and Loki are more or less ancient gods. In a superhero film these beings make sense. A change of genre and I argue it easy to see the *Avengers* films, in particular the final dyad, as gothic horror.

In *Infinity War*, in the climactic showdown on the ruins of Titan between Iron Man, Spider Man, Peter Quill, Mantis, Drax, and Doctor Strange on the one side and Thanos on the other, Thanos finally gains possession of the last Infinity Stone and, by snapping his finger, is able to alter reality and end half of all living things in the galaxy. This is represented by characters suddenly melting into smoke and ash, vanishing before the eyes of their horrified friends and colleagues. This event is presented as particularly horrific as those randomly selected to cease existence are aware that something is happening to them. Peter Parker/Spider Man, for example, disintegrates in the arms of his mentor Iron Man/Tony Stark, crying out, "I don't—I don't know what's happening. I don't . . . Save me, save me! I don't want to go. I don't want to go, Mr. Stark. Please. Please, I don't want to go. I don't want to go . . ." and he crumbles to dust. Thanos calls this death a mercy, but the self-knowledge of one's own end is repeatedly shown as a moment of terror before death for its victims.

Infinity War ends with the on-screen deaths of Peter Parker/Spider Man, Bucky Barnes/Winter Soldier (Sebastian Stan), Groot, Wanda Maximoff/Scarlet Witch (Elizabeth Olsen), Sam Wilco/Falcon (Anthony Mackie), Mantis (Pom Klementieff), Drax, Peter Quill/Starlord (Chris Pratt), Dr. Strange, and Nick Fury, not to mention the off-screen deaths of half the galaxy. In other films, the Thanos effect has already been shown, such as the conclusion of *Ant Man and the Wasp* (2018), in which Hope van Dyne (Evangeline Lilly) and Dr. Hank Pym (Michael Douglas) disintegrate after the Thanos snap, which leaves Scott Lang/Ant Man trapped in the subatomic realm, since they no longer exist to pull him out (resulting in a major plot point for *Avengers: Endgame*, as well as a possible solution to the Thanos situation).

All this exploration of death and horror is part of the use of cultural imagination to engage with fears about genocide, the end of the Anthropocene, human extinction, and how to deal with looming environmental catastrophe. At the heart of these fears is Thanos's quest to bring balance to the universe and end overconsumption of resources by ending half the sentient life in the universe, leaving the other half to better manage the resources. Thanos began this quest when he saw and warned his home-world, Titan, of imminent collapse. Thanos explains, "Titan was like most planets: too many mouths, not enough to go around. And when we faced extinction, I offered a solution" (*Infinity War* 2018). Titan exiled Thanos because he demanded immediate and direct action to counter overpopulation. His fears were proven true and by the time of the films Titan is a ruin, devastated, an entire planet embodying the gothic—a haunted ruin, empty, yet pregnant with meaning and warnings.

Martin Premoli notes, "Thanos, in other words, becomes an 'endling.' From this experience, Thanos develops his eco-philosophy of 'balance,' a practice of radical conservation through which he plans to erase half of each planet's population, enabling society to 'prosper' at a proper rate and scale" (2018). There is an irony in that there was collapse, proving Thanos right, but he then becomes the collapse for numerous other civilizations. He does not allow them to reach the tipping point, instead using force to arbitrarily separate the population and then slaughter half of them. He himself is the collapse he fears. Because Titan collapsed, Thanos assumes every planet will eventually have this problem and go the same way. The problem with Malthusian thinking is that it does not account for other factors. Thanos not only removes agency from the worlds he visits. He no longer warns; he simply ends life to save life without giving any other option.

In a sense, Thanos is a truly gothic figure: haunted by the past (the collapse of Titan), spurred to action to prevent the horror from happening again, but in doing so becomes the horror himself. And as Premoli then surmises:

> Embodied within this ambivalent depiction of Thanos are various key tensions of the Anthropocene: What economies and political systems might arise under the shadow of resource finitude? What methods might be developed for the responsible management of population growth? What issues and limitations are tied to geo-engineering? What is the appropriate scale for potential solutions? And how does one determine who has the power to make those decisions? (2018)

Thanos thus, in his own words, "offered a solution" to these questions. He sees his solution as inherently fair. The rich are not privileged, the poor or disenfranchised are not singled out for extermination. Those selected for death are chosen randomly without regard for class, purpose, profession, role in society, or even merit or worthy as distinguished by society. Entire families could be wiped out, or certain members, or none at all depending on the random selection. Gamora's mother is killed, Gamora is not. Drax's wife and daughter are killed, Drax is not. In a sense, Thanos truly seeks to emulate death in a disaster: death can come to anyone, regardless of station, location, or occupation.

This solution obviously is a highly problematic one, in keeping with the trend within MCU films in which a villain identifies a genuine, serious real-world problem but then offers a solution that is equally problematic. The heroes of the *Avengers* films, however, fail to demonstrate what Timothy

Morton calls "ecological awareness" (2016, 6). Their fixation is upon "saving lives" and bringing back their dead friends and associates. Thanos, on the one hand, is attuned to "ecognosis," which is "like knowing, but more like being known"—the needs to the environment in response to the destruction and degradation caused by civilization (2016, 5). He, however, can only implement an unimaginative solution: the instantaneous death of half the galaxy. In the face of his solution, the heroes can only react against him and not respond to the actual problem he has indicated. Thanos must be defeated and destroyed, but the challenge of Anthropogenic change to the planet/galaxy and the coming Malthusian catastrophe get ignored. Not once in any of the films do the hero engage or even discuss the underlying issue Thanos's admittedly abhorrent solution addresses.

YOUR CHOICE: IMMEDIATE OR SLOW DEATH OF THE PLANET

Two conversations in *Infinity War* take place between hero characters and Thanos, in which he presents the problem and his solution. In neither is the problem actually addressed. Thanos brings Gamora, his adopted daughter to Vormir, "a dominion of death . . . at the very center of celestial existence," as Nebula calls it in *Endgame*, and they discuss the evolution of his approach to the dangers of a species becoming a telluric force, overpopulating and overconsuming:

Gamora: I was a child when you took me.
Thanos: I saved you.
Gamora: No. We were happy on my home planet.
Thanos: You were going to bed hungry, scrounging for scraps. Your planet was on the brink of collapse. I'm the one who stopped that. You know what's happened since then? The children born know nothing but full bellies and clear skies.
Gamora: Because you murdered half the planet.
Thanos: A small price to pay for salvation.
  It's a simple calculus. This universe is finite; its resources are finite.
  If life is left unchecked, life will cease to exist. It needs correction . . .
  I'm the only one with the will to act on it. (*Infinity War* 2018)

Gamora's response is simply that Thanos is wrong. She never directly addresses the issue. Instead, she (correctly) accuses him of murder and atrocity. Because Thanos killed half her people, she does not and cannot listen to his justification. This exchange is emblematic of the *Avengers* films. The goal is to stop Thanos at all costs, but because he is the one raising the argument of collapse of both environment and civilization the "good guys" need not engage or even pay attention.

On Titan, Thanos, ever reasonable even in his mad approach, attempts to explain to Iron Man, Spider Man, and Doctor Strange why he arrived at his solution. In the midst of the ruins that provide the very evidence of at least his underlying concern, the response from the Avengers is again not to address the issue but the man and his solution to it:

Doctor Strange: Genocide.
Thanos: At random. Dispassionate, fair to rich and poor alike. They called me a mad man. And what I predicted came to pass.
Doctor Strange: Congratulations, you're a prophet.
Thanos: I'm a survivor.
Doctor Strange: Who wants to murder trillions!
Thanos: With all the six stones, I could simply snap my fingers, and they would all cease to exist. I call that . . . mercy.
Doctor Strange: And then what?
Thanos: I finally rest, and watch the sunrise on a grateful universe. The hardest choices require the strongest wills.

Thanos is obviously out of touch with reality. No planet that he has visited has yet been "grateful" for his services. Actually, most people from those planets (like Drax and Gamora) want to kill him. Like all megalomaniacs and self-appointed messiahs, he raises himself up as the only one with the vision and will to make the worlds into the paradises they could be, even though it is obvious his solution is unnecessary and causes more and different problems than it solves. Thus, at every moment the films are couched as an existential fight against an insane, genocidal, godlike alien, ignoring his very real point.

By the end of *Infinity War*, Thanos has all six stones, and on the verge of defeat by the Avengers (Thor has his newly forged battle ax buried in Thanos's chest), he snaps his fingers, and half the universe's sentient beings disintegrate, including, as noted above, about half of the Avengers. The film concludes with Thanos's victory and the Avenger's defeat. They failed to stop the snap, and thus trillions have died. But, in theory, the problems created on Earth by living in the Anthropocene have been solved. The survivors now have enough resources and will damage the planet significantly less. (Although admittedly Thanos does nothing to prevent the cycle from occurring again and in time, no doubt, all of the planets will again reach the point of overpopulation with limited resources. There is a reason why all the known civilizations in the MCU have gotten to this point where Thanos finds his work necessary on a galactic scale).

Avengers: Endgame begins with the idea that catastrophe is reversible. Thanos ensures that it is not by destroying the infinity stones that would allow the superheroes to alter reality in the same manner he did. This, however, being a superhero film, the heroes discover a way to travel through time to acquire all the stones before Thanos, brings them to the present, bring back the dead without changing anything else, and then return the stones to their proper moments in time. At the heart of this "it's-kind-of-crazy-but-just-might-work" plot is the idea that the dead can be returned to life without losing any of the changes (or the people born) in the last five years. This conceit is, at best, problematic in a number of ways.

First, a population cut in half five years ago has substantially decreased its food supply as well as its stored resources. A society does not need as many dwellings, as much stored water or electricity, or labor when you halve its population. When that population is immediately doubled, as John Halstead argues:

> The short-sightedness of the heroes is manifest when they restore everyone to life who had been killed five years earlier, instantaneously doubling the universe's population. As numerous critics have pointed out, after Thanos cut the population in half, the production of food and other necessities for sustaining human life would have been correspondingly reduced over the intervening five years. We're supposed to be glad that all those people got restored to life at the close of Endgame, but who's going to feed them all? You can't just ramp up the world's economy fast enough. Billions would die of starvation! (2019)

And it is here where the crux of the problem for the Avengers films as model of the Anthropocene lies. We can solve certain problems, but in the end, we are doomed to death on a massive scale no matter what. Ultron, in his first confrontation with the Avengers in Stark Tower in *Age of Ultron* tells them, "You want to protect the world, but you don't want it to change." This is the heart of the problem in the *Avengers* dyad: protect the world, but don't let anything change. Those are the only terms under which Stark will help the others change time and fight Thanos.

It is indeed a selfish reason. Since Thanos has halved humanity, Stark has had a daughter. He does not wish to lose her, and thus will only work on a solution that does not change the timeline in which she exists. If time travel is possible, rather than return to a moment when they could stop Thanos and ensure the continuation of the timeline as it was, Stark wants to have the world as it has continued, just with all the missing back and no other changes. He wants to have a world without consequence or change, other than bringing the dead back to life.

The Avengers seek to practice "de-extinction" in Premoli's term, borrowed from Kate Marshall. This is defined as "the partial resurrection of extinct species"; however, in the Avengers films humanity is not extinct, per se, just reduced by half (Premoli 2018). The loss of that half, however, is presented by *Endgame* as an unimaginable catastrophe, an unbearable tragedy and the beginning of a different kind of end. The film shows the powerlessness of the heroes to do much of anything. Black Widow takes over the leadership of the Avengers and grows frustrated with the others for not investigating an earthquake in the Pacific. "It's an earthquake," Okoye tells her "There's nothing for us to do." A simple geological event does not require superheroes. In some ways, Thanos has made superheroes unnecessary. Captain America now leads a grief support group. The others attempt to solve an unsolvable problem and clearly feel at a loss.

Thanos will not find a grateful world. The collapse of civilization as well as the resulting mass destruction of life on Earth that Thanos sought to address is not a significant issue for the Avengers. In that sense, perhaps they are indeed an effective metaphor for humanity, as we, too, confront climate change and its obvious and devastating effects (as I write this the air quality near my home is poor due to large incident wildfires throughout California where I live and throughout the American west. Flooding is occurring in Germany and China, while the ice on Mexico's mountains, centuries if not millennia old, is melting). When the heroes launch a plan to travel through time and retrieve the stones to reverse the snap, Black Widow reminds them, "If we do not get that stone, billions of people stay dead." If *Infinity War* concerns stopping Thanos, *Endgame* is concerned with bringing the dead back to life without thought of consequence, as noted above.

Perhaps most problematic, however, is the idea that catastrophe is reversible and is done so with a literal snap of the fingers. The ecological crisis of the Anthropocene cannot be solved by such wishful thinking. After gathering the stones, the heroes manufacture their own gauntlet, bringing Thanos to Earth to retrieve all the stones at once in this new timeline. Hulk is able to snap and bring back the dead. Thanos retrieves the stones and seeks to end them again, but the stones are taken from him again and Iron Man is able to snap and disintegrate Thanos and his allies. The first sign the dead have returned, Laura, Clint Barton/Hawkeye's wife calls his cell phone and is identified by text and picture. He answers and hears her voice. The dead heroes all begin to emerge from gates created by Doctor Strange. The dead, both heroic and nonheroic, do not reset; they do not go back in time and stop the snap. The billions who died suddenly reform and reappear, many clueless that they have been gone for five years and the world has changed.

When the dead superheroes return, they return to immediately join the fight against Thanos and his forces. Though literally dead for five years, mostly having perished at the end of a long, exhausting and painful battle, they emerge, like zombies, immediately ready to unquestioningly attack their enemies. It is not a stretch to see this moment as one in line with other essays in this volume: a moment of un-dead revenge, striking back against the forces that killed them.

CONCLUSION: DEATH IS NOT THE
PROBLEM, AVOIDING DEATH IS

This concept brings us full circle back to the idea that the Avengers dyad is an ellipse centered on the twin centers of the dead returning to life and the concern of Malthusian catastrophe and humanity and metahumans as telluric forces, both of which at heart display a return from catastrophe—dead back to life, a planet on the brink somehow saved and able to continue without cost. The things we fear are reversible, the films say, without cost or even effort on the part of the ordinary person. And yet the films also force us on some level to confront the unfortunate facts of both our own demise and the end of the Anthropocene. It will not take Thanos to bring about the end of much of humanity, simply a continuation of overconsumption and over population. Premoli reminds us that *Infinity War* "unsettles and expands the parameters that shape our understanding of this tragic reality, asking that its audience meditate on the permanence of loss of life" (2018). *Endgame*, however, tells us we do not have to meditate on it too much—everything will be okay at the end and with only minimal effort.

Taking a different view, John Halstead concludes that the films demon-strate that, "Our enemy isn't death, it's our attempt to avoid death, the myth of human exceptionalism, uncritical techno-optimism, and a Christian savior complex" (2019). By attempting to continue without changing, defeat death without cost, and that somehow, we can escape what happened to Titan because our own endemic anthropocentrism and sense of exceptionalism, we bring about the very catastrophes and collapses we fear. In *Avengers: Age of Ultron*, Ultron, the AI inadvertently created by Tony Stark who seeks to bring about human extinction, remarks of humanity, "They're doomed," thus prophesying not only Thanos, but the inevitable end of the people and the planet (*Age of Ultron* 2015). Vision, however, responds that it is the very transience of life that makes it wonderful, remarkable, and valuable. "They're doomed" might refer to humanity as a species, which, admittedly, Ultron had just tried to destroy through an extinction-level event. It could also, however, refer to humanity individually, as can Vision's answer. We're all doomed to die, but that is not only part of life, but the very thing that makes life special and significant. It ends.

In the dyad that follows that film, however, not only is Vision destroyed by Thanos, as the Mind stone is what indeed makes Vision Vision, but that conceit is reversed. Neither humanity nor individuals are doomed (at least not immediately—no promises on the long term). The dead are made un-dead, but at the cost of the planet. The deaths of Thanos and Iron Man, with nothing else put into place to stop the Malthusian catastrophe the films seem to suggest still might lurk in humanity's future also thus seems to imply the Anthropocene will come to an end with humanity's end. But at least all the Avengers and their friends and family are alive and together at Iron Man's funeral. It is an odd ending in a series (and cinematic universe) that has always implied (often through mid- and post-credit sequences) a continuation of the story and on ongoing need to battle the coming threat. There is no coming threat at the end of *Endgame*. With Thanos's defeat, the job is done. He might have been death himself, and inevitable, but in defeat he is no longer a threat, and thus death is no longer a threat or inevitable. The irony, of course, as noted above, is that with his defeat and the return of billions to Earth with an increased population and decreased resources and food, the threat now looms much larger and much more imminent. But it is one heroes can neither solve with superpowers, despite their powers being a telluric force as Okoye notes, nor do they seem to particularly care about. Death was always the threat, not the end of the Anthropocene, the heroes never recognizing those two are actually one and the same.

WORKS CITED

Halstead, John. 2019. "The Avengers Won the War, But Lost the Argument: How Our Heroes Doom Our Future" *A Beautiful Resistance*. 28 May. https://abeauti fulresistance.org/site/2019/5/8/the-avengers-won-the-war-but-lost-the-argument. Accessed May 12, 2021.

Hamilton, Clive, François Gemenne, and Christophe Bonneuil. 2015. "Thinking the Anthropocene" in *The Anthropocene and the Global Environmental Crisis: Rethinking Modernity in a New Epoch*, edited by Clive Hamilton, François Gemenne, and Christophe Bonneuil Routledge, 1–14.

Johnston, Joe (dir.). 2011. *Captain America: The First Avenger*. Burbank: Walt Disney Studios Motion Pictures.

Morton, Timothy. 2016. *Dark Ecology*. New York: Columbia.

Premoli, Martin. 2018. "Avengers in the Anthropocene," Exploring the Environments of Modernity. 6 June. https://ppeh.sas.upenn.edu/field-notes/avengers-anthropo-cene. Accessed May 12, 2021.

Reed, Peyton (dir.). 2018. *Ant Man and the Wasp*. Burbank: Walt Disney Studios Motion Pictures.

Russo, Anthony and Joe Russo (dirs.). 2018. *Avengers: Infinity War*. Burbank: Walt Disney Studios Motion Pictures.

———. 2019. *Avengers: Endgame*. Burbank: Walt Disney Studios Motion Pictures.

Whedon, Joss (dir.). 2012. *The Avengers*. Burbank: Walt Disney Studios Motion Pictures.

———. 2015. *Avengers: Age of Ultron*. Burbank: Walt Disney Studios Motion Pictures.

Chapter 9

"To Remember Forever to Forget"

Into Eternity *and the Anti-Anthropocene*

Mikaela Bobiy and Kristopher Woofter

THE WORLD WITHOUT US

Midway through Michael Madsen's speculative documentary film *Into Eternity: A Film for the Future* (2010) occurs an image of quiet dread. Miles deep in cavernous darkness, two workers pause from chiseling the sides of a tunnel, faces illuminated only by the bluish light of their construction headgear. The shot is rendered in slow motion, the only sound that of the film's plangent piano score. One of the workers turns toward the other, in profile, his dirty cheek streaked with tears caused by dust and debris. He offers a few words, a quiet smile; his coworker responds by wiping the tears with a finger.

It is a small, moving gesture—a delicate act of empathy, and an acknowledgment of the pain experienced by someone who may not be aware he is suffering. Yet the film doesn't linger long on this moment, and its resistance to doing so is part of a broader strategy in *Into Eternity* that undercuts the conventional affect of such moments to decenter the place of humanity in the film, even as it explores one of humanity's most egregious "achievements."

Into Eternity is an amalgam. In part motivated to document the construction in northern Finland of a colossal repository for that country's nuclear waste, Madsen's film is first and foremost a philosophical thought experiment—what Paul Ward calls a "conditional tense" (2006) documentary[1]—asking spectators to contemplate "deep future," or a sense of deep time projected far into a future that may or may not include humanity (at least as we know it).[2] The film's explorations revolve significantly around the issue of both temporal and physical scale. The Onkalo facility will require a century of blasting, digging, widening, and finally backfilling, to complete; its waste storage vaults will be cut into five kilometers of rock below the surface; it must endure for 100,000 years to safely contain the harmful radiation's

Figure 9.1 A Moving Moment, Decentered. *Into Eternity* (2010, Films Transit International).

interminable shelf-life; its designers must consider how to either mark the site with a dire warning that will be legible as such far into the future, or leave it buried and hidden in hopes that it will never be discovered; and—in perhaps one of the most futile elements—its builders must do all of this with the knowledge that the facility itself can hold only a finite amount of the nuclear waste produced by Finland, suggesting the need for "many more Onkalos," as Madsen's narration puts it. Even the massiveness of the undertaking here is dwarfed by the implications that made it necessary (if absurdly ill-advised). In short, Onkalo (which means "hiding place") is a feat of construction being built as a future ruin not-to-be-discovered. It is a necessity due to a lack of foresight around producing sustainable, clean energy, and it is *itself* evidence of a lack of foresight. It, like the future its very presence intimates for human-ity, is a grave.

Into Eternity builds its speculations around paradox. Madsen's film is a treatise on human folly—evoking the coming exigencies of the Anthropocene, up to and including human extinction. Yet it is also an ahumanist thought experiment on the idea of futility, exposing the self-centeredness of anthro-pocentrism in the very notion of an Anthropocene.[3] The film points to an "indifferent" cosmos (Thacker 2015, 125-26), intimating a future already haunted by the egregious—yet also ultimately nugatory—acts of humanity in its march towards scientific dominance over nature. The vision of humanity that *Into Eternity* laments is less tragic than pathetic. And the odd enthusiasm Madsen's film has in throwing out speculation after speculation suggests a queer form of resistance that looks more like active resignation than intervention. Madsen himself appears on occasion throughout the film to address current and future viewers directly.

He appears in shadow, striking a match to illuminate his face in a kind of existential quiver as he asks questions such as "Did that happen? Are there forbidden zones with no life in your time?" and "A hundred thousand years is beyond our understanding and imagination. Our history is so short in comparison. How is it with you? How far into the future will your way of life have consequences?" (Madsen 2010). And as his face fades in the flickering, ephemeral match-light, the viewer feels Madsen's curious stare in two embodiments—as a "you" who is part of Madsen's historical moment, helpless to stop humanity's terrible legacy; and as an imaginary, even fantastical "you" who may never exist, or may exist in such a radically altered form or in such a radically different time that Madsen's film could never communicate its message. There is no redemption here, the film seems to suggest—only the intimations of what we have done, and of a creeping sense of "what [we] don't know that [we] don't know" (Madsen 2010).

Madsen's film is an experiment in pessimism. As much as it is a warning to its viewers to look around them, it is less a call to action than a call to ruminate. Not despite, but especially because of, his darkly comical and often darkly whimsical treatment, Madsen aligns himself in some ways with what Weird author Thomas Ligotti calls the "morbid man" (2015, 184). Ligotti might be speaking of the philosophical stance of *Into Eternity* when he writes: "Madness, chaos, bone-deep mayhem, devastation of innumerable souls—while we scream and

Figure 9.2 An Existential Quiver: Madsen and His Match. *Into Eternity* (2010, Films Transit International).

perish, History licks a finger and turns the page" (2015, 185). Though Ligotti's pessimistic despair is rather more upfront than Madsen's, the philosophical ruminations of both are characterized by the sardonic humor and an odd sort of "euphoria" (Thacker 2018, 127) of the pessimist. Madsen's comes in his many direct addresses to viewers, current and future; in his aphoristic mythmaking; in his open-ended questions; in his seemingly naive, yet playfully pointed inquisitiveness; and in a kind of resigned calmness—all forms of resistance, to both the answers given by his interview subjects (a couple of them quite endearing), and any final truth to be found in his subject matter.

In *Into Eternity*, the "shadowy incomprehension" and "futility" (Thacker 2018, 20) of pessimism turns us to thoughts of what Eugene Thacker calls "the world-without-us" (2011, 5). That is, not the world created in our own image (the "world-for-us"), or the scientific world (the "world-in-itself," which we probe and analyze and exploit for knowledge and superiority in creating the "world-for-us"), but instead the "cosmological" or "planetary" view (2011, 7) that includes the "impossible thought of extinction" where, without human thought, *Earth* becomes *planet* (2011, 17). In short, *Into Eternity* pushes into a place of unthought—not a state of negativity, albeit one of a kind of resigned enthusiasm that leads us to unthinkable dead-ends, to anti-order, and to uncategorizable post-anthropocentric realities.

Into Eternity undercuts the world-for-us at every turn. As the film progresses, the human becomes more and more decentered, such that by the end we have crossed over into something anti-humanist, or even ahuman. If we return to the scene of the two tunnel workers above, in this context even a shared "human" moment becomes more evidence of the absurdity of the underlying circumstances leading to and including the creation of Onkalo—human aspirations to superiority over nature as a kind of sick joke.[4] The film resists being read as redemptive in this way, with a moment of human connection between two workers feeling less tragic than grotesque—striking the spectator with a sense more of dread or outrage than of pathos. It tells us that the lessons history has taught us about humanity amount to trying to save ourselves from our own destructive impulses, resulting in perpetual cycles of abuse. The will to death.

In an aesthetics of speculative, spectacular morbidity, *Into Eternity* is a humanist film that decenters the human, forcing us to make the leap from the world-for-us to the world-without-us—an exercise that cannot help but inspire horror. The idea of futurity haunts the entire film. As Thacker writes, "Our own era is one haunted by the shadow of futurity, precisely because there is no future" (2015, 130). As it imagines into the future, *Into Eternity* provokes a cosmic pessimism where any idea of futurity is both false hope and pure fantasy. In this way, *Into Eternity* is not a human redemption story, but a story about obliteration.

MYTH AND HUBRIS

Into Eternity opens on an image that looks out through frost-covered trees onto a 'forest' of electrical transformers (Figure 9.3). A series of tracking shots follows, pressing slowly into the mouth of the Onkalo facility's tunnel, the smooth-formed concrete entrance yielding to the rougher surfaces and blasted darkness of the tunnel's depths. Rounding out the film's opening sequence, the camera peers out of a forest of silhouetted trees onto a lawn leading up to a large, looming estate house, seemingly out of place in this isolated wilderness (Figure 9.4).

Taken together, these images of boundaries and frontiers between "wild" and "tamed" nature reveal an uncanny likeness that betrays the "nature" inherent to human technology—it mimics, it burrows, it nests. The cumulative effect of these images suggests the human-nature dichotomy as an anthropocentric fabrication. While they more explicitly identify an adversarial relationship—a human struggle for dominance over, or domestication of the environment—these images also intimate a quality of human endeavor inextricable from nature. Steven Shaviro tells us, "We must think of nature without any residual anthropocentrism: that is to say, without exempting ourselves from it, and also without remaking it in our own image. Human beings are part of Nature, but Nature is not human, and is not centered upon human beings or upon anything human" (2015, 216). Similar to Thacker's acknowledgement of the "unthinkable" world-without-us, Shaviro sees the human

Figure 9.3 A "Forest" of Trees and Power Lines. *Into Eternity* (2010, Films Transit International).

Figure 9.4 Evoking the Gothic Estate House. *Into Eternity* (2010, Films Transit International).

on a much grander, cosmic scale that decenters and diminishes the human. Shaviro is concerned in part with a tendency to privilege human cognition over other forms of sentience (including other forms of human sentience) by which "biological entities" engage in "reality testing" with Nature (2015, 13). And there is a sense in *Into Eternity*'s opening juxtapositions that humans are not superior to Nature, but evince its processes in everything we do—including paradoxically pursuing our own extinction in the name of transforming Nature's "natural" chaos into increasingly destructive forms of 'order'.

Following these images, Madsen's opening commentary—presented, as throughout the film, in direct-address to the audience—reads like a warning, though as the film makes clear in other parts, it is a warning that may not be decipherable (or even *have* an audience) in so far away a future:

I am now in this place, where you should never come. We call it Onkalo; Onkalo means "hiding place." In my time it is still unfinished, though work began in the 20th century, when I was just a child, where it would be completed in the 22nd century, long after my death. Onkalo must last 100,000 years. Nothing built by man has lasted even a tenth of that timespan. But we consider ourselves a very potent civilization. If we succeed, Onkalo will most likely be the longest-lasting remains of our civilization. If you, sometime far into the future, find this—what to tell you about us?" (Madsen 2010)

As we mentioned earlier, Madsen's address is to multiple spectatorial positions. There is here the "we/us" of Madsen's moment (including all thought leading up to and influencing human exceptionalist ideologies), and the speculative "you/them" of 100, 300, 500, and 100,000 years in the future. In framing this portentous question to its speculative audience(s), Madsen's opening words invoke a sense of deep time and dreadful futurity extending from present malaise. Madsen's question, like his film, does not intend its current audience to consider an answer, but instead opens up a kind of inter-rogatory precipice—an *ellipsis*—that encourages darkly fantastical specula-tion rather than logical hypotheses or teleological projection. Thacker has written of the ellipsis as "the punctuation mark of pessimism. It undermines whatever precedes it . . . ." (2018: 125, author's ellipsis). The sense of an ellipsis—the unfinished, fragmented, or trailing thought—adds an allegorical quality, so that Madsen's question, "what to tell you about us?," begs another: "What will telling you about us tell you about us?"

Madsen parallels this "elliptical thesis" with what might be called a new myth for the Anthropocene, a suggestion that human technology has revealed a fatal flaw in human nature. The film builds into its structure a speculative myth that collapses deep past and deep future into present folly.

> Once upon a time, man learned to master fire—something no other living crea-ture had done before him. Man conquered the entire world. One day he found a new fire, a fire so powerful that it could never be extinguished. Man revelled in the thought that he now possessed the powers of the universe. Then in horror he realized that his new fire could not only create but also destroy. Not only could it burn on land, but inside all living creatures, inside his children, the animals, or crops. Man looked around for help but found none, and so he built a burial chamber deep in the bowels of the earth, a hiding place for the fire to burn—into eternity. (Madsen 2010)

Here, *Into Eternity* could be read as a "mere" Promethean cautionary tale of "mad science" in its centering human efforts to control nature (through nuclear fusion, of course, but also in the construction of Onkalo itself) as absurdly egoistic and misguided. The film itself risks the same folly—and hubris—featuring engineers and scientists speculating how best to convey a warning message to "humanity" 100,000 years from now. Madsen deflects such criticism, however, in creating a "film for the future" that also encour-ages associations with the deep past, and the timeless, placeless universality of allegory.

The myth-as-metacommentary undermines an anthropocentric reading of the film. The atemporal handling of very real and present dangers of humanity's folly in terms of a tale so old it reads as folklore reduces the cur-rent moment to a cautionary tale among so many others about how people never learn. And the reference to humanity's "possess[ing] the powers of the universe" (Madsen 2010), combines the timelessness of myth (about humanity) with the deep time of the cosmos (before and after humanity). The present-ness of the film's focus and events—what to do with the harmful, potentially catastrophic waste caused by atomic science—is thus stripped away, projecting us once again into that "sometime far in the future" (Madsen 2010) of the film's second address: the possibility of human extinction, and beyond.

Madsen's myth making continues some twenty minutes later in the film, following a lengthy discussion of whether to warn the future at all, or instead attempt to hide the site from future discoverers. Discussion here moves from constructing imposing monoliths that would include warnings in all the "major languages" spoken; to the more iconic power of the "low sophistication but . . . robust message" of a cartoon (Figure 9.5); to the "emotional information" rendered by more abstract images of "a landscape of thorn . . . that would get you to feel that this is something which is wrong, this is something not inviting," and works of horror art such as Norwegian artist Edvard Munch's *The Scream* (1893, appropriately originally titled *Der Schrei der Natur*, or *The Scream of Nature*).

Madsen's response to such thoughts comes again in direct address to the viewer, the typical tone of soft-spoken, genuine inquisitiveness in his voice rustling unsettlingly against the negative implications of his questions: "When you opened Onkalo, did you see landscapes of thorn? Did it make you hesitate, or maybe curious? What drove you to enter? Was it the scars we left on the surface, or a rumor?" With the self-conscious melodramatics of such moments Madsen underlines the absurdity of any attempt at warning the

Figure 9.5 Warning the Future. *Into Eternity* (2010, Films Transit International).

deep future by becoming our "horror host," evoking in caricature the many horror shows of yore, such as television's *Twilight Zone* (1959–1964, hosted by Rod Serling) or *Thriller* (1960–1962, hosted by Boris Karloff)—and even more so *Lights Out!* (1946–1952), whose host (Arch Oboler) appeared as an illuminated disembodied head before every episode.

In the quasi-mocking context of horror-host caricature, the continuation of the myth carries even greater portent regarding the active oblivion humanity must court, now and then and forever, to avoid confronting the dark, decentering truth behind human "progress":

> When the burial chamber was complete, man laid his new fire to rest and tried to forget about it, for he knew that only through oblivion would he be free from it. But then he started to worry that his children might find the burial chamber and awaken the fire from its sleep. So he bade his children to tell their children, and their children's children, too, to remember forever to consign the burial chamber to oblivion—to remember forever to forget. (Madsen 2010)

What might be called the film's "epistemology of the paradox" comes out strongly in the last line, "to remember forever to forget," and its multiple implications, from the need to hide something from ourselves, to the need to ignore the suffering of others in the name of human progress, to the sense that humanity's future is essentially a Great Death—an extinction that mirrors the natural death of the body. "Were you warned about Onkalo through legend?" Madsen intones ten minutes later in the film, adding: "Maybe our legends will reach you by being told over and over, from generation to generation, like ancient legends have reached us. . . . Did your parents tell you stories about the fires in the burial chamber deep in the bowels of the earth? The chamber you must always remember to forget." A sense of the unspoken and unspeakable comes into play here—that there are things we must push to the edges of consciousness to be able to move forward in the name of "humanity." And yet, in doing so, are we "forgetting" that our primary legacy is one of violence, destruction, and a return to chaos and entropy—a death drive for Freud, a will to death for Schopenhauer?

The film's epistemology is clear in that "Onkalo" comes to represent the greatest "forgetting" of humanity in its epic journey to set itself apart from, and to dominate nature. Onkalo is grave, is death, is futility. A facility like Onkalo, and the reasons it exists, itself must be forced to the margins of thought; the threat to existence of all kinds that it archives—that it embodies—must be allowed to be buried, "forgotten." The film is at its most Gothic in its speculations of a future society (of whatever sort) potentially unearthing the site and seeing it as some form of burial site full of import and possible riches. The "sins of the fathers" revisited upon the children. What the Onkalo burial site does/will archive is the portent of extinction left to the future by the past. Onkalo is therefore an archive of trauma resulting from a criminal lack of foresight. The site is a marker of shortsightedness and lack, and also a kind of reenactment of it. Nuclear energy is not sustainable; it will overwhelm us with its eternal, poisonous waste—it is evidence of the point at which scientific advancement meets the inevitable death of humanity.

TIME AND CATASTROPHE

Any practice of mythmaking requires a negotiation with time and the event. *Into Eternity*'s relationship to time is unique—it does not signal the event in any Lacanian way,[5] nor does it signal any violent rupture; it is instead a kind of waiting game. It marks our experience of temporality as the anticipation of a catastrophe projected far into the future. In her book *Enduring Time* (2017), Lisa Baraitser makes a psychoanalytic examination of time, articulating a kind of rupture-time, which includes abrupt change and the Lacanian "event"; as well as unravelling-time, which is about diffuse change; and deep time, the time of climatological change. Baraitser argues, though she is not the first, that contemporary temporality (or our current time-consciousness) is marked by waiting: "[W]e appear to be holding our breath, *waiting*, not for a pending catastrophic 'event' in the sense that Frederic Jameson suggested characterized post-modern time (1996), but for a diffuse catastrophe that has already happened to unpredictably play itself out" (2017, 10, emphasis in original). *Into Eternity* is a film about waiting for the results of a catastrophe (the exigencies of nuclear power) that has already happened.

This reverse waiting is tied to a sense of geological time, and therefore of timelessness. "At the surface," one of the film's researchers tells us, "the clock runs very fast, while in the rock, it goes very, very slowly" (Madsen 2010). Taken together, both the speeding up and slowing down of time are countervailing. Though Madsen asks us to think about deep time, many of the film's shots seem out of time, something it has in common with David McMillan's eerie photographs of the abandoned regions around Chernobyl (discussed below).[6] Stills of the Finnish forest under snow-cover, quietly buzzing power lines, Gothic mansions nestled at forest's edge, all point to something frozen in time, or perhaps beyond (or transcending) time. While snow, human structures and even forests are all ephemeral, they point to something else—something primal, a need and a process that extends beyond the human animal to other animals, and the planet itself. Additionally, the shots of forest and powerlines are washed out and abstracted—recalling the film's extreme close-ups of the pristine, monochromatic metallic surfaces of radioactive rods and other nuclear apparatus—giving the illusion of some future irradiated landscape. Whether representing a fantasy of past, present or future, these shots make it seem as if time has stopped altogether. Considering the film's constant circling around uncertain events and causal chains, ineffable beginnings and futures beyond human thought, such imagery also suggests space trapped or stranded in an entropic temporality representing primal pasts, present futility, and future chaos.

This waiting, and its parallel experience of timelessness, is not benign, but is instead marked by violence, what Baraitser refers to as a "prolonged or chronic violence well into 'the deep future'" (2017, 10). *Into Eternity* also brings this violence into the *near* future, as engineers worry about the instability and unpredictability of "above ground" nuclear waste storage, whether in the form of war, natural disasters, or another ice age. Images of the Fukushima Daiichi Nuclear Power Plant meltdown in Japan in 2011, the result of an earthquake and subsequent tsunami, underscore these anxieties. There is violence as well in the unravelling of deep time, about which *Into Eternity* invites us to think; Onkalo is but a band-aid, a papering over of a more sustained and prolonged violence. This prolonged violence makes it difficult to think into the future. Baraitser writes that, "alongside speed theory," a theory which sees time in terms of capitalist production and the development of technologies that accelerate and proliferate,

> we have seen the emergence of a different kind of articulation of the vicissitudes of time in the early twenty-first century, overshadowed by a collapse in twentieth century modernity's belief in progress and mastery over the future, that has given way to a sense that the future is now imagined or at least routinely narrated as uncertain, unpredictable, and for some simply "cancelled" or foreclosed. (2017, 11)

As *Into Eternity* frames it, the interplay between mastery (harnessing nuclear energy) and folly (its "eternally" harmful waste and potential for catastrophe), has similarly brought us beyond an uncertain future and into the realm of "foreclosure."

The prospect of foreclosure brings about a kind of dazzling giddiness in the film, a reveling in the absurdity of such an undertaking as Onkalo, and the "impossible" future it provokes us to imagine. Early in the film, one of the research directors discusses the possibility of sending our nuclear waste in a rocket to the sun; a brief additional mention of the possibility of even one malfunction on the launchpad renders this as no less absurd than burying it underground for 100,000 years. Elsewhere in the film, Madsen's self-seriousness gives way to a theatre of the absurd that might be the only response to an uncertain, or potentially foreclosed future. Early in the film, on-screen text informs us that there are currently 250,000 tonnes of nuclear waste in the world and that it will take at least 100,000 years for this waste to become harmless. These revelations are accompanied by slow-motion shots of technicians in white lab coats and red protective gloves, handling the interim storage of Finland's nuclear waste—all underscored by postpunk band Kraftwerk's irreverent, satirical 1975 single, "Radioactivity": "Radioactivity / Is in the air for you and me. / Radioactivity / Discovered by Madame Curie. / Radioactivity / Tune in to the melody. / Radioactivity / Is in the air for you and me." Cosmic pessimism is often met with a kind of resignation, a shrugging of the shoulders that opens up space for bleak ruminations and predictions. This film approaches its subject almost sardonically, skewing its humanist tendencies in later scenes of loneliness and isolation among Onkalo's builders. We follow one worker back to his spartan apartment where he sleeps off his night shift. His solitude is accompanied by the voiceover of a theologian associated with Sweden's National Council for Nuclear Waste, who speculates that just as the Roman Empire grew, flourished, and died, so too will the West; here melancholy and futility commingle. This melancholy persists in the bleak emptiness of Onkalo's break room—a tone that is absurdly, even hilariously undercut by a bulletin-board pin-up calendar, boobs staring out at the audience, presiding over what's left of an abandoned meal, while the few workers move through the adjacent locker room like ghosts. Interstices like these pull us out of the realm of science and speculation and into the realm of absurd gallows humor.

The film's sense of absurdity is further underlined by the interplay of human mastery, hubris, and imprudence—the certainty with which any future is discussed becomes an act of recklessness. The majority of the scientists and engineers interviewed speak with conviction about the safety of the repository, and the belief that should anyone in the future reach the repository, it will be a civilization just like ours that will understand nuclear waste and the danger it presents. Others are more uncertain: "That might be the most probable scenario, but I'm not so sure. It could be . . . another situation. I think if someone found a facility like that in the future, they might interpret it as something religious, a burial ground, or a treasure" (Madsen 2010). Gone is the conviction that human intrusion is an unlikely, yet predictable or manageable scenario.

Likewise, the questions surrounding the transfer of knowledge of the facility point to an epistemological absurdity. Madsen asks the engineers and scientists of Onkalo to imagine how we might communicate the dangers to/with the deep future. Do we leave a marker? And if so, what kind? Or do we leave nothing with the hope that nature overtakes the site with Onkalo a mere unmarked grave to human aspiration? It is the responsibility of the Finnish government that knowledge of Onkalo and its purpose be passed on to future generations, or at least put forth in some permanent manner. That this transfer of knowledge should be universally understandable, yet is written only in Finnish, a language spoken by roughly five million people, is not lost on the scientists. Madsen's lens focuses on the engineers' and senior managers' faces—by turns serious, smiling, bemused—as they acknowledge the absurdity of even featuring this message in *multiple* languages, underscoring this idea with the comment: "We will leave written information for you in all the major languages of our time. Will you understand any of them? Can you read?" (Madsen 2010). Even the engineering markings on the tunnels leading down to the repository have the appearance of runes, or some other pictograph imbued with ritual importance. The close-ups of the tunnel walls provide glimpses of blast markers, "mysterious" calculations that are not unlike the prehistoric art of the caves of Lascaux, further disorienting us in time. Comparisons of Onkalo to the Ancient Egyptian pyramids occur several times throughout the film, by Madsen and the scientists and engineers, suggesting a site readable in the future in multivalent ways: tomb, treasure trove, place of magic, place of danger—all of the above. *Into Eternity* underscores this future illegibility in featuring the participants' signatures (including that of its director) superimposed on the screen when they are introduced. Including the signatures is a double-edged gesture: it highlights the individual identity, the individual humanity, of these subjects; yet each inscribed signature is already a hieroglyphic, and will certainly be so in 100,000 years, a gesture as pointless as these individuals are meaningless in the film's cosmic scheme of deep time, where, as one of the engineers of Onkalo acknowledges, "the darkness thickens."

DEATH AND THE ABCANNY: BEYOND CHERNOBYL

Into Eternity occurs at the site of a tomb, Onkalo, that "hiding place" marking the human drive towards mastery and superiority writ large as catastrophe. The film forces us to confront the possibility of our own extinction (potentially at our own hands), suggesting a kind of collective death drive.[7] In Freud's early formulations, the death drive is that which propels us back toward a state of the inorganic; likewise, Madsen's film opens an interrogation into the possibility of a collective push toward eradication. In *Beyond the Pleasure Principle* (1920), Freud asks, what if we aren't driven by the pursuit of pleasure, but instead the pursuit of self-destruction? What if, rather than a drive toward reproduction, there were a drive toward entropy? While many took this to mean a further examination of aggressivity in the human subject,[8] for the cosmic pessimist it is this return to the inorganic or inanimate that is the most compelling. Thacker, for example, notes Freud's comment that the "question of the purpose of human life . . . does not admit of" an answer (quoted in Thacker 2018, 181), prompting Thacker to suggest that "what keeps us going is certainly not 'us,' not anything inherent in our psyche or our convoluted rationalizations for our motives and actions, but something more nebulous" (2018, 73), like the return to primordial chaos described by the death drive. The death drive is a drive toward stasis, a state of non-being. And for Freud, this state of non-being is a *return*, a kind of circular extinction; yet another way to think about the repetition compulsion. Unlike speculative works that attempt to imagine possible human futures, asking us to, as Matthew J. Wolf-Meyer puts it, "choose our future" (2019, 14), *Into Eternity* propels us to our end and beyond. Its space of recuperative possibility is the world beyond thought, the world-without-us.

It is this return to the inorganic that haunts David McMillan's Pripyat and Chernobyl photos, which, in many ways, function as an inverse to Madsen's film. While *Into Eternity* encourages us to *think* about the world-without-us, David McMillan's photographs *show* us a version of this world; it is the death drive made manifest. For his photo series *Growth and Decay: Pripyat and the Chernobyl Exclusion Zone* (2019), McMillan photographed the exclusion zone over a period of twenty years, documenting nature's gentle reclamation of the land. McMillan's Chernobyl photographs are haunted by visible absence of humans and the invisible presence of the radiation, that suffuses every aspect of the environment. In *Hallway, Village School* (October 1998), we are confronted by an abandoned school with peeling paint, overturned desks, and a faded Lenin smiling benevolently from a propaganda poster. What is uncanny is less the objects in and of themselves and the human lives to which they allude, but the encroachment of the world-without-us (of which radiation is a part). Like *Into Eternity*'s still-lives of forests and wildlife, what stares back at us through McMillan's photos is the planet's indifference to an invisible killer.

This indifference is most striking in two photos of the same rooftop view taken twenty-three years apart. *View of the Nuclear Power Plant from Pripyat Rooftop* (1994), shows concrete communist apartment blocks, tree-lined streets, and the power-plant in the background. Taken nearly ten years after the evacuation, these photos evince the city as a quiet, sleeping giant. In *View of the Nuclear Power Plant from Pripyat Rooftop* (2017), the apartment blocks are hardly noticeable, most of them completely overtaken by forest; glimpses of gray concrete in the small gaps of thick forest growth are the only signs of civilization. The power-plant, once a sight of horror, now wrapped in its protective white-gray cocoon, blends into the cloudy skies. Likewise, *Hotel Room* 1996, 2004, and 2013, through an unsettling time lapse, witnesses the cycle of growth and decay of a miniature forest taking root in an abandoned hotel room. Beyond the cracked hotel window, gray cement buildings are similarly overtaken by nature. This is one engineer's hope for Onkalo—that it, too, will disappear into the forest.

While the deep future of Madsen's film unsettles because of its ineffabil-ity, the "present-future" of McMillan's photographs show us scenes that are familiar (even from the confines of the capitalist West)—a schoolroom, an apple orchard, an abandoned helicopter. What render the photos uncanny is not just the absence of humans and the dominance of creeping, patient nature, but also the invisible threat or shadow (radiation) that is added—nature's double. For Slovene philosopher Mladen Dolar, the uncanny feeling brought about by the double is an incursion of the Lacanian Real (1991). It is something familiar made unfamiliar, by a shadow or mark, a rupture expos-ing that which cannot be spoken or conceived (the unthought). McMillan's photographs evoke an invisible double in the visual presence of nature, the once familiar. Because *Into Eternity*, unsettles us with imminence, the dreadful speculation of what's to come, it is less uncanny than *abcanny*. The uncanny is the disturbing return of the once-known, what is available to our ken though perhaps forgotten or unconscious; it carries the mark of traumatic past-ness. The abcanny, however, *confronts* us with the *unknowable*—it is, like the world-without-us, a radical possibility or otherness that is inconceiv-able and not yet encountered by humanity. The abcanny is strange, weird, foreign. More than a radical alterity, there is an antimeaningness at the heart of the abcanny, a refusal to submit to thought or understanding (2012: 6). China Miéville writes: "The monsters of the abcanny are teratological expressions of that unrepresentable and unknowable, the evasive of mean-ing" (2012: 5). Radiation is such a monster, and Onkalo a foolish cage. Though radiation is a known quantity—detectable and measurable—it is pushed to its abcanny limits in Madsen's film as a metaphor for the ultimate amalgam, the ultimate shapeshifter, in that it is both inside and outside, both present and absent, and the product of both human achievement and human failure. Near the end of the film, Madsen imagines a future trespasser into Onkalo's depths: "You have now gone deeper into the tunnel, and you have reached a place where you should never have come. Down here, radiation is everywhere. You do not know it, but something is happening to your body right now. It is beyond your senses. You feel nothing. You smell nothing. An invisible light is shining right through you. It is the last glow of my civi-lization that harvested the powers of the universe." (Madsen 2010) This is the abcanny caused *by us*, but not *of us*, in any convenient way that attaches to historical trauma or "bad acts." It is worth noting that the experience of the abcanny is not unidirectional. Again, as the film remarks: "It is possible that we will not be understood by the future, especially the distant future." The abcanny works both ways; both past and future are unknowable. Yet if anything unites the unsettling elements in both McMillan and Madsen, it might be something like the futility of thought in contemplating deep-future subjectivity, or "deep ecology" (see, e.g., Zapffe 1993 [1933]).

The suggestion of a future "without us" is more than uncanny; it is unthinkable, it is of the unthought, or as Miéville terms it, the "unknown unknown" (2012, 385). Nature keeps going, and we are of nature, no matter how much we attempt to achieve mastery over these processes. In this way, Madsen's film exposes the anthropocentric nature of the uncanny, pushing us to consider something less anthropocentric: the abcanny as the cosmically indifferent.[9]

CONCLUSION: A SPECTACLE OF NOTHING

Where McMillan's Chernobyl photos retain some of the concerns of the world-for-us in showing us the world-without-us, Madsen's film wants to shake us like the earthquake at Fukushima, dislodging us with a further sense of our own catastrophic insignificance. The final scene of Madsen's film becomes weighted and operatic.[10] Workers move in the dark depths, approaching the rune-like markings on the cavern walls. A large protective curtain and steel-gridded gates act as a membrane to catch debris from a recent explosion, moving them forward in their goals, plunging them deeper into the earth. The workers open the gates and curtain as though for an unveiling, but the spectacle that meets the eye is nothing but roiling grey clouds of dust ceding to further darkness. The two workers wander inside and are swallowed up in the whorling dust of an uncertain future. As earlier in the film, the humanist element here is equally swallowed up by the allegorical theatrics of the moment.

If Onkalo's builders cannot grasp the futility of their response to humanity's lack of foresight in splitting the atom, then why, the film asks, trust a future humanity (or version thereof) to heed the message attached to Onkalo's purpose: *Danger! Do not enter!*? In the terms set out by *Into Eternity*, these words are an invitation to think the unthinkable, to explore the limits and failure of thought itself. The prospect of having to imagine ourselves 100,000 years into the future, as *Into Eternity* asks us to do, exceeds the limits of logical/rational thinking and forces us into the realm of the imaginary and the fantastical. What will future humanity look like? What specters will remain? What of ourselves can we project forward? Even the Kantian sublime requires that we have the capacity to imagine. What happens when we enter the realm of the unthought?

This ineffability can be extended to the exigencies of nuclear power. Radiation is the *undead*; it is that which survives the harshest conditions. It is everywhere, but invisible, recognizable only by its effects. It passes through organic matter, like a specter, but leaves its physical mark by altering the genetic makeup of cells.[11] Perhaps the "specter haunting Europe" is not communism, as per Marx, but nuclear fallout leading to extinction of human and nonhuman animal life on the planet.

Into Eternity asks us to think about the paradox of what it means to be haunted by the future of a world-without-us, and in doing so, it pushes past the human to the cosmic. Implicit here is a critique of the idea of the Anthropocene, which, while it admits to the devastating impact of two-hundred years of industrialization and scientific/technological "advancement" on the planet, is yet another evocation of the world-for-us, made in our own image. Ultimately, *Into Eternity* comes with a set of speculations that any impact humanity has on the planet, devastating or not, becomes a mere process of nature on a more cosmic scale—the return to entropy, to forgetting.

NOTES

1. Ward explains, the "conditional tense" documentary features "an engagement with an attempt to represent historical events in such a way as to draw attention to their provisional or conditional nature" (2006: 272). They are about "what is imagined, wished, demanded, proposed, exhorted, etc." (2006: 271). Where a "conditional tense" documentary such as *The War Game* (1965) or *The Day Britain Stopped* (2003) actually show a speculative future, however, *Into Eternity* leaves such a future—the *effects* of a particular *cause*—in the realm of the ineffable. Apocalypticism is often the driving orientation of such films. We are indebted to a 17 March 2015, lecture by Papagena Robbins, who discussed *Into Eternity* in the context of "future-tense" documentary.

2. A literalization of such a thought experiment comes in the Long Now Foundation's 10,000 Year Clock. Designed and conceived in 1995 by Danny Hills and Stuart Brand, the project, carved into a mountain in western Texas, is one of several initiatives by the Long Now Foundation to "to foster long-term thinking in the context of the next 10,000 years." See the article "Clock in the Mountain" by Kevin Kelly, at https://longnow.org/clock/.

3. Philosopher Eugene Thacker frames the paradox succinctly: "The anthropocene: an accomplished ruin" (2018, 196).

4. The workers' goal in this detail is ostensibly to smooth the rough outcroppings of a structure that is being built over many years as a repository for nuclear waste—a landfill—only to be backfilled and re-buried as soon as it receives its deadly store. In this way, the excavators are nothing more than gravediggers.

5. That is, as something radical and transformative.

6. The German television series *Dark* (2017–2020) also makes connections between nuclear power and time. In *Dark*, portals to different time periods, as well as alternate universes, exist below a nuclear power plant deep in Germany's Black Forest. Again, links are made between nuclear power, radiation, and deep time. Likewise, David Lynch's *Twin Peaks: The Return* (2017) depicts simultaneous realities tied, in some way, to the atomic age; an irradiated landscape, intermittently

illuminated by the unearthly glow of a gas station in the desert, is witness to monstrosities of alternate temporalities.

7. As a site of contemporary resistance, the Freudian death drive has had something of a resurgence in the last ten years. See, for example, Benjamin Y. Fong's *Death and Mastery: Psychoanalytic Drive Theory and the Subject of Late Capitalism* (New York: Columbia University Press, 2016).

8. Vis à vis itself, and others; see the work of Melanie Klein.

9. In a May 12, 1986, comment in *The New Yorker*, Jonathan Schell writes, "It's a peculiarity of the end of the world, which human beings threaten to bring about with their nuclear arsenals, that until it happens it leaves us almost wholly undisturbed" (accessed via www.newyorker.com, n.p.). See also Thacker, *Infinite Resignation* (London: Repeater Books, 2018), 33, 53.

10. Literally so, as it is underscored by Edgard Varèse's 1906 composition for voice and piano, "Un grand sommeil noir" (translated as "A Deep Black Sleep" or "A Long Black Sleep"), with lyrics from Paul Verlaine's poem.

11. At present, we have no way of detecting radiation using our human senses, but it is not entirely inconceivable that far into an increasingly nuclear future, human beings might develop such a sense.

WORKS CITED

Baraitser, Lisa. 2017. *Enduring Time*. London, UK: Bloomsbury Academic.

Dolar, Mladen. 1991. "'I Shall Be with You on Your Wedding-Night': Lacan and the Uncanny," *October*, Vol. 58, Rendering the Real (Autumn), 5–23.

Fong, Benjamin Y. 2016. *Death and Mastery: Psychoanalytic Drive Theory and the Subject of Late Capitalism*. New York: Columbia University Press.

Madsen, Michael (dir). 2010. *Into Eternity: A Film for the Future*. Copenhagen: Magic Hour Films.

Kelly, Kevin. (n.d.) "Clock in the Mountain." *The Long Now Organization*. Accessed April 19, 2021. https://longnow.org/clock/.

Kraftwerk. (Ralf Hütter, Florian Schneider, Emil Schult). 1975. "Radioactivity." Track 2 on *Radio-Activity*. EMI, Kling Klang.

Ligotti, Thomas. 2015. "Professor Nobody's Little Lectures on Supernatural Horror." *Songs of a Dead Dreamer* and *Grimscribe*. London: Penguin Classics. 183–188.

McMillan, David. 2019. *Growth and Decay: Pripyat and the Chernobyl Exclusion Zone*. Gottingen, Germany: Steidl.

Miéville, China. 2012. "On Monsters: Or, Nine or More (Monstrous) Not Cannies," *Journal of the Fantastic in the Arts*. 23.3 (2012), 377–392.

Robbins, Papagena. 2015. Lecture. "'Caging the Monster that Will Live for 100,000 Years in the Future-Tense Gothumentary." Theorizing Horror, Part 2: Horror and Sensation. *Miskatonic Institute of Horror Studies*. March 17. https://www.miskatonicinstitute.com/events/theorizing-horror-part-2-horror-and-sensation/.

Thacker, Eugene. 2011. *In the Dust of This Planet: Horror of Philosophy, Vol. 1*. Alresford, UK: Zero Books / John Hunt Publishing.

———. 2015. *Tentacles Longer Than Night: Horror of Philosophy, Vol. 3.* Alresford, UK: Zero Books / John Hunt Publishing.

———. 2018. *Infinite Resignation.* London: Repeater Books.

Schell, Jonathan. 1986. "The Terrible Truth About the Chernobyl Disaster," *The New Yorker*, May 12. Accessed April 15, 2021. https://www.newyorker.com/magazine/1986/05/12/comment-the-terrible-truth-about-the-chernobyl-disaster.

Shaviro, Steven. 2015. *Discognition.* London: Repeater.

Ward, Paul. 2006. "The Future of Documentary?: 'Conditional Tense' Documentary and the Historical Record." *Docufictions: Essays on the Intersection of Documentary and Fictional Filmmaking*, edited by Gary D. Rhodes and John Parris Springer. Jefferson: McFarland. 270–283.

Wolf-Meyer, Matthew J. 2019. *Theory for the World to Come: Speculative Fiction and Apocalyptic Anthropology.* Minneapolis: University of Minnesota Press.

Zapffe, Peter Wessel. 1993 (1933). "The Last Messiah." *Wisdom in the Open Air: The Norwegian Roots of Deep Ecology*, edited by Peter Reed and David Rothenberg. Minneapolis: University of Minnesota Press. 40–51.

Part IV

THE DISANTNROPOCENE

IS NOT ALL ABOUT US

Chapter 10

"You're Next!"

The Enemy Within and the End of the Anthropocene as Seen in Adaptations of "Who Goes There?" and The Body Snatchers

Andrew J. Wilson

When considering the end of the world, we almost always frame this in terms of the demise of humanity rather than the destruction of the planet itself. In other words, our focus is on the end of the world as *we* know it, that is, the Anthropocene, the proposed geological epoch defined by the measurable impact of human activity on the environment. While estimates of the start of this period vary from as long as 50,000 years ago to as recently as 1950 (Biello 2015), the issue at hand is when and how the Anthropocene will finish.

According to Robert Frost, "Some say the world will end in fire, / Some say in ice" (1920, 67). However, over the past century, a variety of works of speculative fiction have explored another possibility: What if another lifeform attempted to take over the planet by usurping or destroying human beings first? If they succeed, would these alien cuckoos in the nest inherit the Earth, or would they in fact configure an expression of a larger planetary environment restoring biological balance and reintegrating the planet into a more organic, galactic whole? With consummate irony, the Anthropocene could be brought to a close by pretenders who look and act exactly like us.

The invasion narrative has been a fertile strand of Victorian speculative fiction reaching its apotheosis in 1898 with H. G. Wells' *The War of the Worlds*. Before this, the enemy aliens threatening the Home Counties had generally been French or German. However, inspired by a discussion with his brother, Wells subverted the established tropes, and modeled his Martian invasion on the British Empire's Tasmanian genocide. During the twentieth century, a more insidious form of alien attack would reflect Cold War paranoia, and in particular, the intertwined American fears of communist subversion and the witch-hunts of the McCarthy era. However, the foundational text for the enemy within story is "Who Goes There?" a novella by John W. Campbell that was originally published pseudonymously in *Astounding Science-Fiction* in 1938. A pen name was used for this appearance because he had assumed the editorship of the magazine.

The original version of the novella was divided into twelve chapters, but subsequent appearances favor a longer one. In 2018, author Alec Nevala-Lee found an earlier, novel-length manuscript among a box of Campbell's papers held by Harvard University. This was published the following year as *Frozen Hell*. However, for the purposes of this discussion, it is the best-known, fourteen-chapter expansion of the novella that will be our focus: a story that begins in ice and ends in fire. An American Antarctic expedition investigating a magnetic anomaly discovers the wreckage of an extraterrestrial spacecraft that has been buried under the blue ice of the South Polar Plateau for twenty million years. An attempt to excavate the ship by detonating a thermite bomb backfires, but the scientists manage to recover the remains of a three-eyed, blue-haired, and green-blooded creature that had survived the crash—the suggestion being it might be extremely evolved flora rather than fauna.

Despite concerns being raised about the possibility of the creature carrying dormant alien diseases, the decision is made to thaw out the body for further investigation. As Blair, the expedition's pathologist, says with unwitting irony, "never in all time to come can there be a duplicate!" (Campbell 2011, 13). However, the creature is not dead, but in a state of suspended animation. The alien, simply referred to by the men as the Thing, can replicate itself like a virus working on the macroscopic scale, and assume the guises of other forms of life. By the time they discover that it has come back to life, the creature has already begun its program of infiltration. The destruction of a partially assimilated sled dog only serves to expose the existential threat that this represents:

> There's nothing that can reach the sea from this point—except us. We've got brains. We can do it. Don't you see—*it's got to imitate us—it's got be one of us—that's the only way it can fly an airplane—fly a plane for two hours, and rule—be—all Earth's inhabitants.* A world for the taking—*if it imitates us!* (31, emphases in original)

Having posed the problem, Campbell complicates matters. The members of the expedition quarantine themselves by disabling their aircraft and other vehicles. However, attempts to come up with a way of identifying who might actually be an alien counterfeit are repeatedly thwarted. The Thing is telepathic, and able to mimic behavior as well as appearance: it can invade their minds and read their thoughts.

Science-fiction scholar Sam Moskowitz attributed the origins of the idea to Campbell's childhood experiences. His mother was a mercurial woman with a volatile temper who had an identical twin:

> John's aunt treated him with such abruptness that he was convinced she thoroughly hated him [. . .] [He] would come running into the house to impart something breathlessly to a woman he thought was his mother. He would be jarred by a curt rebuff from her twin. Every time his aunt visited the home, this situation posed itself until it became a continuing and insoluble nightmare. Was the woman standing in front of him "friend" or "foe?" (Moskowitz 1974, 28)

This idea embedded in the story, where the alien found in the ancient ice of the South Pole is not so much from the stars above, but rather, a "monster [. . .] from inner space [. . .] It had lived in Campbell's childhood home, in the heart of his family" (Elms 1994, 104).[1] Whether by conscious design or unconscious impulse, "Who Goes There?" is a Pandora's box of sublimated anxieties. Campbell's subtext is not simply fear of the other; it can be read as fear of the *hidden* other, that which seems secure but is suddenly deadly; people we know, places we inhabit and even the world we live in. The Thing wants to assimilate, reveal its true nature and have its wicked way with its victims, and all at the same time. Its vicious attacks on those whom it would convert disturbingly parallel sexual assaults and biological penetration and mutation. A human-immunity serum test using a sled dog fails when it becomes clear that one of the supposedly human donors is actually a Thing—or part of it. McReady realizes that the creature is actually an utterly ruthless gestalt entity: "Selfish, [. . .] *every part is a whole*. Every piece is self-sufficient, an animal in itself" (Campbell 2011, 65).

After a conceptual breakthrough, McReady dips a red-hot wire into blood samples taken from the members of the expedition. If the specimen reacts to the challenge, then the donor is proved to be a Thing, and therefore, must be killed. The last test has to be performed on Blair, who had been locked in an isolated cabin for several days because of his erratic behavior. The men discover that the Thing that has taken his place has used its time in isolation to build an atomic-powered antigravity machine. As McReady had speculated earlier, "It doesn't fight. I don't think it ever fights. It must be a peaceable thing, in its own—inimitable—way. It never had to, because it always gained its end otherwise" (55). It is like a force of nature in that its expression of life will always persist no matter what seeming setbacks it might suffer in the short term. The survivors do make a stand, of course: McReady flushes out the last iteration of the Thing and destroys it with a blowtorch. While Robert Frost may have wondered whether the world might end in fire, according to Campbell, this is what will save it. However, the lingering impression left by the story, and of course, its subsequent cinematic adaptations, is that you can never really know if it has been completely destroyed, has assimilated an as-yet-unknown host or is just biding its time under the ice again.[2]

The novella became the title story of Campbell's eponymous first collection. This was published in 1948, the year after the pilot Kenneth Arnold's famous UFO encounter, which was the first of the post-war era. The stars were coming into alignment, and the novella would attract the interest of Hollywood. *The Thing from Another World* was the first of the three feature films that have been based on "Who Goes There?" to date.[3] Directed by Christian Nyby under the auspices of producer Howard Hawks, it was released in April 1951.

The screenplay by Charles Lederer, with uncredited contributions from Hawks and Ben Hecht, simplified the story considerably. The events now take place within the Arctic Circle rather than in the Antarctic. The alien craft is a flying saucer that has only just crash-landed. Most significantly, the Thing is no longer a creature that hijacks the bodies and personalities of the members of the expedition. In a press release quoted by George E. Turner, Hawks stated that:

> It is important that we don't confuse the *Frankenstein*-type of film with the science-fiction picture. The first film is an out-and-out horror thriller based on that which is impossible. The science-fiction film is based on that which is unknown, but given credibility by the use of scientific facts which parallel that which the viewer is asked to believe. (Turner 1991)

Ironically, as Turner points out, "the creature became a giant, hairless, humanoid vegetable which somewhat resembled Universal's Frankenstein monster" (ibid). Furthermore, the Thing's appetite for blood evokes that other classic horror character, Count Dracula. Nevertheless, the threat that this hybrid of gothic archetypes presents is on a par with Campbell's original: seedlings taken from a severed limb and nourished on blood plasma grow at an alarming rate, and plant life becomes an active agent in humanity's demise; no longer our food, but an apex predator whose favorite meal is mankind. The implication is clear: as in "Who Goes There?," if the creature can make its way out of the Arctic, then it can propagate an army of replicas and colonize the world: *every part is a whole*. The Anthropocene will end in an orgy of bloodletting, and what we might term the Xenocene will begin. Of note in this cinematic adaptation is that the attempt to incinerate the Thing by dousing it in kerosene fails, but a trap involving an electric arc works. This suggests that human technology will be our savior, even if it was responsible for releasing the creature from the ice in the first place.

The contagious nature of the creature continued to apply to the film—it became the most successful science-fiction film of the year, and one of the most influential ever made—and Campbell's novella as well. "Who Goes There?" is a clear influence on a novel published later in 1951, Robert A. Heinlein's *The Puppet Masters*. This is a breathless account of American secret agents fighting an invasion of slug-like alien parasites from Titan, Saturn's largest moon. Set in the aftermath of a limited nuclear exchange between the Western democracies and the Soviet Union, Heinlein's themes of duplicity and enslavement are cleverly established from the outset. Agents investigating reports of a flying saucer fail to report back from the landing site. When others follow up under cover, what they find is an obvious fake. However, this tourist trap is a double cross: the real spaceship lies underneath the replica. Anyone who enters the attraction will become an alien puppet and leave carrying one of the slugs on his or her back—this notion of something formerly hidden emerging into plain sight and changing the familiar into the deadly is one that is inherent in many eco-horror/eco-revenge narratives.

Beyond the core premise of a malignant invasion by infiltration, *The Puppet Masters* and "Who Goes There?" share two other elements. First, both Campbell and Heinlein's characters speculate that the alien species whose space vehicles have been hijacked encountered the parasites somewhere other than on their home worlds, which implies that a much more widespread occurrence on a galactic or even universal scale. Secondly, Campbell's non-normative subtext begins to surface in his prodigy's variation on the theme: "Heinlein's characterization of the slugs as communists/homosexuals coincides with [his] overt allegorization of the slugs as communist invasion" (Brown 2008, 18). Here we find that a correspondence is formed between ecological and nonnormative (subversive) themes that more clearly equates the apocalypse not with the death of humanity, but the end of patriarchal heteronormative ideologies. The aliens among us are signaling a future beyond such ideologies, which is then necessarily shown as monstrous.

Sam, the protagonist, is possessed by a slug, which allows Heinlein to describe the twilight world that the hag-ridden victims of possession are condemned to inhabit. They are conscious but without a will of their own anymore. Even as Sam and his colleagues move against the enemy, the slugs counter their every step in a war of nerves. The irony within the story is that the capitalist ideology of America in the 1950s Sam so desperately clings to demands he "conform and lose autonomy[, which] is done precisely to differentiate oneself from a Soviet society that demands conformity and loss of autonomy" (Brown 118). As in "Who Goes There?" and *The Thing from Another World*, the end of the mankind's exploitation of the earth is averted at the eleventh hour, when humanity mounts a revenge attack on Titan.

Two years later, in the summer of 1953, the Manx writer Nigel Kneale would offer a very British response to the subject in a BBC drama serial. It seems certain that, even if he had not read Campbell or Heinlein, Kneale must have seen *The Thing from Another World* because it was one of only four science fiction films that had been released in the UK since the Second World War that had had large enough budgets to involve special effects of any note.[4] Kneale wrote three stories around the character of Professor Bernard Quatermass: *The Quatermass Experiment, Quatermass II* and *Quatermass and the Pit*, all variations on the theme of an alien force taking over human beings. Here we will focus on *The Quatermass Experiment* since it is an important counterpoint to *The Thing from Another World*.

In an eerie echo of the V-2 ballistic missile attacks of World War II, a three-man probe launched by the British Experimental Rocket Group crashes into a row of houses in London. Believed lost until radar contact was re-established, the spaceship had travelled far beyond its planned orbit and entered deep space. When the capsule is finally opened for the first time since the launch, only one astronaut, Victor Carroon, remains inside. A fungal alien entity has infected Victor and absorbed his fellow astronauts. It will go on to impel him assimilate things as diverse as a potted cactus plant, a pharmacist, and various animals at London Zoo. Eventually, Carroon's grossly mutated form will take refuge in Westminster Abbey in order to spore, and thereby, take over the world.[5] While this *modus operandi* does emulate that of Hawks's *The Thing*, Kneale renders the process as tragic as it is horrific. Carroon is a victim rather than a malign agent, and however doomed he is, his struggle with the entity that is taking him over is heroic. Furthermore, Quatermass is a thoughtful and compassionate man who bears a burden of guilt for putting his astronauts in harm's way. This gives him the gravitas and moral authority that carries Kneale's bravura but necessarily theatrical ending. Quatermass sets no trap for the monster, but rather pleads with the men trapped inside it instead. As Kim Newman observes, "Quatermass tries to talk to the monster—only, in Kneale's universe, the monster listens" (2014, 21). The three men that have been assimilated by the fungal life-form commit suicide by sheer force of will, destroying the fruiting body of their host in the process. Older and wiser, a chastened Quatermass will live to fight another day. It provides an unusual ending in that mankind might be able to save itself through understanding, self-sacrifice, and learning from past mistakes, a scenario that is often missing from Hollywood where a more black-and-white, them-or-us solution is favored.

The idea of nonhuman invaders having more plant-like origins continues in *The Body Snatchers* by Jack Finney, originally published as a serial in *Collier's* magazine at the end of 1954, and then in paperback in 1955. It shares aspects with Campbell's green-blooded monster, but is far more organized and rhizomic in its invasion strategy, and subsequently became one of the most influential science-fiction novels of the twentieth century. To date, it has been continuously reprinted and adapted for the screen four times. Numerous other works also owe an unacknowledged debt to it, such as the 1998 film *The Faculty* and Stephanie Meyer's 2008 novel *The Host*. As with the works that have been previously discussed, the biological, vegetative alien begins as a parasitic infection, but soon becomes an autonomous entity which uses humanity as a kind of fuel to power their invasion of the Earth—the invasion itself being part of a wider galactic assimilation.

The Body Snatchers is set in Santa Mira, a small town in Northern California. Local doctor Miles Bennell receives reports of people claiming that imposters have taken the place of their relatives. What seems like a mass delusion proves to be a low-key invasion. Alien seed pods have drifted to Earth and are duplicating human beings. The invaders steal their sleeping victims' memories as well as their appearance, reducing the template to dust in the process, literally sucking them dry of all they were as humans. The replacements are emotionless and have a lifespan of only five years. The body snatchers' program of assimilation will progress exponentially until it is completed. Then they will move on again, leaving a dead—de-humanized—planet behind them.

Like *The Puppet Masters*, *The Body Snatchers* can be interpreted as a warning about a communist fifth column, a condemnation of the McCarthy witch-hunts, or "a signal text that satirized the creeping conformity of the Eisenhower era" (Nayman 2018, 152). However, from a twenty-first-century perspective, it seems very prescient of more ecological readings of an environment that is no longer willing to put up with an all-consuming humanity and so assimilates us into itself. Bennell and his girlfriend, Becky Driscoll, become increasingly isolated as the population is supplanted, but finally manage to escape the town. As they try to reach the highway, they find a field full of the pods, and set fire to it with tractor fuel. Although the gesture seems futile at first, the surviving pods, to escape the existential threat of fire, float off and return to outer space:

> And so now, to *survive*—their one purpose and function—the great pods lifted and rose, climbing up through the faint mist, on and out toward the space they had come from, leaving a fiercely inhospitable planet behind, to move aimlessly on once again, forever, or . . . it didn't matter. (Finney 2010, 203)

While Finney's upbeat ending might have been a commercial necessity, it now reads like a cop-out, an emotional appeal to the American ideal of rugged individualism. Perhaps this can be forgiven considering when it was published, which was at almost the exact time that resistance to McCarthyism was turning public opinion against the senator and his witch-hunt. However, later adaptations would not take the easy option of restoring the existing order.

The 1956 film of Finney's novel expanded the title to *Invasion of the Body Snatchers*, but followed the plot of the book closely until the climax. Director Don Siegel's film noir approach further darkens the story. The original script by Daniel Mainwaring saw a sleep-deprived Miles Bennell lose both Becky and his mind. Actor Kevin McCarthy breaks the fourth wall by yelling "You're next! You're next!" into the camera as trucks carrying pods hurtle out of Santa Mira, and other drivers ignore him. The threat of human extinction that gives all the works discussed dramatic tension was finally realized. This was the end of mankind's dominion over the world and signaled the final act of the Anthropocene.[6]

This was not necessarily a scenario that was wholly acceptable to popular audiences at the time, and related works that appeared throughout the rest of the decade often presented more human-centric conclusions. In 1957, Hammer released *Quatermass 2*, a remake of the second installment of Nigel Kneale's trilogy of works mentioned earlier. The story involves events following a disastrous ground test of his eponymous nuclear rocket, and Quatermass has to abandon his plans to establish a permanent human presence on the Moon. He is then asked to investigate the showers of meteorites landing near a top-secret industrial plant, only to discover that this is a copy of his proposed moon-base. The artificial meteorites carry protean, ammonia-breathing lifeforms that possess any human beings unlucky enough to find them.

The alien creatures form a gestalt entity with a collective consciousness. Quatermass discovers that a program of subversion has, in fact, been in progress for several years at various locations around the world that has infiltrated the highest levels of government. The film ends with the destruction of the ammonia-filled pressure dome housing the protoplasmic alien hive mind. As the gas escapes into the night sky, the "Hail Mary" launch of Quatermass' faulty atomic rocket destroys the creatures and their home asteroid.[7]

Quatermass and the Pit, the third part of Nigel Kneale's trilogy, was transmitted by the BBC between December 1958 and January 1959. It had the biggest budget, best staging, and largest audience of all three serials, and serves as the writer's definitive statement on the themes that he had been exploring. Quatermass, who has lost control of his rocket group to the military, is asked to investigate after pre-human remains and a suspected unexploded bomb are discovered at a building site. However, the buried rocket is not a German V-weapon, but in another echo of *The Thing From Another World*, a crashed Martian spaceship.

Kneale's final twist on his perennial theme is that an invasion actually succeeded five million years ago. Like the protoplasmic monsters of *Quatermass 2*, the insectoid Martians could not colonize Earth themselves when their planet was dying. However, they were able to genetically modify captured ape-men, and inculcate them with their own telepathic, warlike and genocidal traits—as with *The Thing* there is the faint suspicion that such remains have been purposely left so that, once humanity has gained the technological ability to find them, they are ready to be "culled" for the safety of the planet's eco-system (see also recent narratives such as *Life* [2017], *The Meg* [2018], and *The Silence* [2019]). The excavation of the Martian ship reactivates its dormant systems, and the machine draws energy from the power cables that have been strung inside it. London descends into chaos as any citizen with a strong Martian genetic component becomes part of a hive mind, and ethnic cleansing begins. A second Martian Xenocene will end the Anthropocene.

Kneale masterfully constructs a science-fictional rationale for the legends of demons and witchcraft. He also skewers reactionary, insular and racist attitudes, the products of an inhuman and insectile mindset. Nevertheless, he shows that few people—not even his beloved Professor Quatermass—are entirely free of this programming. One can equally read this as the kind of galactic biological life force mentioned earlier, and that witchcraft and earth-magicks are ways to reconnect humanity to the wider ecosystem around them—a form of anti-modernity that is more often termed as regressive in twentieth-century thought.[8] This is confirmed by the ending of the story: the threat is negated, but with the knowledge that a large amount of the population of the Earth carry the alien "genes," a connection to an anti-human past that is just waiting for the right circumstances to be re-energized.

By the 1970s, and in the wake of the American fuel crisis, a need for energy production alternatives and a greater awareness of environmental issues—the term "Anthropocene" was first used in English in the mid-1970s[9]—alien invasion narratives were in a place where the inevitable could finally be more explicitly tackled. The future no longer belonged to humanity as we know it. Writer-director Philip Kaufman tackled the theme in 1978 by reimagining *Invasion of the Body Snatchers*. Part remake and part sequel, the screenplay by W. D. Richter shifts the setting from the small town of Santa Mira to the big city of San Francisco. Kaufman retrospectively outlined his approach: "Could it happen in the city I love the most? The city with the most advanced, progressive therapies, politics and so forth? What would happen in a place like that if the pods landed there and that element of 'poddiness' was spread?" (Wiener 2018). The film can be read as a product of the "me" decade with its focus on urban paranoia and the hangover after the end of "the long sixties," although it can equally be seen as a commentary on the toxicity of capitalism at the end of the twentieth century. The pod people can exemplify the monstrosity of capitalist ideology that turns everybody into mindless consumers while simultaneously representing ecological revenge on mankind.

From the outset, the characters seem uncomfortable in their own skins. Donald Sutherland plays the protagonist, health inspector Matthew Bennell, whose first name and profession have both been changed from the original. The film subtly acknowledges the essential nature of a remake: the Miles Bennell of the 1950s has already been replaced. The point is underscored by a cameo from Kevin McCarthy, the star of the original film, as a lost soul still screaming "You're next!" at passing traffic. Original director Don Siegel also appears in a crucial vignette as a cab-driving pod person. Kaufman discussed the compromised ending of the original with Siegel and McCarthy, and they all agreed on how to improve it. The first frames of the film show the alien germ seed drifting into space, foreshadowing the end of our own world:

> We were able to create that sense, essentially, of a planet that could be our planet in the future where all living matter has been devoured. It's a barren, Martian-like planet and the pod ectoplasm is escaping from it, looking for fresh hunting grounds, flying through space and arriving in San Francisco. (Kaufman 2018)

The ending is uncompromising. The pods have taken over the city and are well on their way to conquering the world. No one is spared: Bennell reveals himself to be a pod person when he betrays an old friend by calling to the collective with an unearthly scream. It has taken nearly a quarter of a century, but the pod people have finally won. Despite a valiant struggle, the Anthropocene is well and truly over. A point of note within Kaufman's film is that, while humanity is the main focus of the vegetative invaders, it also suggests that a broader agenda of biological reintegration is possible when we are shown an image of a hybrid human/canine pod creature that has somehow produced a dog with a human face. Intimated here then is not just the end of humanity or even eco-revenge, but the unstoppable forces of "life" itself that have no respect for distinct species, just organic evolution and hybridization (see *Annihilation* [Garland 2018]).

The unstoppability of the forces of life and the ability to fully realize adaptations of source material arguably reached their apotheosis in 1982 with director John Carpenter's *The Thing*. An avowed fan of the Hawks–Nyby adaptation, Carpenter had initially been reluctant to direct a remake. However, after reading Campbell's original novella, he was intrigued by the possibilities of a version that grappled with a shape-shifting nemesis. Bill Lancaster's screenplay retains much of "Who Goes There?" including an all-male cast, although a significantly reduced one. It also nods to *Horror Express* (1972) by Eugenio Martín, which also featured a shake-shifting alien that, like Kneale's Martian insectoid's, had been on the Earth for hundreds of thousands of years. The claustrophobic setting and relentless build-up of tension make this the definitive adaptation of Campbell's story.

The film begins with two survivors of a Norwegian base pursuing a dog that has been assimilated. One accidentally blows himself up, and the other, who is firing a rifle at the animal, is shot by the American commander. Having already wiped out one research station, the Thing has now invaded another. If you are prepared to accept the initial premise of an alien life form being retrieved from underneath the ice, then the plot unfolds with remorseless logic. As in "Who Goes There?" attempts to identify who has been replaced are continually frustrated. As the number of uninfected human beings dwindles, Kurt Russell's R. J. MacReady (note the extra "a" in his surname) reasons that the Thing intends to return to hibernation until a rescue party arrives. To prevent the creature taking over anyone else, he blows up the research station. However, another apparent survivor, Childs, appears as MacReady watches the ruins burn. While MacReady is not wholly convinced by Childs' explanation of his movements, they both recognize that their mutual suspicion is pointless, and share a last bottle of whisky. Carpenter's ending becomes less ambiguous when you realize that only MacReady's breath is condensing in the freezing air. Childs is the Thing, and it has won. At the very least, the events at the Norwegian and American bases will repeat themselves at McMurdo Station. In all probability, the Thing will assimilate the world, and end the Anthropocene for once and for all.

In many respects, Carpenter's *The Thing* completes the journey begun by Campbell in honoring and updating the original source material, and showing the inevitable end of mankind's dominion over the Earth. Over the next few decades, there would be other remakes and homages, but arguably little new ground would be broken—the 2011 prequel can be seen to more clearly adapt the story for an age of pandemics and contagion, but humanity is still doomed. However, what is of significance is that, even though the Cold War has ended—the conflict that provided much of the imaginative impetus for the earlier incarnations of the two stories under discussion—the trope of the vegetational, ecological invader persists. This can be read in various ways. In terms of Jungian analytical psychology, the things—or Things—that steal our faces and attempt to supplant us should not be read as extraterrestrial entities, but as expressions of our id; we are literally, individually and collectively, our own worst enemies. The "other" that we fear is, of course, that repressed dark part of ourselves—the shadow archetype—that we project onto our chosen scapegoats in a spectacularly foolish act of denial. We are the greatest threat to our own environment, and therefore, ourselves: having created the Anthropocene, we now seem to be hell-bent on ending it by facilitating our own demise. Linked to this is the idea that what we have repressed in terms of our interactions with the ecological consciousness.

Mankind has sublimated the needs of the environment around us to satiate our own desires above all else. Therefore, alien doppelgängers are not so much mirrors that show our own darkness to ourselves, but the environment revealing that we are no different to the plants and insects around us; we are all made of the same stuff. Until we recognize this—a MacReady and Childs sharing a drink moment—the end of humanity is inevitable, and rather than being a part of what life will become, our reckoning will be abrupt and violent.

NOTES

1. It should be acknowledged that Campbell's reputation has significantly diminished over time, not least because of the extreme views around race that he expressed in his later editorials for the magazine that he renamed *Analog Science Fiction/ Science Fact*.

2. "Who Goes There?" would prove to be an enormously influential story. A. E. van Vogt credited it as the inspiration for "Vault of the Beast" (1940), the first science-fiction story that he wrote, and the second he sold to *Astounding*.

3. At the time of writing, an adaptation of *Frozen Hell* is being developed by Jason Blum's Blumhouse Productions for Universal Pictures.

4. The others were *Destination Moon* (1950), *The Day the Earth Stood Still* (1951) and *When Worlds Collide* (1951).

5. In this aspect, it precedes a similar scenario seen in *The Girl with All the Gifts* (McCarthy 2016).

6. This was too much for the studio, of course. A reluctant Siegel and Mainwaring were ordered to add a framing sequence suggesting that there was still some hope: "The film was nearly ruined by those in charge at Allied Artists who added a preface and ending that I don't like" (quoted in Lovell 1975, 54). Fortunately, contemporary viewers can watch the director's cut by simply skipping the interpolated scenes.

7. Asteroids and comets are popular tropes in apocalyptic invasion narratives, often forming a kind of cosmic regulator of life on Earth with cyclical appearances in the skies above the planet throughout history.

8. Nigel Kneale also wrote the screenplay for Roy Ward Baker's adaptation of *Quatermass and the Pit* (A.K.A. *Five Million Years to Earth*), which was released by Hammer in 1967, and largely followed the original narrative and its denouement.

9. This was used by atmospheric scientist Paul Crutzen.

WORKS CITED

Biello, David. 2015. "Did the Anthropocene Begin in 1950 or 50,000 Years Ago?" *Scientific American*, 2 April. https://www.scientificamerican.com/article/did-the -anthropocene-begin-in-1950-or-50-000-years-ago/. Accessed October 1, 2021.

Brown, Joseph F. 2008. "Heinlein and the Cold War: Epistemology and Politics in *The Puppet Masters* and *Double Star*." *Extrapolation* 49, no. 1 (Spring), 109–121.

Campbell, John W. 2011. "Who Goes There?" In *Who Goes There?* London: Gollancz, 1–75.

Campbell, John W., Jr. 2019. *Frozen Hell*. Cabin John, MD: Wildside Press.

Crutzen, Paul J. and Eugene F. Stoermer. 2000. "The 'Anthropocene'." *International Geosphere-Biosphere Programme Newsletter* 41 (May), 17–18.

Elms, Alan C. 1994. *Uncovering Lives: The Uneasy Alliance of Biography and Psychology*. Oxford: Oxford University Press.

Finney, Jack. 2010. *The Body Snatchers* [1954]. London: Gollancz.

Frost, Robert. 1920. "'Fire and Ice,' A Group of Poems by Robert Frost." *Harper's Magazine* (December), 67.

Heinlein, Robert A. 1987. *The Puppet Masters* [1951]. London: New English Library.

Lovell, Alan. *Don Siegel: American Cinema*. London: British Film Institute.

Moskowitz, Sam. 1974. *Seekers of Tomorrow: Masters of Modern Science Fiction*. Westport, CT: Hyperion Press.

Nayman, Adam. 2018. *The Coen Brothers: This Book Really Ties the Films Together*. New York, NY: Abrams.

Newman, Kim. 2014. *Quatermass and the Pit*. Basingstoke: Palgrave Macmillan.

Turner, George E. 1991. "The Thing from Another World." *American Cinematographer* 72, no. 1 (January). https://ascmag.com/articles/the-thing-from-another-world-1951. Accessed October 1, 2021.

Van Vogt, A. E. 1940. "Vault of the Beast." *Astounding Science-Fiction* 25, no. 6 (August), 50–69

Weiner, David. 2018. "Why 'Invasion of the Body Snatchers' still haunts its director." *The Hollywood Reporter*. 20 December. https://www.hollywoodreporter.com/movies/movie-news/invasion-body-snatchers-ending-still-haunts-director-1170220/. Accessed October 1, 2021.

Chapter 11

Nonconsensual Eco-sex

A Guided Meditation to the Permeable Membrane

Sarah Lewison

In 2008 I lived in Yunnan, China, on a family farm near the Yangtze River headwaters. At that time the Chinese government was putting forward a "New Countryside" policy that aimed to entice smallholders to abandon subsistence farming and enter the market as consumers. There was a construction boom and tree-covered mountains were sculpted into new luxury resorts and phantom cities. That same summer, the nearby glacial springs that had been maintained for centuries began to languish, their flow turning to a trickle. Older residents who paid attention to such things observed this was because too many holes were being dug into the ground, and that the mountain spirits were displeased. The peremptory warning of the mountain spirits gestured to the degree to which human mining, drilling, boring, paving proceeded with a studied ignorance of what's lost when what mining companies cynically call the "overburden," the dense mesh of life that is the planetary surface, is removed. When humans disturb and destroy habitat, the lives of countless others are thrown into chaos. They must find another place to live, and one of the places they run to are humans themselves.

In this chapter, I consider the spread of Lyme, a bacterial infection spread by ticks in relation to the eradication of habitat and consequent biodiversity loss. The United States Centers for Disease Controls estimates nearly half a million diagnoses of the Lyme infection per year, although fewer incidents are actually reported to the agency. Tests for the disease are unreliable. The bacterium, which is a spirochete much like syphilis, evades detection once an infection has progressed, and its symptoms are indistinct from other chronic conditions. Lyme roils in medical and popular controversy. Some contend the disease originated from a federal biological weapons laboratory and claim that incidents are undercounted as part of a coverup. Regardless of origins, it is acknowledged that Lyme's rapid spread within the last fifty years is associated with biodiversity loss and habitat fragmentation, and that, as an infectious agent, it has, in the parlance of biologists, "spilled over" from forest mammals to humans. Environmental infection encourages us to see our relations with more-than-humans as co-evolutionary, and as defined by an array of perspectives that include the more-than-humans who make us who we are. Through regimes of environmental scale that reveal the parallels between the earth body and our own bodies, Lyme makes palpable the perils of development and gestures toward both the problems and possibilities of co-inhabitation on a limited planet.

Although the mass of humans by weight on our planet is small in comparison to all other life, in 2020 we crossed the point where human-made, anthropogenic stuff exceeds the weight of all other living planetary biomass (Elhacham, Ben-Uri, Grozovski, Bar-On, et al., 2020). More to the point, the biomass of our mere warm-blooded bodies is now eight times greater than that of other wild mammals (Bar-On, Phillips and Milo, 2018). This little fact alone statistically increases our chances of becoming a destination for ticks which depend on the presence of mammals to complete their reproductive cycle. In becoming a vector for the tick, we humans become their new ontological target, along with forest-dwelling white-footed mice, deer, and opossum. Humans who become infected by the Lyme bacteria experience symptoms similar to long-term Covid that might include muscle aches, fever, tiredness, brain fog, memory problems, severe arthritis, carditis, and terrible pain. If Lyme is a form of ecological revenge, it is because, as it takes refuge in humans, it has potential to change and, in its own way, domesticate us.

SUBURBAN TICKS AND BACTERIAL HITCHHIKERS

Ticks are tiny, nearly sightless arthropods, like tiny crabs with sticky legs that live in the rich ecological matrix of North American forest. They lay eggs that hatch in the spring, after which the larvae need mammalian blood to continue development to the nymph stage. They need a blood meal for each life stage: larvae to pupae to maturity, when the adults will feed once more to reproduce. Jakob von Uexküll, a twentieth-century zoologist and early ecological theorist, wrote about how the tick's limited sensory organs constitute their life world, a sensitivity to heat and the smell of butyric acid, which is present in mammalian sweat (Agamben 2004, p 84; Uexküll 2010, pp. 44–51). They also detect carbon dioxide concentrations and will flock to dried ice placed on a sheet. Ticks cling to grass blades and tree branches until an animal brushes past they might snag or drop on to. Once landed, they crawl around to find a protected hairless spot where they can latch on with a resinous chemical cement and penetrate the skin with their saw-like mandibles. They inject an anticoagulant into the wound site causing the blood to make a pool from which they will drink with a straw-like proboscis. Over days, they swell to many times their size before dropping off. Some ticks carry the bacteria that causes Lyme disease in their hind gut, and it does not affect the tick. If *Borellia burgdorferii* is present when the tick is feeding, the spirochetes sense a chemical change inducing them to move from the tick's gut, through the feeding mouth, into the mammal. The corkscrew shaped bacteria twirl through the tick's mouth into a mammal's bloodstream and tissue, literally drilling forward. They slide through collagen, mucus, and connective tissue between the joints, around the eyes, the brain and heart, any viscous media which resemble the ancestral home of all spirochetes, the mud (Margulis, 2004, p. 119). If not detected, they begin to multiply and to express custom-ized genetic sequences that match immune patterns of the host animal: mice, dog, deer or humans, assuming a ninja-like camouflage. This hacker-like ability to disguise their genetic signature is why Lyme is difficult to detect after the first few weeks of infection. A further disguise allows them to seal themselves off from antibiotics as an inert cyst. (Brorson, 2009).

Spirochetal bacteria like Borelia have been around for millions of years. In Central America, their corkscrew shape has been observed in the intestines of both fossilized termites (Brorson, 2009) and ticks (Gannon 2014). The Lyme bacterium has been in North America at least 60,000 years (Caccone, 2017; Walter 2017), but was not identified until the 1970s, when a woman in Lyme, Connecticut, noticed disabling arthritis, rashes, and swollen joints in her children. Over the summer, as other residents in the neighborhood, a new subdivision by a forest, began to exhibit the same spreading bullseye rash, the woman called the State Department of Health (Walter, 2017). It's rare for children to develop arthritis, and more unusual still for it to appear in a population cluster. Where did it come from and what caused it? A Yale rheu-matologist agreed to treat the afflicted residents and subsequently published an article on what he called "Lyme arthritis." The outbreak was so localized that some linked it to an accidental or deliberate release from a nearby bio-weapons research lab. But, within a few years, Alan Steere, the doctor, heard of hundreds of similar cases from Wisconsin, California, New Jersey, and throughout the northeast. Although geographically dispersed, all illnesses were found near fragmented woodlands, where two species of black-legged ticks were present. In 1982, a medical etymologist named Burgdorfer identi-fied the spirochetal bacterium being hosted in these ticks.

Since then, the range and number of tick-transmitted Lyme infections have increased exponentially, correlating with both development and cli-mate change. As forests are removed or reduced to patches, there are fewer wild mammals to act as hosts or vectors for the ticks, and even fewer predators to keep the numbers of small mammals with ticks down. Furthermore, the ticks live longer and travel farther as the climate warms (Caccone, 2017). As Katherine Walter, an infectious disease expert who studies the biological implications of human practices writes, ticks are not entering into human territory; humans have moved into tick-land (2017). When there is a scarcity of the usual hosts: mice, opossums, shrews, foxes, and squirrels, ticks will find the random passing human or dog. As land continues to be cleared, and as the climate continues to warm, their range expands, they reproduce more, and the number of ticks carrying *Borrelia burgdorferi* increase.

The bullseye-shaped skin rash that some humans exhibit after being bit suggests the wake of the spirochete's spinning motion, a visual metaphor for how screwed it is. Dogs, deer, mice and humans provide an environment where *B. burgdorferii* continues its reproductive functions, just as we produce spaces as part of our own life cycles. I think of Lyme infection as nonconsensual eco-sex, for its intimacy is psychologically horrifying; it finds lubricated regions you do not know yourself, and it knows how to work with these parts, to open them up like a fork bomb. Its extraction of resources for its own reproduction leads us to feel pain, and to become not ourselves. Without going too far into the bleakness of chronic disability, I wonder what we can learn from Lyme. I feel like it is screaming that we have dug too many holes in the mountains. And I wonder if it could change us to actually become or to act otherwise by getting us in touch with the ways our bodies and ourselves are stranger than we think.

THE ONTOLOGICAL AMPHIBIAN

I draw from anecdote, science, and speculative fiction to contribute to the work of reframing the human and more-than-human relationship to imagine possible futures in the Anthropocene. Speculative fiction offers one compassionate way to imagine the life world of others. It is the kind of tale making that follows the flight of birds, informed by observation and imagination, trading in transformations of scale and function; transformation itself. It is used alike by naturalists, anthropologists, indigenous elders, and bedtime storytellers. I'm especially inspired by *Testimony of a Spore*, in which Anna Tsing (2014) tenderly narrates the hypothetical subjectivity of a spore, offering a vicarious experience of the fungal reproductive gamble through an exhilarating aerial journey that culminates, hopefully, in mushroom sex. Speculative fiction is also the storytelling of science when ideas are in formative but untested stages.

The anthropologist and cyberneticist Gregory Bateson who, in his own peremptory warnings about human habits, wrote, "the organism which destroys its environment destroys itself" (1972, 451) In considering pathways to avoiding this, he proposed the flexible organism-plus-environment as the fundamental "unit of life." Flexibility, to Bateson, was rooted in the group's genomic diversity and possibilities within and for the co-cultivation of environment. His "organism-plus-environment" formula challenged the evolutionary primacy of genes, both individual genes and those of an individual species as determinants of survival. When a habitat is wiped out, communities unable to adapt to alternative spaces become extinct while those that can continue living, by adapting a different configuration. Part of the "success" of humans is arguably due to our skill in adapting spaces to our use, but in an era of climate change, we are all going to have housing problems, from humans to the unicellular critters who depend on others for habitat. It's a biopolitical conundrum, as housing problems for humans become housing problems for others and are tightly connected to survival and reproduction. For humans, the flexibility to move and adapt leads to wars, immigration, and refugees. What about the refugees of the forest?

Forced migration does not always lead to the end of a species. Maybe the critters are just hanging out in the patches, waiting for us to leave. During the first months of the coronavirus pandemic, many mammals who had been hemmed in by highways and traffic began to take to the human streets. Their presence reminded people of how closely we live. In *The New Wild*, Fred Pearce describes the adaptations made by species that have been moved to new environments, that even fill essential habitat or food needs. (Pearce 2015, 4) We are familiar with destructive introductions of nonnative species, such as, say kudzu which simply take over, but the displacement of species also leads to functional configurations in ecological systems which are simply different. The contradictions within adaptability gesture toward how many ways the puzzle of habitat, human intervention and political ecology fit together.

If we could observe an evolutionary path in fast motion reverse, it would reveal an organism in a multi-scaled dance—or maybe fight!—with other species within its environment (Stern, 2020, p. 160). Lichens, which are symbiotic unions of fungi and algae offer one example of how organisms that are encroached upon by others sometimes emerge as new lifeforms. There are also species who simply provide a space cum habitat for viruses and bacteria to which they are immune. Ecologists call these reservoir hosts—bats in the case of corona and other viruses. (Quammen 2012, 23) Julieta Aranda and Eben Kirksey use the conceptual metaphor "ontological amphibian" to describe an organism that can flexibly adapt to different environments by changing its form or through its world making. Amphibians, of course, are species that survive in both water and land. As the metabolic speed of environmentally destructive activities continues apace and climate change side effects intensify, legions of displaced organisms will search for new environments. Some have the potential to become ontological amphibians, just as humans might someday live on the rising tides in floating buildings that provide cool shade to corals.

To say that we are all connected is a truism that gains strength and meaning a time when viral and bacterial agents are increasingly being unleashed by figurative holes dug in the forest. Relationship is by definition the foundation of functioning ecosystems. The problem of habitat loss is not only about distant rain forest or ice shelf; it is an intimate matter because ecological complexity is everywhere, and when it is diminished, organisms are orphaned into everyday spaces like our backyards. Often, such infectious agents live within reservoir hosts, which like the tick are vectors, but are not themselves sickened. Coronavirus, caused by a virus that has possibly migrated from a reservoir host species—perhaps bat—into humans, should come to mind. When habitats are diminished, or when domestic animals are in proximity to reservoir hosts, opportunities are created for infectious bacteria and viruses to "spillover" into new populations as a zoonosis, a species crossing infection (Quammen 2012, 20–21). Our connectivity is grounded in this strange reality that we are all bound tightly into environment, which performs as foreground and background for each other in complicated ways (Morton 2010, 28-30). We form environments for each other, but there also are kinds of boundaries. Boundaries are like membranes, expressed in diverse ways. It is difficult to predict what happens when boundaries are crossed, but not so hard to imagine that something will happen. We may need the imagination of the elders in mountainous Yunnan, China, who forecast that when too many holes are dug, there will be repercussions. In the 1997 animated movie directed by Hayao Miyazaki, *Princess Mononoke*, the forest gods take revenge upon the humans who have pillaged the forest for their technologies. If the spirits of the forest are disturbed, unsettlement will reverberate. *B. burgdorferii*, a spiral inhabiting the gut of some ticks, is a shapeshifting spirit of the forest.

Like many Lyme stories, mine is from personal experience. It was summer and I got a flu; achy, fevered, back and head pain, confused and couldn't think. I didn't feel like myself, had no energy and felt displaced from myself. This sense of derangement is common with Lyme; it's also familiar for sufferers of "long Covid," who experience persistent brain fog, and memory loss. My county health department said it was unlikely to be Lyme because "there wasn't much here." The test was nonconclusive however my doctor agreed it was a good idea to prescribe a thirty-day course of antibiotics. I learned that my state was not (then) tracking local cases, and that owing to the patchy profit-based medical system, there was little research being done on the condition. I met local people, outdoorsy-type men in particular, who claimed to have had multiple infections, and to be living with the symptoms. It was the first time I heard the term "brain fog." They shrugged it off, as in "this is what men do." I wondered if there were others like them. The symptoms are similar to arthritis, so maybe they just take painkillers. I began to marvel at how close this little organism was to humans, how we have become a landscape to a microscopic monstrosity that was a marker of development itself as a phenotypic expression of human interactions with environment.

That summer I got a cheap microscope and started looking at microorganisms, learning to identify arthropods, bacteria, fungi, and some protists, all of which are found in a drop of puddle water. Once something big raced across the stage. Refocusing, I saw a tardigrade, which looks like the Michelin man's padded arm, with eight plumped up legs, tiny claws, and a jagged maw for a mouth. Its popular name, water bear, conveys its weird cuteness. This ultra-durable organism can be desiccated into a freeze-dried fleck that withstands irradiation and hypoxia, to be rehydrated years later to carry normal functioning. It is an ontological amphibian. The tardigrade's ability to persist without an environment poses a stark contrast to we mammals, with our limited tolerances of diet, temperature, stress, water, and light. There are many creatures, from single-celled organisms to tiny arachnids, who live upon and reproduce within us; we are their habitat. Each has its own biological trajectory contributing to a nested bundle of interlocking lives that somehow, in the end, resembles a human person, or a wolf, or otter. The tiny organisms living on and in us are the subject of shrill graphic banners on the internet. "Thousands of insects are secretly living in your eyebrows! They're eating, mating and laying eggs all over our faces!" (Cummings 2015). The banner-ad's headline illustrates the atrocious squatter through the quotidian: a photograph of an attractive woman sporting a fashionable thick eyebrow which is supposedly teeming with bugs. Microscopic arthropods such as the *Demodex* mites that inhabit the sebaceous glands at the base of our eyelashes and eyebrows are an obligate species, meaning their sole home is eyebrows and eyelashes, where they also perform a grooming function for us. As long as their population is in balance, their presence is unnoticed. My son calls them eyebrow lobsters; we think of them as having a kin or sim (for symbiotic) bond with us.

FEMINIST SPECULATIVE SCIENCE (FICTION)

Symbiosis, writes evolutionary biologist Lynn Margulis, is "the living together in physical contact of organisms of different species" (1998, 33). Margulis' most important work was the construction of a theory demonstrating how symbiotic relations evolve over time into new, more complex organisms. Up to 90% of the cells that make up humans can be traced to have ancestors in single-celled organisms that once lived independently (Gilbert et al 2012). Because these once independent organisms are incorporated into, and now compose our functioning organs, these strangers fall below notice; they have literally become us. Its easier to visualize *Demodex* rummaging around in our eyebrows, and to get bothered by it. People get itchy just thinking about it. Maybe this itchy bother can be enlisted to reimagine environment and nonhuman lives. Our bodies are not simply environment for a few eyebrow lobsters living out their lives and deaths; the human biome is a composite mashup of environments-within-environments for ten thousand species.

Complex life forms such as animals, plants, algae and fungi are eukaryotes, which means our cellular DNA is contained within the membrane of a nucleus—a structure that is maintained and repaired to protect the organism's integrity. Bacteria are prokaryotes and lack a nuclear membrane to protect their DNA. Unprotected, their genes flow, "connecting them with a planetary genetic miasma." Margulis analogizes the radical mutability of the bacterial cell with its unprotected DNA to a person jumping into a swimming pool with brown eyes and emerging a few minutes later with blue ones (Margulis and Sagan 2000, 96). Suspended in plasma rather than contained within a membrane, the DNA freely responds to its environment by exchanging DNA and genetic information. It is having—or doing—sex. Lynn Margulis' revelatory speculations into how life creates habitats, is expelled, and then recombines and emerges in new forms is based on her study of bacterial sex between organisms with different characteristics, sometimes consensual, sometimes not. Her hypothesis was that complex, highly differentiated organisms combine, Frankenstein-like, through the co-evolutionary assimilation and adaptation of multiple different organisms. It is now accepted that our own gut-living mitochondrial DNA are such symbionts. These organelles (diminutive organs within cells) which regulate energy production and immune reactions within us were once independent organisms that joined forces through a serialized co-evolutionary process.

One of the organisms that she learned this from is the sea slug, which she dubbed a "green animal" for the way it is able to photosynthesize chlorophyl like a plant. It is both plant and animal, a real chimera, a co-evolutionary symbiont. It inspires speculation, but we've already met lichens, that collusion between fungi and algae which exemplify the evolutionary merging of once autonomously living species, algae and fungi. As evolutionary composites, humans are then both human and not human. Like all mammals, we have developed our complexity through a long series of events in which cells have become incorporated into another until, like the green animal, our composited organs accomplish multiple tasks. The incorporation of one cell into another is not necessarily nonconflictual. Margulis describes how an aggressive spirochete might repeatedly attack a slower moving bacterium. One cell could get killed off and ingested, or one could encapsulate the other in its cellular walls. It is a dramatic struggle, dance or fight—or eventually merge. Margulis' conclusions about symbiotic evolution at the bacterial level destabilize the idea of organismic individuality, identity, and even species.

Through such destabilizations, which were long resisted by the scientific community, Margulis' scientific work bears comparison with science fiction, which she herself acknowledged (Margulis and Sagan 2000, 96). Her take on each organism being more than what it seems, and her invitation to see reproduction as multiple and various reads especially well as feminist speculation, but as a scientist Margulis does not dwell on affective nuances of such reproductive alliances. What can we learn about harm and conflict in the context of ecological balance?

In her science fiction, Octavia Butler, perhaps more than any other twentieth century writer, explored intimacy in relationships between humans and non-human others. A number of her stories are set in worlds where humans have been rescued from an unlivable earth by an alien species, and where the continuity of both aliens and humans rest upon the challenges of cooperation and the possibility of sexual intimacy. In her Xenogenesis series, the protagonists are urged to forge unions and bear children with non-human extraterrestrials. Rather than downplaying the ambivalence we feel toward those who don't look like us, Butler stays steadfastly with that trouble.

The short story *Bloodchild* (1995) embarks upon this precise biopolitical negotiation between humans and a society of intelligent insect-like creatures who have lost their ability to bear young without the aid of warm-blooded surrogates. Butler wrote *Bloodchild* to reconcile her anxieties about the human botfly (*Dermatobia hominis*), an insect common to Peru, before traveling to that country to do research for Xenogenesis. The botfly needs a warm-blooded animal host to incubate its larvae. Not catholic at all in choice of host, it will bite a cow, horse, bird, or human, first to feed, and then to deposit its larvae in the wound. The larvae quickly burrow in below the skin where they grow for up to eighteen days before emerging and falling off (Hill and Connelly 2008).

In *Bloodchild*, Butler adopts a similar reproductive premise, while bestowing sentience and intelligence upon the parasitical other, so that the matter of surrogacy becomes a brokered negotiation between humans and the aliens. In this respect, she humanizes the aliens, attributing to them the ability to love, individualize, and to cultivate consensual long-term relationships, including close-knit families. Mature aliens, or "Tlics" are, at three meters long, larger than humans, with segmented bodies, over a dozen limbs, a velvet underside, and a tail with a stinger that delivers a sedative with a euphoric effect on humans. They have an advanced, intelligent, hierarchical society. They have rescued the humans from an uninhabitable Earth, and their own reproductive futures have also been damaged; few Tlics bear fertile eggs. Fertile Tlics need a warm-blooded host to incubate their eggs, for which they once used four-legged animals, but they prefer humans for their emotional responsiveness. Humans, or "Terrans," live under Tlic surveillance in a gated "preserve" resembling a refugee camp. They are protected and provided for, and they are also expected to form family units with reproductive Tlics. Butler calls *Bloodchild* her male pregnancy story, for males are preferred as egg incubation surrogates. Tlics cultivate relationships with a chosen host, so he will feel safe, and later, protective toward Tlic young. This leaves female Terrans to have their own human babies.

The story follows Gan, an adolescent Terran whose time to incubate his first clutch of eggs for his Tlic-kin, T'Gatoi, has come. His Tlic-kin, a kind of relative: part sister, part mother, and part betrothed, will sleep in his room, sedate him, and deposit her eggs inside him. It is a procedure the family has accepted and planned for Gan's whole life. Unexpectedly, however, he is forced to witness the horrifying surgical intervention he himself will have to undergo once the eggs hatch. The surrogate is cut open and each grub must be removed before they eat his flesh from the inside out. The procedure is understood as a necessary sacrifice benefitting both his human family and the Tlic "mother," who is responsible to ensure he feels no pain, is sutured, restored to health, and cared for within their mixed family. In crisis, he questions this relationship based on debt and power that will use his body for the incubation of these "bugs." Having obtained a weapon, he brandishes it as he tentatively withdraws consent, refusing to cooperate with the reproductive process. As Butler explores valences of emotional bonds between "aliens" and humans in a world they share, she also reveals a yawning gap between their perspectives based on their species differences and power differentials.

The vocalized practice of giving and withdrawing consent in the context of sexual intimacy has, in recent years become an important part of sex education for the role it plays in preventing sexual violence. In the conclusion of *Bloodchild*, Butler establishes consent as a foundation upon which a new society might be able to go forward after the end of the world. The adolescent Gan ultimately re-commits to the alien-human mixed family by consenting to an act of ecosex, providing a womb to another species to sustain the only world they both have. Butler also shows how mutualism, and for that matter, entanglement, which is currently a popular word, is not necessarily pretty or easy. Entanglement demands sacrifice and the relinquishment of control, and sometimes withdrawal. Butler's ecosexuality is consensual, albeit coercive given the circumstances. In contrast, Margulis' theory of serial endosymbiosis, in which aggressive cells repeatedly attempt to invade another cell until one is either killed or engulfed, could be seen as nonconsensual ecosex. Likewise for the infectious invasion of Lyme—*B. burgdorferii*. In all accounts, intimacies negotiate difference, and species strive, each in their own world views, toward habitat and survival. As the borders, or membranes—between humans and beyond-human others mutate and reshape, we might speculate on new frameworks of coexistence and habitat provision that diminish our capacities to lay waste to the planet. What are the chances that a human might agree to become the reproductive habitat for the beyond-human other because there was an incalculable benefit?

THE ENTANGLEMENT AND OUR TERRA BODY

For environmental artists, filmmakers, and theorists, Elizabeth Stephens and Annie Sprinkle, ecosexuality is their neologism to describe passionate and intimate love for the earth and the full functioning of its biological systems and ecological relationships. Their exuberant performance art includes elaborate publicly staged weddings—to clouds, to the earth, specific lakes, rivers, and dirt. Their films bring together politics and pleasure to address ecological crisis, such as mountaintop removal, through sensuality, joy, and care. Their book "Assuming the Ecosexual Position" is a manifesto for earthly pleasure. As advocacy for intimacy with beyond-humans and ecological systems, their activist work offers new ontological metaphors for coexistence and respect, love, and sexual pleasure. The title of their recent film, *Water Makes us Wet!* is a cheeky word play on our earthly entanglements. The suggestive ambiguities Sprinkle and Stephens enlist in their titles might be a way to communicate about the relations we have with the Lyme spirochete and its vectors, relations that are *too* close because we have loved "nature" so much that we've forced it into our backyards. (Walter 2017, Dauphinais 2019) To connect habitat loss and Lyme, and the inflammation of heart tissue in cases of advanced Lyme, we could offer the peremptory proclamation, "Logging makes us lose heart!" I like to imagine declaring, "Habitat destruction makes me lose my mind!" a pun-like ambiguity in speculative ecological imagining that relays the real impacts of Lyme on the human nervous system.

We are at a fork in this political and ecological journey. Going one direction, we accept Lyme as an infectious agent that we've coaxed out of the forest and attempt to regain control through vaccination and species eradication. Perhaps scientists can genetically reengineer the spirochete, but the chances are it will just turn around and re-edit itself. In another direction, we simply continue to be oblivious to the factors underlying the disease's proliferation and make more subdivisions and painkillers. Maybe some people will attain immunity or forge new talents with the spirochete. Perhaps more people get sick, and ambition will fade because it's too much work. The weeds will grow back. Young trees will retake the lawns, each sprout an act of poetic justice as increasingly disabled humans lose the energy and will to dominate. After all, the disablement of the forest's systems has led these once concealed organisms to human hosts. Maybe the spirochetes change too, and start using less aggressive, "greener" practices, becoming more human?

We could close the hole that has been rent by suturing habitats: invite back predators, shrink back into more compact cities, and relinquish the attempt to control, develop and extract from land as a critical public safety measure. Our culture could scour old stories and adopt new ones that, like the elders in China, posed precautionary warnings and eco-regulatory measures to be shared in song and on Tiktok. Or we could lose control and become other in an evolutionary stream, not as parasitical invasion, but as a release from individuality that gestures toward different frameworks of co-existence; symbiosis, dematerialization, and the habitat provision for others.

One of Margulis' most extreme ideas was that the capacity for perception, awareness, speculation, thought, memory, and knowledge always already existed in the microorganism. Spirochetes are a phylogenetically distinct bacteria that, owing to their slim profiles and flagellate curls, move quickly. Margulis believed that movement itself was a trait descending from bacterial ancestors. She speculated that thought "is a kind of cell movement" (Margulis and Sagan 1997, 122). Hypothesizing that the brain is assembled from cells that long ago engulfed fragments of highly active spirochetes, she wondered whether encapsulated fragments of spirochetes or spirochetal DNA could be producing the intense spasms of connection we experience as thinking. Her speculation: "the origin of thought and consciousness is cellular, owing its beginnings to the first courtship between unlikely bacterial bedfellows who became ancestors to our mind-brains" (Margulis, 1998, 118) invites my own; is spirochetal DNA at the root of something that we have heard of, that is called a soul? Plato believed the soul was outside the body while Aristotle thought the soul is produced by or emanates from the body. Spirochetal DNA is, arguably both.

Some years ago, the public radio featured an interview with Sam Parnia, a doctor of resuscitation medicine who brings patients in cardiac arrest back from death. Some recalled their deaths and reported seeing their lives pass before them, an omniscient awareness of their surroundings, and described entering into a brilliant white light or encountering a luminous being. Parnia describes brain death as a slow process during which cells that suffer from lack of oxygen stop communicating. I imagine that the semi-permeable membrane must start to collapse. Margulis herself died in 2011 before she could prove her theory of spirochetal fragments within brain cells, but I speculate about her fantastic hint that each one holds a spark of awareness. I imagine fragments of DNA no longer trapped within the cell membranes; the symbiotic arrangement has disintegrated. But they are thin and hardy, and in the instant when the cell membrane collapses, their pulsive firings are freed. They coincide in an orgasm of connectivity, as the environment containing them collapses.

WORKS CITED

Agamben, Giorgio. 2004, *The Open, Man and Animal,* trans. by Kevin Attell. Stanford: Stanford University Press.

Aranda and Kirksey. 2020. "Toward a Glossary of the Oceanic Undead." *E-flux Journal.* Issue 12, October. https://www.e-flux.com/journal/112/354965/toward -a-glossary-of-the-oceanic-undead-a-mphibious-through-f-utures/. Accessed October 1, 2021.

Bateson, Gregory. 1972. *Steps to an Ecology of the Mind.* New York: Random House.

Butler, Octavia. 2005 *Bloodchild and Other Stories* [1995]. New York: Seven Stories Press.

Brorson, Øystein et al. 2009. "Destruction of spirochete Borrelia burgdorferi round-body propagules (RBs) by the antibiotic tigecycline." *Proceedings of the National Academy of Sciences of the United States of America* vol. 106, 44, 18656–18661. doi:10.1073/pnas.0908236106

Cummings, Jack. 2015. "Thousands of insects are secretly living in your eyebrows," *The Tab.* https://thetab.com/2015/08/03/thousands-of-bugs-are-secretly-living-in -your-eyebrows-47759. Accessed October 1, 2021.

Dauphinais, Jennifer. 2019. *The Precariousness of the Non-Human Other: Situating Lyme Disease Within a Multispecies Framework.* Unpublished Thesis. Waterloo, Ontario Canada. https://uwspace.uwaterloo.ca/bitstream/handle/10012/14882/ Dauphinais_Jennifer.pdf?sequence=3&isAllowed=y. Accessed October 1, 2021.

Elhacham, E., Ben-Uri, L., Grozovski, J. et al. 2020. "Global human-made mass exceeds all living biomass." *Nature* 588, 442–444. https://doi.org/10.1038/s41586 -020-3010-5

Caccone, Adalgisa. 2017. "Ancient History of Lyme Disease in North America Revealed." Yale School of Medicine. August 28. https://medicine.yale.edu/news -article/15651/. Accessed 1 October 2021.

Fresh Air. 2013. "'Erasing Death' Explores The Science Of Resuscitation." *NPR.* 20 February. http://www.npr.org/2013/02/21/172495667/resuscitation-experiences -and-erasing-death. Accessed October 1, 2021.

Gannon, Megan. 2014. "Ancient Lyme Disease Bacteria Found in 15-million-Year-Old Tick Fossils." *Live Science*, 30 May. https://www.livescience.com/46007 -lyme-disease-ancient-amber-tick.html. Accessed October 1, 2021.

Gilbert, Sapp, and Tauber. 2012. "A Symbiotic View of Life: We Have Never Been Individuals." *The Quarterly Review of Biology* Vol. 87, No. 4 (December), 325–341.

Hill, Stephanie K. and C. Roxanne Connelly. 2008. "Human Bot Fly." *Featured Creatures: Entomology and Nematology.* July. http://entnemdept.ufl.edu/creatures /misc/flies/human_bot_fly.htm. Accessed October 1, 2021.

Kilpatrick AM et al. 2017. "Lyme Disease Ecology in a Changing World: Consensus, Uncertainty and Critical Gaps for Improving Control." *Philosophical Transactions of the Royal Society B.* 24 April. 20160117. http://dx.doi.org/10.1098/rstb.2016 .0117.

McMenamin, Mark. 2012. "Lynn Margulis. (1938–2011) Pioneering American Biologist and Geoscientist." *21st Century Science and Technology.*24 (4), 26.

Margulis, Lynn. 2004. "On Syphilis and the Nature of Nietzsche's Madness." *Daedalus.* Fall. https://www.amacad.org/publication/syphilis-nature-nietzsches -madness. Accessed October 1, 2021.

Margulis, Lynn and Dorion Sagan. 1997. *Slanted Truths. Essays on Gaia, Symbiosis and Evolution.* New York: Sprinter-Verlag.

Margulis, Lynn and Dorion Sagan. 2000. *What is Life.* Berkeley. University of California Press.

Margulis, Lynn. 1998. *Symbiotic Planet. A New Look at Evolution.* Amherst: Sciencewriters. Basic Books.

Morton, Timothy. 2010. *The Ecological Thought.* Cambridge: Harvard University Press.

Pearce, Fred. 2015. *The New Wild: Why Invasive Species will be Nature's Salvation.* Boston: Beacon Press.

Quammen, David. 2012. *Spillover: Animal Infections and the Next Human Pandemic.* New York: WW Norton and Company.

Stern, Lesley. 2020. *Diary of a Detour.* Durham: Duke University Press.

Tsing, Anna Lowenhaupt. 2014. "Strathern Beyond the Human: Testimony of a Spore." *Theory, Culture and Society* 31, no. 2–3 (March), 221–241. https://doi.org /10.1177/0263276413509114.

Uexkull, Jakob von. 2010. *A Foray into the World of Animals and Humans with a Theory of Meaning,* trans. By Joseph D. O'Neill. Minneapolis: University of Minnesota Press.

Walter, Katherine. 2017. "What We Get Wrong About Lyme Disease." *Nautilus.* Monsters. Issue 53. 5 October. https://nautil.us/issue/53/monsters/what-we-get -wrong-about-lyme-disease. Accessed 1 October 2021.

Yinon M. Bar-On, Rob Phillips and Ron Milo. 2018. "The Biomass Distribution on Earth." *Proceedings of the National Academy of Sciences.* June, 115 (25), 6506–6511; DOI: 10.1073/pnas.1711842115. https://www.pnas.org/content/115 /25/6506.

Chapter 12

Back from the Dead

Tailings Ponds in the Albertan Oil Sands Mining Operations

Aaron Bradshaw

Unfolding deep in the Albertan boreal forests is one of earth's most destructive industrial projects: just below the surface topsoil of these pristine and densely biodiverse ecosystems lies the largest proven reserve of oil in the world. For the oil companies, however, there is an important catch: this oil is mixed with coarse sand, fine clay and silt, and small amounts of water, forming what are commonly termed as "tar sands" or "oil sands." These tar sands are referred to as "unconventional" oil deposits, meaning they cannot be tapped by ordinary means, such as drilling, but must instead be stripped from the earth's surface in huge mining operations. The process of separating bitumen from the sandy deposits poses its own set of technical problems, resulting in the generation of billions of liters of toxic water that is then stored in tailings ponds that, quite frankly, no one knows what to do with (McIntosh & Bruser 2018). This chapter is about the tar sands mining operations, their associated tailings ponds filled with toxic byproducts, and the biogeological unfolding of these ponds over the vastly incongruous temporalities of the human and the geological. I focus on the evolution of microbiological processes within the tailings ponds, as well as ongoing attempts to "restore" these sites to previous ecological conditions, suggesting that both can be read as features of a kind of "undead" landscape that is intimately connected with some of the central issues of the Anthropocene.

Mining of the tar sands began in 1967, although reports of natural bitumen deposits in the area go back to the 1700s when the area was first being explored by settlers (Chastko 2004, 2). The commercial viability of the tar sands has been in flux since their inception, and profitability has been intimately tied to ongoing technological development and geopolitical turmoil, such as the Iraq war, which produce fluctuations in the global price of oil. Despite this volatility, the tar sands mining operation has grown massively over the past half-century and is now visible from space, forming what appears to be a blemish on the surface of the earth and resonating strongly with our conception of the Anthropocene as an era in which the agency of humanity is registered in the very makeup of the earth itself.

The oil component of the tar sands is primarily bituminous - composed, that is, of the organic material left over after millions of years of microbial degradation of dead plants and animals (Head et al. 2003; Aitken et al. 2004). As these compounds are liberated by machine-driven mining operations and set into motion through pipelines, they begin to propel yet other machines and assemblages, moving people and objects within and between places. As it enters into the life cycles of globalized production and distribution, dead matter becomes the very stuff which sustains the life of petrocapital society.[1] The mobilization of oil within society, and the mobilization of that society by oil, then, points to our contemporary era of the Anthropocene itself, at least inasmuch as it is dependent upon fossil fuels for its being and becoming as, in a certain sense, undead (Trevatt n.d.).

Rather than the downstream transformations and mobilizations of their components within globalized circuits of production and exchange, and their relationship with undeadness, however, my focus here is localized to biogeo-logical effects of the tar sands mining operations themselves and how they evoke a "life" after "death" that is intimately tied to the disruptive activities of the Anthropocene. This undead-ness is linked to the material processes by which the oil sands are mined, the corresponding production and distribu-tion of toxic waste products, and the presence of lifeforms within this waste. What follows, however, is not just about the emergence of life forms within a geological background that serves as a "stage" for such organisms, but how these organisms compose and recompose this very stage through their metabolic activities. But before we get there, we need to look at the process of bitumen extraction from oil sands, and the makeup and storage of its waste products.

As indicated by their name, oil sand deposits are composed of bitumen/ oil (up to 14%), the "desirable" component, which forms a film over coarse sand grains (50–60%), that is mixed with fine clay, silts, and a small amount of water to form a viscous semi-solid substance. The nonbituminous compo-nents represent the "undesirable" fraction of the tar sands and are separated from the bitumen in a process called "upgrading" after these deposits have been stripped from the earth. Extraction of oil from the sand is an energy-intensive process that produces an inordinate volume of toxic byproducts that are difficult to deal with and notoriously persistent in environmental, ecologi-cal, and biological systems.

This process of separation essentially consists in pumping very large volumes of heated water—taken from the Athabasca River—into these deposits to produce a slurry. The components of this slurry are then separated out from one another by gravity flotation: as the slurry is passed through a large, inverted cone-shaped tank, bitumen floats to the top while clay, silt, and sand settle to the bottom. These leftover components—water, sand, clay, as well as residual bitumen and other hydrocarbons—are referred to as "tailings" and are shuttled out from the bottom of these cone-shaped tanks and collected into huge open ponds. These storage sites are referred to as "tailings ponds"—although they are more like huge lakes than ponds—that are now estimated to contain, in total, roughly one trillion liters of toxic water. The ponds themselves are the sites of exhausted mines—areas that have been stripped of their vegetation, topsoil, and subsurface oil sand deposits and which now serve as sites for the storage of the very matter from which they were once composed (minus the bitumen, of course).

Drawing from Giles Deleuze and Felix Gautarri, Nigel Clark and Myra Hird (2013) characterize the Anthropocene era as one of accelerated stratifications and destratifications of the earth's successive layers or strata. The movement of large masses of material between the layers of the earth and the accompanying creation of new routes through which novel mixtures may flow, percolate, and concentrate characterizes the Anthropocene across the geological, biological and social registers. Extraction of oil sand deposits, for instance, is a process of destratifying, over just a couple of centuries (at most), an organic layer that developed in the earth's crust over millions of years. Importantly, Clark and Hird also highlight the opposite movement—the anthropogenically catalyzed reinterment of materials, and their transformed byproducts and waste, from the upper layers to the lower layers of the Earth. They point to underground landfilling—the process of burying waste underground—as a key example of this "haphazard restratification" (2013, 49). The tar sands operations also emphatically follow this dynamic of destratification followed by "haphazard restratification[s]," in which deposits stripped from the earth are, following processes of physical separation and chemical refinement, returned back to the earth in the form of tailings ponds.

For my purposes here, the operations in the Albertan tar sands serve as a microcosm of human transformations of the earth system in general, and of their ongoing consequences across the social, biological, ecosystemic, and environmental registers. This hugely disruptive project, I suggest, represents a well-defined empirical site from which to express a notion of the Anthropocene and to begin thinking about the makeup of a post-Anthropocene future.[2] The reality of the tar sands allows us to think about the extent of human disruption of the earth, without becoming overwhelmed by the sheer globality of that disruption.

In what follows I discuss the biogeological makeup of oil sands tailings ponds and suggest that they are "undead" on two accounts. The first concerns the ponds themselves and their present ecological functioning: while generally considered to be "dead" and completely inhospitable, tailings ponds actually provide a plethora of ecological niches for certain forms of bacterial and microbial life that thrive through metabolizing the concoction of organic molecules present there. These newly identified forms of microbes are evolving to digest the abundance of matter-energy released during the mining operations and are proliferating in unexpected ways. The second account focuses on the proposed longer-term plans and goals for these tailings ponds: the aim of the oil sands industry, responding to pressure from governmental and other stakeholders, is to "return" these tailings ponds to their "original" ecological condition, essentially by reversing the processes of water-storage, surface mining, topsoil clearance, and vegetation removal. I argue that, in attempting to recover these ponds, actors in the tar sands are subscribing to a linear and reversible view of ecological time, and suggest that although these lands are indeed likely to "thrive" again, it is unlikely that this thriving will be in the image of a plan imposed upon them. It is in this speculative and unexpected vitality, I suggest, that these landscapes typify a post-Anthropocene undead-ness.

TAILINGS PONDS: DEAD OR ALIVE?

Oil sands tailings ponds are an almost clichéd apocalyptic scene; vast expanses of oily water are set amongst pollution-billowing refineries and barren mines. What's more, the landscapes these scenes have replaced are densely biodiverse, lush green boreal forests that are home to lifeforms from the microorganism to the charismatic megafauna. The ponds themselves, however, are not just sheets of homogenous wastewater but, like the forests that preceded them, form an internally differentiated system with a specific structure. Add to this a burgeoning ecosystem. This structure is produced through geophysical and microbiological processes that give the oil sands tailings ponds, like freshwater ecosystems, the ocean, and earth systems in general, a stratified makeup.

These processes are the interlinked unfolding of sedimentation and microbial metabolism as they come into contact and reconfigure the structure of the oil sands extraction fallout: The "tailings" coming from the process of bitumen extraction contain not only water, but also the sands and clays that were also present in the reserves. As such, the ponds which now house these leftover components are stratified into horizontal layers of increasing density: as the oil sands process affected water is pumped into the ponds, residual sand settles out relatively quickly, forming a sediment on the bottom of the pond. The fine clay and silt, however, settles out much more slowly, remaining suspended and forming a colloid-like mixture with the water. This colloid acts like a gel; it does not flow and yet does not have any kind of shear strength. Surface charges on the clay molecules cause them to repel one another, preventing them from sticking together and keeping them suspended in the water. It is estimated to take upwards of a century for the solids in these colloidal strata to settle enough to form what is termed a "trafficable" surface—one that can support vegetation and organisms without them sinking. Above this colloid is the water layer: oil sands process affected water, containing low amounts of solid particles, but relatively high amounts of hydrocarbon chemical contaminants coming from the separation process.

This top layer, generally termed "oil sands process affected water" (OSPW), and its contaminants are linked to acute and chronic toxicity in aquatic organisms. The water is rich in compounds that interfere with numerous biochemical pathways to produce unexpected biological outcomes. A lot of the evidence for the toxicity of OSPW has come from highly controlled lab experiments that expose specific organisms to selected doses of water containing well-defined constituents. In the "real world" of the tailings ponds themselves, and the hydrological connections they inevitably make with surrounding rivers and wetlands, however, the biological effects are all but unpredictable as these compounds begin to make new mixtures, concentrate in food webs, and intersect with the life cycles of various organisms. Reports from those who sustain themselves off the nearby land, including First Nations peoples of Canada, report witnessing deformities in fish, fewer fish in general, and express a generalized and growing mistrust of the health of the land in connection with the mining operations. The tailings ponds and the industries (mis)use of water have been at the center of these concerns.

Bolstered by aerial images of the tar sands mining operations and continuing reports about the unsustainability of the operation, the toxic nature of these ponds has also been clearly established in the public imaginary.[3] A widely publicized event, and a major hit to the oil sands public relations image, occurred in 2006 when a flock of ducks, diverted from their usual migratory pattern by a storm, were forced to make a stopover on tailings ponds owned by Suncor and Syncrude. Unable to escape from the oily, bituminous water, a large number of these birds died (over 1500). Syncrude were held to account for this widely acclaimed "tragic" event, but when it was repeated again in 2008, no companies were held liable after an independent report indicated the "unpredictable nature of the causative factors (again, a storm)". The longer-term effects of coming into contact with the OSPW for those birds that survived is not known—one could say "unpredictable"—but clearly demonstrates routes by which some of the toxic contaminants there may be trafficked around the globe.

The above considerations—the toxicity of OSPW and the death of wildlife at the hands of this toxicity, coupled with the absolute absence of fish and vegetation in the ponds themselves, have, quite rightly, securely established the image of these ponds as dead and toxic within scientific, environmental, and, increasingly, public discourse. It is not my aim to argue against the clear violence these operations and the tailings ponds are inflicting on wildlife, as well as indigenous cultures, but rather to highlight an alternative discourse that has been gaining momentum in public and scientific circles, and to put this discourse in a critical perspective. In what follows I focus on the microbiological vitality of the tailings ponds and attempt to offer a critical perspective on what this vitality may indicate for a post-Anthropocene future as it intersects with anthropocentric imaginaries about "regeneration" and "reclamation."

MICROBIOLOGICAL VITALITY IN
THE TAILINGS PONDS

Bitumen, the primary "product" of the oil sands is, at base, the fallout of microbial metabolism—the long chain viscous hydrocarbons that are resistant to bacterial hydrolysis as it catalyzes the decay of dead plant and animal matter. Just as microbes were key players in the production of the bitumen deposits in the oil sands, moreover, microbial agency is also a key component in the trajectories of the "waste" products and their biogeochemical cycling after the bitumen has been extracted. Indeed, microbial life has emerged as a vital force with an ability to not only survive, reproduce and proliferate in the tailings ponds, but also to metabolize some of the most toxic compounds found in them; microbial communities are thriving in these regions, and they exist in complex, interconnected and symbiotic networks and webs. It is this latter property of microbial life—its ability to degrade compounds toxic for other forms of life, and thereby produces the conditions for life to flourish—that complicates any interpretation of their presence in the tailings ponds.

What this suggests then, is that in addition to the apparently "dead" landscapes of the tailings ponds being filled with life, they are filled with a form of life we cannot appreciate, let alone understand—a form of life on which all other life depends both ontogenetically and phylogenetically. Microbes literally transform the matter energy of the sun—and its storage in the earth—into forms that are usable by other organisms. Moreover, they are, evolutionarily speaking, the metabolic base upon which all other life on earth is based. As these microbes engage with the matter-energy of the oil sands tailings ponds then, they are performing a function that is at once inconceivably ancient and unfathomably novel: they are in the process of creating new environments and ecologies of which we cannot predict the trajectory and content, but within which we have always been held and enmeshed. In a very fundamental sense, the recent "emergence" of these microbes is nothing surprising—it is precisely what bacteria have been doing for the past 4.3 billion years.

In addition to their adaptation to and thriving in the toxic spaces and externalities of petro-capitalism, microbial life also actively composes and recomposes these spaces. The geophysical capacities of microbes are not to be underestimated, and microbes residing in the colloidal strata of the tailings ponds accelerate the process of particle sedimentation, producing solid ground where there was once a viscous gel (Siddique et al. 2014). Microbes literally make the earth upon which other organisms may root, walk, forage, hunt and many others. Ultimately, these miniscule agents are key components of the earth system,[4] spanning the boundary between life and non-life, existing at the interface of the geological and the biological and regulating the transit between these strata.

It is these properties of microbial life, their "world building" capacity, that has made them central stars in ongoing discourse about "bioremediation"[5] in the oil sands. The oil sands industry is facing increasing pressure on all sides to clean up its tailings ponds, which are widely viewed as one of the most destructive aspects of its operation. There are two key accounts on which reclamation of the ponds represents a huge technical problem: one is the toxicity of the OSPW top layer, and the second is the painfully slow sedimentation of the colloidal strata, which inhibits "reclaiming" the wet land as a dry, "trafficable" surface. Through their ability to both detoxify the OSPW and catalyze the sedimentation of suspended clay particles, bacterial life may appear as a perfect "remedy" to this spiraling problem. Indeed, these biogeochemical processes have been configured—by the oil sands industry, academic collaborators, and public engagement—as a "natural" solution to the growing problem of tailings ponds. In this context, ongoing research into the metabolic potential of microbial life indigenous to the oil sands tailings ponds serves as a promise and a hope for the "regeneration" of these lands.

There exists a deep tension, however, between these discourses of promissory bioremediation and the actual ontology and biological trajectory of microbial life. In *Life as Surplus*, Melinda Cooper (2008, 15–30) characterizes the biotechnological boom—of which bioremediation is a key component—as one fueled almost entirely by venture capital and underwritten by promises of future technologies and applications, not by their actual functioning in the present. In her theoretical analysis of the intersection between biotechnology and capitalism, the ability of microbes to detoxify the fallout of petro-capitalist expansion—such as tailings ponds—is proffered, by the prophets of "green capitalism," as a means by which the limits to (capital-ist) growth can be overcome. What Cooper's account makes clear is the disjunction, in the biotechnological imaginary, between the way biological things "are" and the way they are represented for their recuperation into the networks and flows of capital (i.e., invariably under the "control" and "direc-tion" of human agency). Something peculiar is at play though—although the generative potential of microbes upon which such promises are based *is* in fact representative of their nature, it is this same generativity that ensures the fulfillment of such promises are frustrated and evaded. Because there is no sense in which microbial activity is "for us," any "promises" that their properties may engender for our survival and growth are merely that—human derived projections onto an indifferent and (grotesquely) productive "nature."

RECLAMATION IN THE OIL SANDS TAILINGS PONDS

How do the small worlds and lives of microbes fit into the larger picture of what has been termed "reclamation" and "restoration" of the tailings ponds? The official discourse of tailings ponds reclamation is one in which, suc-cessively, the stages of deforestation, topsoil removal, mining, and tailings storage is reversed. The logic is simple: firstly, detoxify the top-layer OSPW of its deadly toxic naphthenic acids and return this water to the natural water-sheds of the region. Next, either pump out the viscous colloidal clay layer (to another pond . . .) or accelerate its sedimentation to the base of the pond. Next, refill the now empty pond with the sand and topsoil that were removed from it originally, plant indigenous shrubs and trees, and let "nature take its course." The stated goal of reclamation is to restore the tailings ponds to eco-systems with the same levels of "productivity" as that which they replaced. Videos produced by oil companies thematize and visualize this process, with "simulations" projecting that by the year 2025, the previous sites of certain tailings ponds will be visually indistinguishable from the surrounding vegeta-tion (zoom out one more level and the scar of the oil sands industry is clearly visible on the earth). Interviews with oil-site workers in these videos are cut with frequent close-ups of deer roaming between trees in the areas surround-ing the tailings ponds, exemplifying the flourishing of large fauna and coding this as the endpoint of the reclamation project.[6]

Technical difficulties abound, however, in such reclamation efforts. The rate-limiting factor for the majority of efforts is returning the ground to a "trafficable" surface—that is one which will support the weight of plants and animals rooting and roaming on top of it; the ground where the tailings have sat tend to be squidgy because of the slowly settling colloidal clay and silts, as noted above it takes centuries for these particles to settle naturally.

Some companies opt to simply squeeze this out of the ponds and into new ones. Beyond these relatively technical issues, researchers have pointed to some deeper geological and ecological[7] factors limiting the "restoration" of these ponds to lands of "previous productivity." For instance, amongst the landscapes lost to mining and tailings ponds are peatlands which pose their own specific set of problems for regeneration, as explained by ecologist Lee Foote (2012):

> Peat accumulation is a complex nonlinear process . . . dependent on simultaneous accumulation and decomposition with a positive balance [and] requires stable and calcium-rich groundwater of low salinity flowing into low gradient areas with a fairly stable climate and low fire frequency. Even with these exacting conditions, at 1 to 3 mm of peat accumulation per year, approximately one to three centuries would be needed to generate the 30 cm minimum of accumulated peat to technically qualify as a peatland.

The accumulation of peat is, by definition, a slow process occurring over an extended period of time, suggesting an inherent limitation to what can be reclaimed and "restored." Indeed, it is this geo-biological limitation that takes us back to an appreciation of microbes and their complex socio-cultural mediations in terms of the tailings ponds reclamation: Yes, bacteria produce solid ground from colloidal strata. Yes, bacteria "detoxify" chemicals. Yes, bacteria provide the conditions for other life to flourish. But bacteria express such capacities on their own terms. The difference between the immanent properties of bacteria and how these properties are represented in the discourses of bioremediation and biotechnology is that the latter appellate bacteria not as agents doing what they have been doing for billions of years, but as doing so "for us" and on "our terms"—to degrade toxins more rapidly and with greater "efficiency" and so on. It is in this sense that reclamation efforts are grounded in views of a linear and reversible temporality, as well as one that somehow places the human as "outside" of the flow of time. "We" can push out the wildlife, uproot the trees and remove the topsoil, but we can also perform the reverse functions, somehow erasing the time between these two events.

In this sense, reclamation as proffered by the oil sands industry embodies a paradoxical temporality: while it looks *forwards* to an improved state of a particular ecosystem, it finds the model for this improvement by looking *backwards* to a past state of that system. Where anthropogenic effects are implicated in the destruction of the original ecosystem (as they invariably are in the tailings ponds), the paradox runs deeper: what is hailed as an improved state of a particular ecosystem is one which removes human influence from its trajectory through time, while simultaneously relying on such influence to produce the conditions for the new one. In addition to this, reclamation in the tailings ponds implicitly and explicitly calls upon the function of organisms, as well as geological processes to "hurry up" signaling a lack of respect and knowledge for the very lands they are attempting to "restore."

POST-ANTHROPOCENE?

Within the discipline of geology, the Anthropocene has been conceptualized as a precisely dateable era, the inception of which may be inferred from stratigraphic marks in the Earth's crust. The onset of the Anthropocene is indicated by the presence, in the layers of the earth surface, of material deposits that have human activity as their source. This layer is composed of plastics, heavy metals, radionuclides, and other such "fossils" of industrial society, as well as changes in its chemical and biological (in terms of fossils) makeup. From this viewpoint of stratification and sedimentation, does a post-Anthropocene indicate a new geological era in which the layers of anthropogenic input are covered over by a new pattern of sedimentation? And would this newer layer be one that does *not* implicate human activity? By extension, would the interpretation of this new layer, as seen from the vantage point of a subject existing eons in the future, draw a necessary link between its deposition and that which preceded it? Or, in other words, does a post-Anthropocene necessarily indicate the absence of humanity *per se,* or the absence of humanity only as we know it? Could a future society, (whatever that may look like), through the analyses of bacterial genetic and epigenetic marks, reconstruct the global patterns and networks of fossil fuel extraction and distribution that animate our own era? Will traces of human activity reside in the topographic patterns of clay and silt as they pack together to form the ground of novel ecosystems?

The aim of reclamation and regeneration in the oil sands is to bring ecosystems "back from the dead." As noted above, however, these tailings ponds never really "died"—they are teeming with a microbiological vitality that cannot be contained. The model of reclamation of the tailings ponds given above, I suggest, relies on a static and essentialist view of ecosystems that is atemporal at base, an attempt to *undo* the Anthropocene through erasing its effects. In keeping with the conceptualization of the Anthropocene through the geological processes of sedimentation, stratification, and destratification, however, the bio-geological makeup of the oil sands has been irreversibly altered by the processes of mining and bitumen extraction. Leaving its residue in the local geological, environmental and biological registers through the liberation of persistent hydrocarbons, the alteration of hydrology and habitats, and the forging of epigenetic marks in organisms. In other words, the tar sands operations will "live on" in these registers long after they have ceased mining. More precisely, these registers bring into question in what ways it is even possible for these operations to cease, to leave, and to move on. One thing, however, is for sure: Microorganisms have lived through countless planetary upheavals—sometimes producing those upheavals—and the relatively minor convulsions of the Anthropocene are business as usual for them. The question, then, is not whether they will come out the other end—it will be the other end that comes out of them—but whether, and in what form, we will come out with them. Microbiological vitality is not only *undead*, in the sense of its incessant return within desolate and inhospitable environs, but is *undying* in that its extension into the future, albeit in radically unimaginable forms, is all but assured.

NOTES

1. For all heterotrophic organisms life is always sustained by dead matter. The distinguishing mark of petro-centric society, however, is the accelerated consumption of dead matter, and, critically, its consumption at a rate greater than its deposition.

2. By "makeup" I am referring, primarily, to a biological/ecosystemic makeup that has its origins in these operations. The Anthropocene is not "one," and different people have lived through and are living through different Anthropocenes. I use the term here in its geological and biological senses, parenthesizing these important social components.

3. See, for instance, https://www.theguardian.com/environment/gallery/2015/aug/03/canadas-tar-sands-landscape-from-the-air-in-pictures

4. Or, in Isabelle Stengers terms "Gaia's co-authors."

5. "Bioremediation" refers to the harnessing of those biological processes that catalyze the metabolism of toxic and waste chemicals in a given environment. Bioremediation can involve the stimulation, by certain nutrients, of microorganisms already present in a certain site, the addition of microorganisms to a site, or the bio-technical engineering of a specific metabolic pathway into a bacterial strain that is then introduced to a native site. In the context of the tailings ponds and the OSPW their key goal is to detoxify the naphthenic acids present in the water, as this is the most toxic contaminant that is known about. In the tar sands tailings ponds the idea is that the OSPW can be decontaminated and then returned to either the Athabasca River or for reuse in bitumen extraction. The colloidal strata of the ponds are then pushed out of the pond or settling is catalyzed in one way or another. Following this, what is termed "reclamation"—reclaiming wet land as dry land—shrubs and trees are planted, and wildlife moves "back in." Remediation, followed by reclamation and restoration.

6. For instance, see *Reclamation of Tailings Pond 1—Suncor Energy.* available at https://www.youtube.com/watch?v=PbmIFiM9lCY&ab_channel=SuncorEnergy [accessed January 4, 2021.]

7. As well as other "thresholds" across the social and economic registers.

WORKS CITED

Aitken, Carolyn M., Martin Jones, and Steve R. Larter. 2004. "Anaerobic hydrocarbon biodegradation in deep subsurface oil reservoirs." *Nature* 431, 291–294.

Chastko, Paul. A. 2004. *Developing Alberta's Oil Sands: From Karl Clark to Kyoto.* Calgary: University of Calgary Press.

Clark, Nigel and Myra J. Hird. 2013. "Deep Shit." *O-Zone: A Journal of Object-Oriented Studies* 1: 44–52.

Cooper, Melinda. 2008. *Life as Surplus.* Seattle: University of Washington Press.

Foote, Lee. 2012. "Threshold Considerations and Wetland Reclamation in Alberta's Mineable Oil Sands." *Ecology and Society* 17, no.1, http://dx.doi.org/10.5751/ES-04673-170135

Head, Ian M., Martin Jones, and Steve R. Larter. 2003. "Biological activity in the deep subsurface and the origin of heavy oil." *Nature* 426, 344–353.

McIntosh, Emma and David Bruser. 2018. "Alberta officials are signalling they have no idea how to clean up toxic oilsands tailings ponds." *Canada's National Observer*, November. https://www.nationalobserver.com/2018/11/23/news/alberta-officials-are-signalling-they-have-no-idea-how-clean-toxic-oilsands-tailings. Accessed October 1, 2021.

Siddique, Tariq, Petr Kuznetsov, Alsu Kuznetsova, Carmen Li, Rozlyn Young, Joselito M. Arocena and Julia M. Foght. 2014. "Microbially-accelerated consolidation of oil sands tailings. Pathway II: Solid phase biogeochemistry." *Frontiers in Microbiology.* March. https://doi.org/10.3389/fmicb.2014.00107. Accessed October 1, 2021.

Stengers, Isabelle. 2018. *Another Science is Possible: A Manifesto for Slow Science*, trans. Stephen Muecke. Cambridge: Polity Press.

Trevatt, Tom. N.d. "The Petrozombie." *Incognitum Hactenus.* https://incognitumhactenus.wordpress.com/the-petrozombie/. Accessed October 1, 2021.

Part V

THE POST-ANTHROPOCENE, THE SYMBIOCENE, AND UNDEAD FUTURES

Chapter 13

Post-Anthropocenic Undying Futures

The Ecocritical Dystopian Posthuman in Lai's The Tiger Flu *and Bacigalupi's "The People of Sand and Slag"*

Conrad Scott

ABSTRACT

This chapter of *The Anthropocene and the Undead* focuses specifically on intersections between ecocritical dystopianism (Scott) and the posthuman in Paolo Bacigalupi's "The People of Sand and Slag" (2004) and Larissa Lai's The Tiger Flu (2018), exploring how the undead, posthuman characters in each storyworld engage with a sense of environment and place as non-human agents who either are immortal or prolong their lives beyond what a human could ever hope to achieve. Bacigalupi's "The People of Sand and Slag" characters were originally human, and therefore subject to mortality, but by ingesting biotechnology that renders them immortal and facilitating accelerated resource extraction for personal gain, these near-future posthumans participate in the irrevocable alteration of the landscapes and ecosystems we might recognize today, while all other life is driven towards extirpation—including humans. Lai's *The Tiger Flu* presents a climate-affected world set after the petrocultural age and further shaped by a zoonotic pandemic ravaging a future Cascadia bioregion populated by various social groups—one of which is a community of escaped female clones who reproduce parthenogenically and extend lifespans by regrowing communally-donated organs while attempting to live in the natural world, outside of technocratic control. Both Bacigalupi's and Lai's posthuman characters ultimately persist the challenges of changed socioenvironments while respectively working to stave off the death that all mortal humans cannot avoid, and thus call for a reconsideration of the Anthropocene term itself.

Recent speculative narratives about the future imagine both the dystopian detriments from ongoing hypercapitalistic models and the utopian possibility for more environmentally aware societies emerging. These outcomes often involve fundamental changes to a sense of place, prompting us to ask what specific real-world places will look like in the near future, and which social elements will inhabit them. Like many other contemporary sf narratives, Paolo Bacigalupi's "The People of Sand and Slag" (2004) and Larissa Lai's *The Tiger Flu* (2018) include such alterations to the world as we know it;[1] these stories extend my argument about a recent development in dystopian fiction, called "ecocritical dystopianism,"[2] which hinges on narrative employment of environmental changes to place. That is, these narratives about the future present alterations to environmental conditions, understandings of places, and social dynamics by imagining that affected landscapes will never be fully returned to what they were before: how will humanity adapt and, if it cannot, which posthuman elements will arise from these changes? Both stories indicate that, while our human legacy in what has been called the Anthropocene will linger stratigraphically for quite some time, humanity itself will fall victim to its cultures of excess. The more-than-human characters that feature in both narratives, however, who can either heal their bodies miraculously or extend their lives past that of normal human longevity, indicate that the inheritors of the earth will be nonhuman as the time of *anthropos* comes to an end through its seeming inability, on its present course, to live in an entangled manner with the nonhuman world.

THE ECOCRITICAL DYSTOPIAN POSTHUMAN

Narratives like "Sand and Slag" and *Tiger Flu* populate a spectrum from "nightmarish" (Moylan 2000, 148) futures to ones informed by hopeful dreaming, and include the generic registers of a distinct subgenre that has arisen within contemporary dystopian fiction since Tom Moylan, Ildney Cavalcanti, Raffaella Baccolini, and Lyman Tower Sargent outlined the terminological framework of the "critical dystopia" for narratives written in the 1980s and 1990s. My intervention with the term "ecocritical dystopia" demonstrates that, sometime after the first critical dystopias, sf writing has been engaging with realism in a manner that entangles social concerns with environmental crises, but also with how near-future societies—and therefore present ones—might engage with a sense of place. The way in which we understand the lands and waters with which we are familiar in the real-world changes as the near-future progresses: as we move forward further into a sense of alterity, and as we imagine a greater future sense of Suvinian "cognitive estrangement," our sense of place alters. These changes are, notably, both ecological and social, and are not merely symbolic of the current sense of society and culture, as with the "critical dystopia." With the *eco*critical dystopia, the changes are also meant to inform our sense of the present, but the relevant near-future narratives, being informed by a sense of place and environment, are tangibly extrapolated forward from a present moment in the real world. My added "eco-" prefix descends from the ancient Greek *oîkos*, denoting a "house," "dwelling," or "residence."[3] Fittingly, Oxana Timofeeva contemporizes the "eco" etymology by reminding us that both "economy and ecology are concerned with nature—either as a living world, environment . . . or as a source and resource. They are conjugate—beyond ecology there is always economy, and vice versa: this is our earthy home, here we keep slaves and exchange oil for money" (Timofeeva 2017). This is appropriate since the *oîkos*/"eco-" of modern times displays a distinctly counterproductive relationship within which environmental disruption is also a destabilization of what might be called home.

With tangible, ongoing disruptions to our home places in this time of unpredictable weather events while rampant resource extraction and fossil fuel use is ongoing, these sf narratives convincingly imagine intersections between ecocritical dystopianism and the near-future perpetuation of economies of labor, which is, respectively, upheld and juxtaposed with the emergence of posthumanism in Bacigalupi's short story and Lai's novel. In part, I am interested in how some characters in each storyworld engage with a sense of place and environment as non-human agents who prolong their lives beyond human capability. In Bacigalupi's narrative, characters who were once human, and therefore subject to the natural rule of living and then dying within the "web of life" (2010, 59) have "transcended the animal kingdom" (2010, 58) by ingesting a worm-like biotechnology called "weeviltech." The story opens within the hellscape of a robotically mined, unrecognizable post-Montana landscape and, while all other flora and fauna are driven extinct—including (most) humans—these near-future beings persist, pushing today's hyper-extraction of resources to new extremes in the name of personal, capitalistically-enabled gratification, all while reshaping and redefining the landscapes of the present day into horrific terrains. Lai's *The Tiger Flu* also presents a dystopian near-future world where vestiges of our current overconsumption linger in the form of elements like frequent "monsoon[s]" (12) and acid rain storms (25), while areas populated by different groups struggle to survive in the face of a capitalistically-driven zoonotic pandemic emanating from Saltwater City and environs—the metropolis once called Vancouver, British Columbia, from which extend "quarantine rings" representing separate worldviews. In one such grouping, more-than-human, cloned women[4] attempt to live in concert with the natural world while extending communal lives through their laborious "starfish" and "doubler" abilities. In both narratives, posthuman characters supersede the efforts of humans to survive in changed landscapes and environments, creating their own niches that respectively exploit or complement the natural world while also prioritizing the longevity of the group's lifespan—thus articulating imagined possibilities for post-Anthropocenic futures functioning in landscapes that are palimpsests of the current day.

LAI'S POSTHUMAN LABORERS

The Tiger Flu highlights Lai's critique of cyberpunk's "separation of mind and body" (Lai 2021), alongside her other distinctly *bio*punk elements, like the "seal bladder and oyster material . . . hydrogen cell" and "transport vehicle" (Lai 2018, 91) "batterkite" (90) that is later fused with the character Kora's consciousness and planted to become the "Kora Tree" and the "Starfish Orchard" (327-328).[5] The physical labor of Lai's posthumans, which involves women who are able to remove organs for donation to the community and then regrow them—hence the "starfish" moniker—and women who reproduce parthenogenically—hence "doubler"—is not the only mode of "economic" exchanges in this near-future, post-petrocultural narrative where the timeframe is, in part, gauged in units of "Time After Oil," or "TAO." There are also the economic interactions of the Saltwater Flats, like the "exchange" frequented by "N-lite junkies stoned on history" (40), who connect what are often infectious "tendril information scales" (12) with their heads. This information accessed through the tendril scales is, notably, controlled by the techno-authoritarian Saltwater City "HöST" corporation, which "has vast powers over the citizenry of Saltwater City and Saltwater Flats" (24). The Saltwater Flats also features a "wet market"[6] with "cans recovered from the time of before," "lush fruits from the [United Middle Kingdom], salvaged coffee from Seattle Before, [and] squashes and fresh rabbit from Houston North" (41). Some of these market-related elements such as the changed place names above connect with the ecocritical dystopianism of the book, like with the "sellers of salmon jerky from the Coast Salish Timeplace" (41), which, in the novel, is a sovereign area located directly "across the Stó:lō" (64-65), or colonially named Fraser River, whose terminus is currently tied to Greater Vancouver.

A further relationship of exchange found in the "wet market" involves the "elk-skin gloves and raw forget-me-do purportedly from the mythic village of Grist" (41), indicating a trade network that might extend across the four Quarantine Rings comprising this loose-knit Cascadian nation (Lai 2021), or bioregion on the North American west coast. But the Grist sisters, who at first try to subsist in what, in an interview with me in June 2021, Lai linked roughly to Beaverdell and the maybe western-Kootenays/eastern-Okanagan region, Kettle Valley area of the future, are also involved in an exchange with both the community and the land upon which they live. Problematically, the community is in danger since both "starfish" and "doublers" have become scarce. Part of the issue here is that, as Lai puts it, "Like many of us, they hold co-operation as an ideal, but they struggle to practice it. They must co-operate in order to survive, but it is hard because they have egos and desires" (Lai 2020). It is only through exchanges with others—that is, the intrepid Cordova Dancing School for Girls of Saltwater Flats, who were at the root of their original ancestral escape from the cloning company Jemini—that the Grist sisters are finally able to move beyond the range of socioeconomic and technological control of the Saltwater City and Flats society, with its continued, pandemic-spreading resurrection of the Caspian tiger and related production of "tiger-bone wine factories"(Lai 2018, 226), which is done to create "a perfect money machine" also featuring "the cure" (229). David Quammen's *Spillover* (2012) explains that most major pandemics are zoonoses, or transferred from animals to humans through contact with and disturbance of the natural world. This includes events such as the Black Plague that Mary Shelley's *The Last Man* references with the 1348 date (Shelley 2010, 169) through to Ebola and SARS in more recent times. But, in *The Tiger Flu*, a deliberate cycling of pandemic is produced in waves as a bid to control and profit from this near-future Cascadian society.

Escaping the influence of this corrupt and failing human social system, the Grist Sisters eventually inhabit a "place in the mountains" including "a well-hidden valley," where, importantly, "the Kainai [have given] permission" to "begin a new Grist Village" (109). It is here, through a productive exchange with the Kainai people—who, in the real-world of today, are the "Blood" tribe members of the Blackfoot Confederacy that have traditional territory including the borders between current-day British Columbia and Alberta—in the Gregorian year 2301 and, in what I will put forward as a *utopian* register to the ecocritical dystopian mode, that the "New Grist Village" (326) community persists parthenogenically through a Saltwater Flats' former resident, who flourishes as the Kora Tree in the Starfish Orchard "that nurtures the great Grist Garden" (328): this labor and exchange is, finally, entangled, regenerative, and communal.

BACIGALUPI'S UNDYING HYPERCAPITALISTS

The "community" we meet in Bacigalupi's "Sand and Slag" is, at first glance, regenerative in a particular way, but this is notably not entangled like the "great Grist Garden," and nor is it symbiotic in the way that trees and ecosystems function in, at the very least, a mycorrhizal manner. Rather, it is one based on *self*-regeneration and *self*-perpetuation—the mathematical equivalent being seemingly asymptotic with relation to mortality, but paradoxically also where a sense of moral limits has been erased and a line already crossed. This narrative involves posthumans who physically perform and embody resource extraction for both survival and as a continuation of individualistic capitalistic excesses. They are the titular People of Sand and Slag because what was once human has been biotechnologically altered to consume the physical stuff of the earth—or

anything else, really. Their name is a link to the *process* of resource extraction
seen through our societal dependence on what is extracted. What should be poisonous, in Bacigalupi's vision, is now nutritious. As the character Lisa ingests
"a spoonful of tailings" (2004, 55), she explains to the narrator Chen why they
can now consume anything but cannot themselves be consumed: after having
swallowed weeviltech, something like "mercury and lead running through [the]
blood" (55) is of no concern. Notably, economic profit is so highly valued that
the trio of main characters in this story work as, ostensibly, destructible-but-
regenerative security guards protecting the value of materials and land they
have no direct personal stake in. They are comfortable with "slamm[ing] into
the ground at hundreds of kilometers per hour" (50) to have a broken "femur
[ram] through [the] thigh like a bright white exclamation mark" (51)—all in the
name of corporate profits and personal bonuses.

The mortal fragility of what it means to be human has been removed in the
name of ongoing resource demand. As Chen explains early on, "[they] ate sand
for dinner. Outside the security bunker, the mining robots rumbled back and
forth, ripping deeper into the earth, turning it into a mush of tailings and rock
acid that they left in exposed ponds when they hit the water table, or piled onto
thousand-foot mountainscapes of waste soil. It was comforting to hear those
machines cruising back and forth all day. Just you and the bots and the profits"
(53–54). Such a lack of connection to environment, ecosystem, and sense of place
is featured in several ways throughout the story—including when the trio of Lisa,
Jaak, and Chen finally end up eating the one living thing they encounter, a miraculously survived dog they had saved to take in as a pet—but also through their
disengagement from environments we might normally value today. This includes
the horrific Hawaiian beach vacation the trio takes, where they frolic in oil-filled
waters and copulate on the rubble and barbed wire littered beach as waves they
lit on fire crash nearby, before they also betray what should be an entangled
relationship with the natural world and consume "man's best friend." The story
does not specify a Hawaiian island, so the suggestion is that the entire area, and
perhaps beyond, has been affected by near-future processes extrapolated from
today, and especially a disregard for the environmental impacts of rampant fossil
fuel resource extraction and general pollution. Bacigalupi's sense of disconnec-
tion for these future beings surely also juxtaposes with our sense of connection to
the landscapes and lost social values these posthumans barely mourn.

If the threat of mortality is gone, if one can have all their limbs cut off but regrow them by the next day, then no environmental conditions are detrimental.
These characters are always, however, caught in a state of horrible fascination
with mutilating the self, with continually ruining a body that will never stay
ruined: in this, Bacigalupi juxtaposes the forever-ruined earthly orb with our
corporeal selves. After we have transitioned into a society where the job of a
biologist is "a dead-end job" (56) because the majority of other living things

are extinct, we might as well be living on the moon for all that a living ecosystem will matter to us. But in this future where we, the people "from the past," might call our descendants "gods" (66), time will trickle by just as slowly as for Tithonus of Greek mythology. As Bacigalupi's "'last mortal poet'" (63) of the future, aptly named Yearly, elaborates in his poem, "Dead Man,"

> Cut me I won't bleed. Gas me I won't breathe.
> Stab me, shoot me, slash me, smash me
> I have swallowed science
> I am God.
> Alone. (62)

Imagine if we, like Bacigalupi's posthumans, had, through an inability to die, lost our "compassion for all things on Earth" (58). We would merely become cruel and uncaring through our lack of fragility, and would spend our days immersed in violence and destruction without end, alone. Though the narrator admits at the end of "Sand and Slag" to missing "when the dog licked [their] face" and crawled onto their[7] bed (67), Lisa, Jaak, and Chen "[roast] the dog on a spit" (67) and consume it instead of healing its wounds (66), even though it trusts them (67). Bacigalupi's future, undying nonhuman is a figure for which no surroundings or other lives matter, and for which there never is an end to either existence or consumption. It is a creature within whose conception the death of humankind is ensured, even as it secretly longs for the uncertainty and thrill of a brief human existence.

TOWARD? A POST-ANTHROPOCENIC GEOLOGIC EPOCH

Both Bacigalupi's and Lai's narratives are ecocritically dystopian in their engagement with understandings of changed places, environments, and societies. Bacigalupi's work does this quite literally and has done so through his several publications, including *Ship Breaker* (2010a) with New Orleans and the Gulf Coast, *The Drowned Cities* (2012) with Washington and its neighboring East Coast cities, and *The Water Knife* (2015) with Phoenix and other locations in the American Southwest. *The Water Knife* imagines the future of the current megadrought (Meyer 2016) and both *Ship Breaker* and *The Drowned Cities* posit the effects of sea-level rise. Notably, both *Ship Breaker* and *The Drowned Cities*, as well as their sequel *Tool of War* (2017), involve the addition of posthumans, but unlike those in "Sand and Slag," these are mortal. In comparison, Lai preceded *The Tiger Flu* with *Salt Fish Girl* (2002), a novel set in the 2040s that also involves clones, disease, and changes to society in a distinctively near-future Pacific Northwest setting. *Salt Fish Girl* is, in part, ecocritically dystopian because of "the Painted Horse Democratic Urban Village located off Highway 10 in the former municipality of Greenwood, British Columbia" (71); other oblique place-based references like those to national currencies (81); indications of socioenvironmental effects like "the Contagion" (76); and the inclusion of "local ferns" (84), which suggests a lower-mainland region for the city of Serenity, and pairs with a mention of "the Fraser Valley" (163), "Langara" College (165), and the use of "an old hotel in what was once downtown Vancouver, the first part to be abandoned after the earthquake of 2017 submerged several metres of the original waterfront of the city, including the Pan Pacific Hotel" (111). Lai again comes at the problems of utopia and dystopia in a very ecocritical dystopian manner in *Tiger Flu* by intersecting the fictional and real worlds: as she explains, "[t]hrough the concept of insurgent utopias I suggest placing worlds in interaction with one another to seek eruptions of the unexpected. For me this is where both hope and danger lie. Something of our present world is also reflected in this thinking" (Lai 2020a).

Fittingly, after my interview with Lai in June for Cappadocia University, my colleague Emrah Atasoy astutely asked about the fixity of utopian and dystopian nomenclatures—and my response in addition to Lai's is that there is, at the very least, a spectrum involved in most recent works. *The Tiger Flu*, as well as Lai's own theorizations, recognizes the necessity for this spectrum and for complicating it, though Bacigalupi seems to take a more straightforward approach, in general. As an author with several dystopias, he commented on social media at the end of January 2017 that he realized he "was overly optimistic" (Bacigalupi 2017a).[8] He had "tried to see the important trends . . . and tried to guess where those trends are leading us"—trends that might "lead us to disaster in fifty years, or a hundred years—sometime further away than right now, at least. Sometime safely comfortably far away" (Bacigalupi 2017a). While he said toward the end of January that he was "having a hard time imagining the future turning out well for us" (Bacigalupi 2017b), he also added at the end of the month that he "didn't understand that those trends were right upon us" (Bacigalupi 2017a). This produces both positive and negative action. Perhaps it is also, as Lai suggested in our interview chat, that we humans are still subject to being "monkeys" with our actions, and that some of the discordance is with our "human" nature.

While Claire L. Evans argues that "[w]e need . . . a form of science fiction that tackles the radical changes of our pressing and strange reality," and specifically that "[w]e need an Anthropocene fiction" (2015), both Lai and Bacigalupi extrapolate their narratives to a point beyond the scope of human concerns. That said, these "fictions" still resonate with realism, as speculative as any near- or far-future thinking tends or desires to be. Much contemporary speculative work is already doing this, and should continue to do so, but the point also stands for the fictions spun about not only what the Anthropocene is and who and what it might affect, but also how we understand it through its roots. There is at least one fallibility in its etymological roots being sourced from Ancient Greek, where the etymology of "anthropo-" incorrectly suggests that women are not even relevant, or perpetuates the false-binary, hierarchical sense of subsuming women (and other gender identities) into subsidiaries of a "higher" male category. The Ancient Greek word "ἄνθρωπος" is currently used as the combining form, and that term in philosophy more commonly referred to men; the descendent Greek word "anthropos" is a masculine noun, but has been adopted in a typical, patriarchal manner to denote all humans (Montanari 2015, 179–180). Moreover, one of the definitions for ἄνθρωπος is also in the derogatory and can indicate a "female slave." While the first overall definition is male-centered and thus, at the very least, exclusionary or assuming that the male gender represents all genders, the second definition is even more offensive, and certainly paints a horrifying picture of the lives of those without rights or agency in Ancient Greek times: here, *The Online Liddell-Scott-Jones Greek-English Lexicon* uses defining language like "contemptuously, of female slaves" and "with a sense of pity" (Pantelia n.d.) and *The Brill Dictionary* says that the feminine usage is "[sometimes] pejorative," and can denote a "servant" or "slavewoman" (Montanari 2015, 179-180). The "Anthropocene" as a term is clearly fraught with gender inequalities that encode and thus extend the cultural mores of a long-fallen civilization that, while producing many inspirational qualities we admire (such as art, infrastructure, and architecture), also degraded countless individuals. In their presentation of perpetuated hypercapitalistic excesses and the effects of pollution and the climate crisis, both "Sand and Slag" and *Tiger Flu* comment on and reinforce what Stacy Alaimo calls a "carbon-heavy masculinity," "a gendered style that contributes to increasing CO2 emissions" (Alaimo 2016), which pervades the Anthropocene as a time period, whatever we name it. But Lai and Bacigalupi's insistence on imagining story worlds pushing past the time of humans at the very least means that more accurate names should be explored for how we affect the geological and natural world.

While the term "Plantationocene" (Haraway 2015, 159-165) is useful since it invokes a continued process of colonialism, and thus how "plantation logics organize modern economies, environments, bodies, and social relations" (Perry and Hopes 2019) and Jason W. Moore's "Capitalocene" sagely probes global economic systems (Moore 2015), I particularly appreciate Donna Haraway's feminist deconstruction and critique of the term "Anthropocene" itself with a suggestion of "Chthulucene" (2015, 160). In the question period of Bruno Latour's keynote talk at the 2016 Under Western Skies conference on "water," I asked him to offer further thoughts on the term "Anthropocene" itself, citing Moore and Haraway's contributions, and a brief comment on gender problematics. He responded that from the purely scientific, geological perspective he was coming from, the term was quite apt, and emerged from that understanding of the changes that have occurred (Latour 2016); here he means the stratigraphic traces (Szerszynski 2012, 167–170, Zalasiewicz 2011, 1036–1055), among other understandings. His work, and that of others, in bringing awareness to and critiquing human processes that contribute to altering the planet's stratigraphic signals is important, of course, but the problematic etymology of "Anthropocene" is quite clear, and if we do indeed mean to indicate a new epoch in which human activity has impacted the earth's geology, then we need another prefix that more completely and accurately incorporates responsible human agents, and the specific aspects with which we have achieved this so permanent of impressions.

In its deliberations on the inciting "event" of when and how human cultures have most impacted the strata of the earth and thus materialized ourselves a new geologic division of time, the Working Group on the "Anthropocene"[9] and similar technoscientific perspectives play a strong role, but, as Christophe Bonneuil and Jean-Baptiste Fressoz argue,

> [t]hinking the Anthropocene also means challenging its unifying grand narrative of the errant human species and its redemption by science alone. . . . It means meticulously listening to scientists and putting their results and conclusions into public and democratic discussions, rather than sinking into a geocracy of technological and market-based "solutions" to "manage" the entire Earth. The less that the science of the Anthropocene pretends to stand above the world, the more solid and fruitful it will be, and the less the seductive concept of the Anthropocene will risk serving as a legitimizing philosophy for an oligarchic geopower. (2016, 288)

To solve the issues associated with the Anthropocene, we may very well need cultural toolkits that are not derived from that system of knowledge; otherwise our solutions will always be playing lip service to extractive, unsustainable processes of organizing, housing, fueling, and legitimizing culture, and these solutions cannot help but ultimately fail as fully as any of the major civilizations that someone like Ronald Wright indicates, in *A Short History of Progress* (2004), as ultimately becoming self-destructive. Two such instances he offers are with Rapa Nui (58–61), which is known to the Western world as Easter Island—though recent counterevidence to this understanding is compelling (DiNapoli et al. 2019)—and the Maya (Wright 2004, 82–84, 97–98, 99–102). Wright suggests both are doomed by their progression (2004, 102–103), and argues that it will be the same for "Western" society.

Others are also discontent with "Anthropocene" as a term, albeit for a variety of reasons. Bernard Stiegler suggests the "entropocene," while the

2015 summer school at the philosophy academy Stiegler founded in Epineuil (France) focused on ideas about the "neganthropocene." The former references Stiegler's idea that we are facing a time of "[the biosphere] becoming entropic (in the sense of a world-wide exhaustion and ruination) . . . due to what he calls a generalized toxification of all the systems that make up the human habitat on this planet" (Lemmens and Hui 2017, Stiegler 2017). The latter "argues for a new form of technological development that allows a so-called bifurcation—a radical change of direction in the sense of thermodynamics and seeks to produce qualitative differences for individuals as well as social groups" (Lemmens and Hui 2017)—where the terminology seems aimed toward affirming a negation of that which constitutes the Anthropocene, whichever term we use. These variations on the Anthropocene are actually rather striking examples that we could consider as valuable, with perhaps "entropocene" resonating as a strong replacement for our current terminology, and "neganthropocene" as a mindset available for adoption. That being said, Edward O. Wilson's term "Eremocene" resonates strongly with not only the human role in affecting the current geological time period, but also with fears about the 6th Mass Extinction. Wilson calls the current time "the Age of Loneliness," and posits his terminology as coming from "a time for and all about our one species alone" (Wilson 2013). The "ἔρημος" ("erémos") from Ancient Greek implicates roots to the eremocene that connote a sense of desolation, loneliness, and the solitary[10]; as James Bradley argues, the eremocene is "a construction that memorialises the victims rather than the culprits" (Bradley 2017). For me, perhaps the Eremocene, of all these suggestions, resonates most strongly in alternative terminology to the Anthropocene. Moreover, the eremocene also points in some way to the fact that loss is not only imminent, but immanent.[11]

But the eremocene is still clearly a human-centered terminology. Haraway's "Chthulucene" is a more applicable non-anthropocentric term for the current epoch: the wording, "even burdened with its problematic Greek-ish tendrils, entangles myriad temporalities and spatialities and myriad intra-active entities-in-assemblages—including the more-than-human, other-than-human, inhuman, and human-as-humus" (Haraway 2015, 160). Her terminology echoes Anna Tsing's suggestion "that the inflection point between the Holocene and the Anthropocene might be the wiping out of most of the refugia from which diverse species assemblages (with or without people) can be reconstituted after major events" (Haraway 2015, 159). But, as Haraway says, she is "a compost-ist, not a posthuman-ist: we are all compost, not posthuman" (161). *The Tiger Flu* and "Sand and Slag" push beyond this mortal human compostability, and also do not really deal with refugia for humanity—which becomes an abstraction, a historical note, some marginalia in each story. In Lai's narrative, though the Grist Sisters find an entangled refuge, they are more properly a "beyond-human" or posthuman assemblage; in Bacigalupi's story, entangled refuge is a *non sequitur*, since those who have ingested weeviltech ravage the earth into a state no human could survive.

A question that remains, by the end of Bacigalupi's and Lai's narratives, is *which* sort of future we, as humans, are interested in pushing toward—though both suggest we would no longer be human and that humans might not survive the centuries and millennia following extraction- and pandemic-for-profit. Some of my students who read Bacigalupi, when asked to debate either ingesting weeviltech or not, chose the narrative's existence of constant consumption; others, who read Lai, could not fathom the alterity of beings so like us who might also reproduce in ways that are currently possible in some biological cases, but not for humans. In a sense, both narratives are posthuman enough to approach the emergence of a post-Anthropocene—though obviously the effects of the related geological epoch, all irrelevant and relevant names aside, have already been stratigraphically ingrained within the geologic record of this world. The human has already made its permanent, measurable planetary mark, as a history of agricultural practices and the proliferation of radionuclides like Strontium 90, Cesium 137, Americium 241, and Plutonium 239[12] (among others from nuclear detonations and industrial accidents) are joined by the other geologic traces of Late Capitalism, such as plastiglomerate rocks (Corcoran, Moore, and Jazvac 2014), and "even the bones left by the global proliferation of the domestic chicken" (Carrington 2016). When the human being is gone, anthropogenic effects will remain in play for a time perhaps unimaginable to us now in the day-to-day—or to those left behind, only through story and myth, as presented in Bacigalupi's narrative and at the end of Lai's, including with "the old communications satellite Eng[, who] lurches along her still-deepening orbit, a long ellipsis that will take her a thousand years to complete" (Lai 2018, 329–330). The human remnants in this world (and beyond) are the elements that will not die out for a very long time, even though Bacigalupi's and Lai's humans may have succumbed to our current ecocidal excesses. From our present moment, we should strongly consider how long the traces of humanity will last—and, more importantly, what kind of record will prevail in our economy with the planet and labor to persist as a node in its history.

NOTES

1. I would like to thank Larissa Lai for her interview with me in January 2021 for Cappadocia University (Turkey), and to Emrah Atasoy for arranging this event. I would also like to thank Paolo Bacigalupi for his correspondence in January 2017, and the permission to reference his social media posting(s) from that month. Various

elements related to this chapter extend from my PhD dissertation, *Here, at the End: Contemporary North American Ecocritical Dystopian Fiction* (2019), and were presented through a variety of lenses at the following conferences and workshops: *The End and the Enjambment: Beginnings in 21st Century Culture* (2013), ICFA 2019, SFRA 2019, ALECC 2020, *Living in the End Times: Utopian and Dystopian Representations of Pandemics in Fiction, Film and Culture* (2021), ICFA 2021, SFRA 2021, and ASLE 2021.

2. The first publication on the "ecocritical dystopia" appears as part of Paradoxa's 2019-2020 special issue on *Climate Fictions*, edited by Alison Sperling, in my article "'Everything Change': Ecocritical Dystopianism and Climate Fiction."

3. "ecology, n.," *Oxford English Dictionary* (Oxford UP, 2016). Franco Montanari, "*οἶκος*," in *The Brill Dictionary of Ancient Greek*, eds. Madeleine Goh and Chad Schroeder (Boston: Brill, 2015), 1433.

4. Larissa Lai, "Familiarizing Grist Village: Why I Write Speculative Fiction," *Canadian Literature* 240 (2020), https://canlit.ca/decolonial-revisions-of-science-fiction-fantasy-and-horror-author-spotlight-larissa-lai/. Lai reminds us that *The Tiger Flu* extends her "interest in the figure of the clone begun in her second novel, *Salt Fish Girl*."

5. Larissa Lai, *Salt Fish Girl* (Toronto: Thomas Allen, 2008). The intersection of trees, clones, and parthenogenesis also appears in *Salt Fish Girl* (2002) with durian trees (256, 257-58) as fertilizers, and "cabbages and radishes" to "[s]upport and strengthen the fetuses" (258).

6. Lai's choice of "wet market" here is quite interesting, given suggestions that the source of more than one zoonotic pandemic has been connected with Chinese wet markets — like SARS (Quammen). While *The Tiger Flu* was published in 2018, before the outbreak of COVID-19, it has also later been argued that this particular novel coronavirus did not originate there (Letzer).

7. Chen's gender is never specified.

8. Paolo Bacigalupi, *Facebook Messenger* message to Conrad Scott, Sept. 11, 2017. Bacigalupi later corresponded that I had permission to use his words.

9. Jan Zalasiewicz et al., "Working Group on the 'Anthropocene,'" Subcommission on Quaternary Stratigraphy (Feb. 23, 2016), http://quaternary.stratigraphy.org/workinggroups/ anthropocene/.

10. See also Montanari's "*ἔρημος*," which also uses "abandoned" in its consideration of places.

11. For a discussion of immanent apocalypse, see Joshua Gunn and David E. Beard's study.

12. CTBTO Preparatory Commission, "Chart 1—Effects of Radionuclides," *General Overview of the Effects of Nuclear Testing* (2012), https://www.ctbto.org/nuclear-testing/the-effects-of-nuclear-testing/general-overview-of-theeffects-of-nuclear-testing/. The Provisional Technical Secretariat of the Preparatory Commission for the Comprehensive Nuclear-Test-Ban Treaty Organization (CTBTO) indicates that these are the radionuclides with the longest half-lives, or longest periods of decay, and would thus affect the strata of the planet for the longest time. The half-life of Plutonium 239 is 24,400 years.

WORKS CITED

Alaimo, Stacy. 2016. "Climate Change, Carbon-heavy Masculinity, and the Politics of Exposure." *Uminnpressblog.com*, University of Minnesota P, 27 October. https://uminnpressblog.com/2016/10/27/climate-change-carbon-heavy-masculinity-and- the-politics-of-exposure/. Accessed October 1, 2021.

Baccolini, Raffaella. 2000. "Gender and Genre in the Feminist Critical Dystopias of Katharine Burdekin, Margaret Atwood, and Octavia E. Butler." In *Future Females, the Next Generation: New Voices and Velocities in Feminist Science Fiction Criticism*, edited by Marleen S. Barr. Lanham: Rowman and Littlefield, 13–34.

Baccolini, Raffaella and Thomas Moylan. 2003. "Dystopia and Histories." Introduction. *Dark Horizons: Science Fiction and the Dystopian Imagination*, edited by Raffaella Baccolini and Thomas Moylan. London: Routledge, 1–12.

Bacigalupi, Paolo. 2010. "The People of Sand and Slag." In *Pump Six and Other Stories*. San Francisco: Night Shade. 49–67.

———. 2010a. *Ship Breaker*. New York: Little, Brown and Company.

———. 2012. *The Drowned Cities*. New York: Little, Brown and Company.

———. 2015. *The Water Knife*. London: Penguin Random House.

———. 2017. *Tool of War*. New York: Little, Brown and Company.

———. 2017a. "I wrote *The Water Knife*. . . ." *Facebook*, 31 January. https://www.facebook.com/permalink.php?story_fbid=10154946832703904&id=120204113903. Accessed 1 October 2021.

———. 2017b. "I'm having a hard time imagining the future turning out well for us," *Facebook*, 28 January. https://www.facebook.com/permalink.php?story_fbid= 10154936558263904&id=120204113903. Accessed October 1, 2021.

Bonneuil, Christophe, and Jean-Baptiste Fressoz. 2016. *The Shock of the Anthropocene: The Earth, History and Us*. Translated by David Fernbach. London and New York: Verso.

Bradley, James. 2017. "Writing on the Precipice." *Sydney Review of Books*, 21 February. http://sydneyreviewofbooks.com/writing-on-the-precipice-climate -change/. Accessed October 1, 2021.

Carrington, Damian. 2016. "The Anthropocene Epoch: Scientists Declare Dawn of Human-Influenced Age." *The Guardian*, 29 August. https://www.theguardian .com/ environment/2016/aug/29/declare-anthropocene-epoch-experts-urge-geolog ical-congress- human-impact-earth. Accessed October 1, 2021.

Cavalcanti, Ildney de Fatima Souza. 1999. "Articulating the Elsewhere: Utopia in Contemporary Feminist Dystopias." PhD diss., University of Strathclyde. http://www.opengrey.eu/item/display/10068/570756. Accessed October 1, 2021.

———. 2003. "The Writing of Utopia and the Feminist Critical Dystopia: Suzy McKee Charnas's Holdfast Series." In *Dark Horizons: Science Fiction and the Dystopian Imagination*, edited by Raffaella Baccolini and Thomas Moylan. London: Routledge, 47–67.

Corcoran, Patricia L., Charles J. Moore, and Kelly Jazvac. 2014. "An Anthropogenic Marker Horizon in the Future Rock Record." *GSA Today*, vol. 24, no. 6 (June). https://www.geosociety.org/gsatoday/archive/24/6/article/i1052-5173-24-6-4.htm. Accessed October 1, 2021.

CTBTO Preparatory Commission. 2012. "Chart 1–Effects of Radionuclides." *General Overview of the Effects of Nuclear Testing*. Accessed 1 October 2021.

DiNapoli, Robert J., Carl P. Lipo, Tanya Brosnan, Terry L. Hunt, Sean Hixon, Alex E. Morrison, and Matthew Becker. 2019. "Rapa Nui (Easter Island) Monument (ahu) Locations Explained by Freshwater Sources." *PLOS One* (10 January). https://doi.org/10.1371/journal.pone.0210409.

"ecology, n." 2016. In *Oxford English Dictionary*. Oxford: Oxford University Press.

Evans, Claire L. 2015. "Climate Change is so Dire we Need a New Kind of Science Fiction to Make Sense of It." *The Guardian*, 20 August. https://www.theguardian.com/commentisfree/2015/aug/20/climate-change-science-fiction. Accessed October 1, 2021.

Gunn, Joshua and David E. Beard. 2000. "On the Apocalyptic Sublime." *Southern Communication Journal*, vol. 65, no. 4: 269–286, doi.org/10.1080/10417940009373176.

Haraway, Donna. 2015. "Anthropocene, Capitalocene, Plantationocene, Chthulucene: Making Kin." *Environmental Humanities*, 6: 159–165.

Lai, Larissa. 2008. *Salt Fish Girl*. Toronto: Thomas Allen.

———. 2018. *The Tiger Flu*. Vancouver: Arsenal Pulp.

———. 2018a. "Insurgent Utopias: How to Recognize the Knock at the Door," *Exploring the Fantastic: Genre, Ideology, and Popular Culture*, edited by Ina Batzke, Eric C. Erbacher, Linda M. Heß, and Corinna Lenhardt. New York: Columbia University Press, 91–113. https://doi.org/10.14361/9783839440278-005.

———. 2020. "Familiarizing Grist Village: Why I Write Speculative Fiction." *Canadian Literature*, no. 240: 20–39, https://canlit.ca/decolonial-revisions-of-science-fiction-fantasy-and-horror-author-spotlight-larissa-lai/.

———. "The Mythic Future: An Evening with Dr. Larissa Lai, Author of *The Tiger Flu and Iron Goddess of Mercy*—Interviewed by Dr. Conrad Scott." By Conrad Scott, online video recording, Cappadocia University, Turkey, June 18, 2021, https://youtu.be/b7tUMdlwMXY.

Latour, Bruno. 2016. "Reset Modernity!" Keynote Address, Under Western Skies, Mount Royal University, Calgary, 29 September.

Lemmens, Pieter, and Yuk Hui. 2017. "Apocalypse, Now! Peter Sloterdijk and Bernard Stiegler on the Anthropocene." *boundary 2*, 16 January. http://www.boundary2.org/2017/01/pieter-lemmens-and-yuk-hui-apocalypse-now-peter-sloterdijk-and-bernard-stiegler-on-the-anthropocene/. Accessed October 1, 2021.

Letzer, Rafi. 2020. "The Coronavirus Didn't Really Start at that Wuhan 'wet market.'" *Live Science*, 28 May. Accessed October 1, 2021.

Meyer, Robinson. 2016. "A Mega-Drought is Coming to America's Southwest." *The Atlantic*, 11 October. www.theatlantic.com/science/archive/2016/10/megadroughts-arizona-new-mexico/503531/.

Montanari, Franco. 2015. *The Brill Dictionary of Ancient Greek*. Eds. Madeleine Goh and Chad Schroeder. Boston: Brill.

———. "ἄνθρωπος." In *The Brill Dictionary of Ancient Greek*, 179–180.

———. "ἐρημος." In *The Brill Dictionary of Ancient Greek*, 818.

———. "οἶκος." In *The Brill Dictionary of Ancient Greek*, 1433.

Moore, Jason W. 2015. *Capitalism in the Web of Life*. London and Brooklyn: Verso.

Moylan, Thomas. 2000. *Scraps of the Untainted Sky: Science Fiction, Utopia, Dystopia*, Westview.

Pantelia, Maria. N.d. "ἄνθρωπος." In *LSJ: The Online Liddell-Scott-Jones Greek-English Lexicon*, Thesaurus Linguae Greacae, The Regents of the U of California. http://stephanus.tlg.uci.edu/lsj/#eid=9236&context=lsj&action=from-search.

Perry, Laura, and Addie Hopes. 2019. "The Plantationocene Series: Plantation Worlds, Past and Present." *Edge Effects*, Center for Culture, History, and Environment, https://edgeeffects.net/plantationocene-series-plantation-worlds/.

Quammen, David. 2012. *Spillover: Animal Infections and the Next Human Pandemic*. Norton.

Sargent, Lyman Tower. 1994. "The Three Faces of Utopianism Revisited." *Utopian Studies*, vol. 5, no, 1: 1–37, www.jstor.org/stable/20719246.

Shelley, Mary Wollstonecraft. 2010. *The Last Man*. 1826. Dover.

Stiegler, Bernard. 2017. *Automatic Society: The Future of Work*. Vol. 1, translated by Daniel Ross, Polity.

Suvin, Darko. 2016. *Metamorphoses of Science Fiction: On the Poetics and History of a Literary Genre*. 1979. Edited by Gerry Canavan. Peter Lang.

Szerszynski, Bronislaw. 2012. "The End of the End of Nature: The Anthropocene and the Fate of the Human." *Oxford Literary Review*, vol. 34, no. 2: 165–184, www .jstor. org/stable/44030881.

Timofeeva, Oxana. 2017. "Ultra-Black: Towards a Materialist Theory of Oil." *e-flux*, vol. 84. www.e-flux.com/journal/84/149335/ultra-black-towards-a-materialist-the-ory-of-oil/.

Tsing, Anna. 2015. "Feral Biologies." Paper for Anthropological Visions of Sustainable Futures, University College London, February.

Wilson, Edward O. 2013. "Beware the Age of Loneliness." *The Economist*, 18 November. Accessed October 1, 2021.

Wright, Ronald. 2004. *A Short History of Progress*. Toronto: Anansi.

Zalasiewicz, Jan, et al. 2011. "Stratigraphy of the Anthropocene." *Philosophical Transactions of the Royal Society A*, vol. 369: 1036-1055, doi.org/10.1098/rsta .2010.0315.

———. 2016. "Working Group on the 'Anthropocene.'" Subcommission on Quaternary Stratigraphy, 23 February. http://quaternary.stratigraphy.org/working-groups/ anthropocene/.

Chapter 14

"'Cause tonight is the night | When two become one"

Stranger Things, *Parasitism, Assimilation, and the Abject*

Daisy Butcher

The struggle between humankind and Nature has long been depicted in popular media. The demonization of Nature can be seen clearly in the wake of industrialization in Western culture as heroic humans are pitted against the monstrous wilderness that is in need of conquering. This tradition has continued in the Anthropocene era, and I argue that there is no better recent example of this struggle than the ongoing Netflix science fiction series of *Stranger Things* (2016–present) created by Matt and Ross Duffer. Set in the 1980s, the show is not subtle about highlighting the rapid increase in consumerist culture in America. More than this, the 1980s are uniquely positioned in the liminal space between analogue and digital, a world where children had less supervision and could get lost in the woods unlike today's world of constant connection. In the series, a small Indiana town called Hawkins is home to a secret government research laboratory which is connected to the Department of Energy. In this facility, they use child test subjects in an attempt to spy on the Soviets during the Cold War. Hawkins comes under threat, however, as a rift between dimensions is accidentally opened by a young test subject called "Eleven" (Millie Bobby Brown) who has telekinetic powers. The ensuing action of the series is focused on the monsters unleashed from the void, an uncanny alternate dimension of Hawkins called "The Upside Down" and the parasitic horror as the alien Other invades the bodies of Hawkins' residents, namely the character of Will Byers (Noah Schnapp). Netflix's *Stranger Things* exploits ecophobia and abjection to incite fear in the viewer. Through the use of parasitic themes, the creators highlight the fear and disgust evoked by sexual bodies and hybridity with an overarching struggle between humans and Nature and the anthropocenic anxieties of society.

INVASION OF THE CHILD SNATCHERS

Parasitism, or bodily invasion, has been a staple in science-fiction horror as the fear of an unknowable and vast universe surrounding us makes our position on Earth suddenly feel vulnerable and open to the outside. This cosmic fear is then manifested as the fear of an alien entity invading our bodies. A prime classic example of this would be *Invasion of the Body Snatchers* (Finney 1955). Finney's novel is a particularly appropriate example to mention for this chapter as the aliens featured are plant-based, much like that of *Stranger Thing's* monster, "The Demogorgon" which abducts and infects Will Byers. The abduction of Will takes place in Season One, Episode One as Will travels home on his bike (*Stranger Things*, 2016). Will is scared off the road by a tall man's shadow, perhaps a nod to the iconic Slenderman (creepypasta.com, 14/01/2010), and is chased to his home. Will attempts to defend himself by loading a gun in the family shed but is gone in a flash, spirited away by an unseen force. As a result, Will is trapped in an alternate dimension (the Upside Down) where he is forced to hide from the monster in order to survive while the toxic air saps his life away. The invasion of the domestic space signifies how nature, in its nightmarish aspect, is capable of bursting or seeping through man-made barriers. Locking the door does not protect him. Indeed, *Stranger Things* features multiple depictions of nature breaking through man-made barriers such as walls, traps, doors, glass etc. Moreover, the monsters of the Upside Down persist until the very last bulwark of defense, and ultimate in man-made barriers, the human body, is penetrated.

The Upside Down itself is a twisted ecosystem of decay and contagion which serves as a mirror image of Hawkins where everything is polluted by nature.[1] The Upside Down version of Hawkins is recognizable as a dark abyss with muted, blue tones and spores constantly floating and swirling. While some theorists have referred to these particles as ash, I argue these read more as spores or pollen as we see Hopper sprayed with them out of a fleshy, plant pod in the tunnels during Episode Five of Season Two (*Stranger Things*, 2017). This distinction is important for a Plant-Horror/ Nature-as-parasite reading of *Stranger Things* and the Anthropocene. As such, the Upside Down itself has an infectious quality where the very air is toxic. One could argue that the landscape is parasitic and works in tandem with its monsters to infect the flesh of its prey and spread its roots into the real world.

Will is not the only victim of the Upside Down in Season One, however, as in Episode Two we watch as Barb (Shannon Purser), a friend of Mike's sister Nancy (Natalia Dyer), who, after being dragged along to a pool party, is left alone by the pool's edge with a wound bleeding into the water. She is surrounded by the dark forest and when the water ripples, she too, is abducted by the monster. In Episode Three Barb wakes up in the Upside Down covered in slime. She is in an alternate version of the pool which is empty and covered in web-like vines. Her abduction scene, as she screams and struggles to escape the monster, is interspersed with shots of her friend Nancy (who left her friend outside by the pool to go inside with her boyfriend) kissing and having sex with Steve (Joe Keery). The juxtaposition of these two events creates a sense of teenage sex as taboo and, more specifically, a young woman losing her virginity is likened to a young woman being pursued and devoured by a monster. Further to this, victimizing Barb specifically after she bleeds, a signifier of menses and thus sexual maturity/fertility, adds an element of eco-revenge in terms of poisoning and monsterizing future human mothers via the Demogorgon's vegetative hybridity. The sexual symbolism in this scene is present from the moment we see Barb covered in slime, as Simon C. Estok's work on slime and the Anthropocene ecogothic illuminates how [slime]:

> can neither be possessed nor controlled, and it should not be surprising that fears about slime are entangled with sexism and misogyny—each, to differing degrees, obsessed with power and control. Indeed, myxophobia, (fear of slime) is deeply enmeshed with the fear of women's bodies and sexuality and with fantasies of violence. (Estok 2020, 31)

Slime provokes Julia Kristeva's concept of the "abject" (i.e., repulsion experienced as a result bodily fluids/functions) when the scenes are edited in this way as it conjures imagery of seminal fluid and vaginal discharge during sex. In an alien horror context, it evokes disgust with its ability to cling to us, seep beneath our skin and transgress barriers (Estok 2020, 15.) As Nancy has consensual sex with Steve above ground, Barb serves as a mirrored reality, sunken below in the Upside Down, and trapped in a waterless pool as a literal fallen woman, trying to clamber her way up and out. In horror film tradition, teenage sex can never go unpunished, even if it is by proxy.

Later in Episode Seven, Eleven stumbles across Barb's corpse in the void of the Upside Down. Her body is entangled with the vegetal/fungal fleshy matter of the Upside Down realm which blurs the boundaries between life and death. This feeling is reinforced further as an alien larva exits Barb's mouth which can be read as a pseudo-birth after an alien impregnation, adding to the overarching theme of fearing the female body. Control over female sexuality and women's bodies, therefore, is yet another theme which is exploited to drive home the horror of humankind's inability to control the natural world. Using Julia Kristeva's concept of the abject/abjection, the image of the larva exiting the mouth clearly signifies the fear and anxiety as a result of the blurring of outside and inside and the all-important borders of the self. Viewing Barb's corpse triggers repulsion and sadness within the viewer as it is an adolescent corpse, something that feels so wrong to comprehend that it is usually banished out of sight. Corpses, blood, flesh, spit, vomit and excreta are all reminders of our corporeality and, ultimately, our mortality (Kristeva 1982, 3). Discomfort is formed when these insides venture outside. Just as the viewer is able to get over the initial shock of see-ing Barb dead, the larva coming out of her mouth conjures strong feelings of abjection as that which we have now deemed dead has something living inside of it. And it is not something human, or with a face, it is an overgrown and slug/leech-like creature which we cannot even begin to empathize with; it is an ultimate Other. Abject substances such as those listed can be seen both literally and metaphorically throughout *Stranger Things* as the larva exits the mouth like an escaped tongue (and is later referred to as a "booger" by Lucas). Other examples consist of the corpse-like gray skin of the Demogorgon and Demodogs and the flayed, exposed flesh of the Mind Flayer.

Returning to Will Byers, in Episode Eight of Season One, he is finally res-cued by his mother, Joyce (Winona Ryder), and police Chief Hopper (David Harbour). They traverse the muted, uncanny landscape of the Upside Down which serves as a mirror image of Hawkins overrun by nature and decay. They stumble across human remains of varying degrees of decomposition, one of these being Barb, a reminder of the child abandoned by her friends in the forest and her terrible fate. Will is discovered trapped inside a vegetal yet fleshy membrane with a vine (or tentacle) down his throat. Victimized and unconscious, like a fly trapped inside a carnivorous plant, Will appears to be feeding or fertilizing the twisted ecosystem of the Upside Down with his body. In a moment of pseudo-rebirth, Will's mother severs him from the alien umbilical cord. The image of a child with a feeding tube, albeit a subverted one where nutrients are sucked out rather than given or, indeed, evil seeds are planted, conjures associations with hospitals and serious or even terminal illness. This association is driven home by the creators as the character of Hopper flashes back to when his daughter was dying of cancer in hospital, unconscious and with a feeding or breathing tube down her throat. This paral-lel between Will's fate and Hopper's child's cancer exploits a real-world hor-ror to emphasize the powerlessness felt when confronted with something out of human control. Abjection is keenly felt as nature invades the human body, rendering it abhuman and therefore unstable. The changeable, susceptible nature of the body upsets out fallacy of control and fixedness as an organic invader's jouissance, whether that's a parasite plant or cancer, has no respect for humanity. Hostility towards the Upside Down and, therefore, nature is encouraged as it is likened to our inability to control the rapid growth and mutations of child cancer.

This helplessness is felt by the viewer as, in a final scene where Will is home and safe for Christmas, he is clearly still infected/corrupted. As he excuses himself to go to the bathroom, we see him stare at himself in the mirror hauntingly, almost as if he no longer recognizes himself after the Upside Down has inspired abject feelings due to the purity and borders of the self being violated and inside and outside having blurred into one another. It is revealed that the Upside Down impregnated Will with its seed as he proceeds to cough up a larva into the sink and causing a flashback so that it appears he's back in the Upside Down realm. To end on this creates a lack of catharsis for the viewer and a sense of impending dread. It is also no accident that this happens in the bathroom, the most common site for abject substances, as the show refuses to allow us to restore comfortable boundaries and distinctly separate outside from inside, Hawkins from the Upside Down and body from parasite.

PSYCHIC PARASITISM: THE MERGING OF MINDS

Continuing with the analysis of Will Byers takes us to Season Two (2017) where it becomes even clearer that he is not out of the woods yet (literally and figuratively) as he is occasionally transported into the Upside Down as though he never left. His consciousness seems to travel there but his body remains topside in a trance like a nonconsensual instance of astral projection. This separation of the mind from the body is the very essence of the abject and it is during one of these moments where Will's psyche is forced back into the Upside Down and his real body is possessed by the shadow monster as it enters through his nose, eyes, and mouth. Will becomes merged with the Mind Flayer, the big bad of the Upside Down, and through part of the hive-mind he is able to see its location and schemes but is too manipulated by it to be an effective spy for the good guys. The corrupting influence of the shadow monster spreads as the season goes on until Will loses his sense of self. When Will wakes up in Season Two Episode Six he has forgotten Bob (Sean Astin), his mother's boyfriend, and Hopper and is becoming more a husk of his former self. He even feels the pain of the vines and monsters as they are burned by scientists proving that the parasitic creature's reach has gone into the very tissue of his human body as well as his mind. By being joined with the Mind Flayer against his will, Will transcends the limits of human consciousness by having access to how this superior being sees and interacts with the world. In this way, Will is an example of Stacy Alaimo's "transcorporeality" as a "contact zone between human corporeality and more-than-human nature

. . . in which the human is always intermeshed with the more-than-world"
(Alaimo 2010, 2). Christy Tidwell and Carter Soles elaborate of Alaimo's
concept, arguing that the anxiety provoked by feeling permeable to harmful
substances and influences inspires delusions that "animals, weather and pollutants . . . can be separated from us, can be conquered" (Tidwell, Soles 2020,
6). The shattering of these delusions creates the terror upon which Ecohorror
thrives. Monsters, aliens or killer plants, serving as extensions of Nature as a
whole, disrupt humanity, making it impossible for us to uphold our fallacies
of separation.

   Will's experience of having his mind inter-meshed with the Mind Flayer
is reminiscent of the contemporaneous Netflix series *The Dark Crystal: Age
of Resistance* (Addiss: 2019–2019) as the Arathim, a spidery parasite race,
latch onto and control the Gelfings; the most prominent of which being Tavra
(Catriona Balfe), a soldier and princess. When asked by her sister why, after
there is a truce between Arathim and Gelflings, the creature will not come
off her face, Tavra responds "We've been merged too long. Our minds have
become one. We are no longer sure where one of us begins and the other one
ends" (*The Dark Crystal: Age of Resistance*: 2019). This moment in *The Dark
Crystal: Age of Resistance*, and indeed in Season Two of *Stranger Things*,
illuminates the deep-rooted fear of humans being assimilated and consumed
by nature. Estok notes how "[t]o lose control of the body to Nature is a
frightening prospect, and in the Anthropocene, Nature has agencies that are
different than in earlier periods, agencies that are terrifyingly unpredictable"
(Estok 2020, 29). Moreover, Jane Desmerais interrogates the role of the plant
monster as an "alien species invading from another country or planet [serves
as] a recurring nightmare image that speaks to deep-rooted insecurities about
identity and 'home'" (Desmerais 2019, 217). Thus, the human body is a
metonym for humanity as a whole, human flesh can be read as territory, or
indeed "home." The fears of sexual violation and xenophobia, therefore, are
exploited in *Stranger Things* through that of human and nonhuman hybridity-
as-invasion rhetoric on a corporeal and therefore global scale. Using the
example of Will Byers (and Tavra), this loss of control, felt by losing one's
own body to a parasite, perfectly encapsulates the anthropocenic anxieties
surrounding human exceptionalism which stem from the failure to domesticate nature and keep the wilderness at bay.

   More than this, the lack of control felt by this irreversible merging of
boundaries creates extreme discomfort and the loss of identity experienced
is mourned by loved ones. It is revealed that the Mind Flayer's claws are
so deep within Will that he is able to convince the boy to betray his friends
and even his species. Losing control of the body and humans being Nature's
drones appears, of course, in Jack Finney's *Invasion of the Body Snatchers*
but also is having a resurgence in modern media with that of *Annihilation*

(novel VanderMeer, 2014; film Garland: 2018) and Naomi Novik's *Uprooted* (2015) both featuring natural threats (both botanical and zoological) and human bodies becoming enmeshed in or taken over by nature.

SYMPATHY FOR THE PARASITE

Where there are drones, however, there is also a master or puppeteer pulling the strings. Much like how *Ophiocordyceps* is an insect-pathogenic fungus which infects and creates "zombie-ants" for its own ends (David P. Hughes et al. 2011), the spores in the Upside Down could signify the threat of *Stranger Things* as part of a human-pathogenic fungus. Indeed, fungus could be the most effective agent of anthropocenic horror in that it is ever present and difficult to categorize. Fungi is both an alien "Other" and also domestic and familiar. It can also be uncomfortably visceral in appearance such as the "Devil's fingers" (*Clathrus archeri*) or "Bleeding Tooth" (*Hydnellum peckii*) varieties. Fungi have an ability to thrive on decay, in natural and urban environments and have even been proved to display problem-solving skills (Hanson et al 2006.) The combination of these traits, along with their parasitic aspects and ability to endure make them an effective monster to modern humans.[2] On this basis, Ed Yong argues against the term "Anthropocene" altogether since "we are still living in the Microbiocene: a period that started at the dawn of life itself and will continue to its very end" (Yong 2017, 273). With this in mind, we can view the Upside Down as a parasitic Microbiocene with its spores floating in the air, the dark, damp surroundings and even reading the Demogorgon as a fungal imitation of a flower (like the *Geastrum Minimum*).

Reading *Stranger Things* as a pathogenic fungal horror, one could argue that the Demogorgon and Demodogs are also under its control. This is then strengthened in Episode Eight of Season Two by Dustin's (Gaten Matarazzo) relationship with pollywog-turned-Demodog "Dart" (affectionately named after D'artagnan) and how he argues that just because it comes from the Upside Down, it is not inherently evil. After passing the tadpole-like creature around to his friends and Lucas (Caleb McLaughlin) claiming "Ugh, he's like a living booger," it is clear his friends do not share his affection for the creature and actively find it repulsive as an example of abjection. After Will recognizes it to be the same type of (if not the very same) creature as the larva he coughed up in the sink, Dustin has a heated exchange with Mike (Finn Wolfhard):

Dustin: No way. If we take him to Hopper, Dart's as good as dead.
Mike: Maybe he should be dead

Dustin: How can you say that?
Mike: How can you not? He's from the Upside Down
Dustin: Maybe. But even if he is, it doesn't automatically mean that he's bad.
   (*Stranger Things*, 2017)

In this scene, Dustin fiercely advocates for Dart and rejects the closed-mindedness of his friends as he insists that he has formed a bond with the creature from the Upside Down. In this classic debate of Nature vs. Nurture, Dustin is of the belief that the creature being from the Upside Down does not inevitably make it evil and necessitate its destruction.[3] The case of Dart in *Stranger Things* goes on to prove this theory somewhat, as it is revealed that the Mind Flayer can summon and control the Demodogs as seen in Episode Eight of Season Two when a group of them uncharacteristically spare Steve and Dustin on the Mind Flayer's command in order to stop the bigger threat of Eleven closing the gate between dimensions. Moreover, prior to this, Dart proves to have a genuine bond with Dustin where Dart seemingly chooses to eat a treat from Dustin rather than attack. While, as Emma M. McMain and JT Torres point out, "there is still an air of human supremacy, nature-as-pet and creature-as-horrifying" (2021, 11–12) underpinning Dustin and Dart's relationship, their bond creates an element of hope in this otherwise damning anthropocenic ecohorror. Dustin proves that humans are capable of compassion and not merely destruction and violence and furthermore, showcases a relationship between humans and nature without an ulterior motive. There is no direct benefit to Dustin in taking Dart into his home and nurturing this stray animal and his intentions seem to be based on the desire for kinship, allyship, coexistence, and tolerance rather than supremacy and exploitation.

THE MIND FLAYER AS PUPPET MASTER

While it is possible to have sympathy for Dart the Demodog as another victim of the parasite, it is difficult if not impossible to sympathize with the arachnoid Mind Flayer. The Mind Flayer serves as master and puppeteer to the lesser monsters of the Upside Down and is proven to be a sentient being through its "mind flaying" of Will Byers. As such, it seems to have an explicit agenda of expansion and destruction and serves as an embodiment of Nature's antipathy towards humanity. Even Eleven herself is not immune from the monsters corrupting influence. In Season Three Episodes Seven and Eight we see a fleshy, slug-like offshoot of the Mind Flayer's body burrow under her skin like a horrific and oversized botfly. As Eleven's leg it caught and the Mind Flayer tries to reel her into its maw and a piston-like tongue (very similar to the xenomorph from *Alien* (Scott: 1979)), it burrows into her skin hoping to add the powerful telekinetic human to its zombified ranks. Eleven finally manages to fight through the pain to extract it and throws it across the mall in a violent act of rejecting the "Other." Her father figure, Hopper, quickly stomps on it as it attempts to crawl away which signifies his paternal role as protector. More specifically, he is protecting or avenging his daughter's body against the phallic invader/corrupter (which is something he seems very concerned about earlier in the season in regard to her physical relationship with Mike). Reading parasitic invasion as an act like sex, Hopper's patriarchal defense of Eleven's virginity serves as an effective metaphor for defending the purity of the self against the alien other, the inside from outside and the ensuing abjection.

Sexually charged language is also seen in Season Two in regards to bodily invasion and horror as Will is infected with the shadow monster. Tendrils of shadows enter his mouth, eyes, and nose as he chokes and is unable to move. In Episode Four of Season Two, he shares the fact that the monster "got him" with his mother, Joyce, saying: "I felt it everywhere. Everywhere. I still feel it" (*Stranger Things,* 2017). The parasitic invasion of the child's body, therefore, has connotations of child molestation as the young, innocent, and sacred body of the child is violated. More than this, events later in the season reveal that the shadow monster is ventriloquizing through Will, using him as a mouthpiece. The monster manipulates Will to protect itself from heat while also forcing him to betray his friends and lead scientists into a trap. Will refers to the monster as a "he" and says "he made me do it" in response to luring men to their deaths. This humanizing of the monster conjures connotations of real-world horror and human evil such as masters and enslaved persons or child abusers who emotionally manipulate, control and groom children and alienate them from their parents. Nature here is positioned as not only a predator, but as an agent of revenge rather than the passive and submissive victim. This creates feelings of shock, outrage, and disgust in the viewer and elicits an emotional response which causes a protective feeling over Will and a righteous hatred towards the parasite and therefore Nature.[4] By attacking and mutating specifically child and female bodies, the Upside Down strategically targets those that patriarchal capitalism undermines, oppresses, and dismisses.

Although Eleven's physical integrity is maintained and Will is saved from the Mind Flayer (in what can only be described as a heat exorcism), the same cannot be said for all hosts of the parasitic monster. Hawkins' violent bully and new kid on the block, Billy (Dacre Montgomery) is attacked and overwhelmed by the Mind Flayer in Episode Two of Season Three. Under the influence of the Mind Flayer, Billy is a stronger host than Will and is used to assist in the abduction of Hawkins residents. As Billy kidnaps a woman from the pool where he worked, he advises her, "Don't be afraid. It will be over soon. Just stay very still" (*Stranger Things,* 2019). Wearing Billy's face, he uses these words to try and calm his victim, like pacifying a lamb before slaughter, no doubt to make the Mind Flayer's job easier as it consumes her. However, these words in particular feel very sexually charged and akin to something an attacker would say before an act of rape. Once again, *Stranger Things* exploits the terrifying reality of real-world horror or trauma to inspire fear and disgust within the viewer and rape is arguably one of (if not *the*) worst and, unfortunately, most common instances of body invasion experienced.

As more sacrifices are taken to the Mind Flayer in Season Three, Episode Four, the tendril turned umbilical cord seen in the first season down Will Byer's throat returns when the big bad of the Upside Down, the shadow monster also known as the Mind Flayer is made flesh as it assimilates with human bodies. As innocents are captured and joined with the parasite, a tendril engulfs their face, fixed on like a large lamprey and at first it is unclear whether something is being sucked out of them or pumped into them. This harkens back to the tendril down Will's throat as we believed it to be siphoning nutrients out of Will to feed itself, and instead it was planting a seed deep within him. The parasitic horror reaches a peak in Episode Six, however, as many residents of Hawkins suddenly become zombie-like drones, marching towards their death. As they reach the monster in the abandoned building, they queue to offer themselves up, in what I can only describe as an assembly line of abjection. One after the other, they spontaneously disintegrate, collapsing into a puddle of blood and guts which is then absorbed by the monster and used as the basis for its own corporeal form[5]. The very name of this episode, "*E pluribus unum,*" a Latin motto used in the United States meaning "out of many, one," twists the concept of human collaboration into horrifying assimilation. Estok touches on this blurring of corporeal boundaries in *Stranger Things* noting how the show:

> [reminds] us that our bodies and identities are permeable to the ecologies around us with "human" as a composting category . . . but they present that reminder in very different ways. The question has never been *whether* we live in symbiosis with the world (neither in total harmony nor total horror). The question we focus on is what we *do,* as ethical stewards of the world, with the realisation that the answer has always been yes. (Estok 2020,17)

This then challenges the anthropocenic fallacy of human exceptionalism and emancipation from Nature by claiming that we were never truly separated from the environment and that the Anthropocene is in a reluctant symbiosis (or toxic relationship) with Nature. Considering this Mind Flayer scene further, Elizabeth Parker explores the dual meanings of "being at one with

Nature" as both a positive, spiritual experience, perhaps like that of Dustin's relationship with Dart, and a horrifying human and nonhuman entanglement (Parker 2020, 77) as seen in the Mind Flayer's farming of the human race. In this vein, *Stranger Things's* emphasis on manicured lawns, 1980s fast fashion, gadgets, toys, technology and even the Starcourt mall which opens in Season Three is contrasted with the other-worldly and overwhelming threat of nature in the form of the floral Demogorgon and Demodogs, the strangling vines which enter the bodies of humans and the fleshy Mind Flayer itself. The show is a perfect example, then, of the ways in which humankind's symbiosis or harmony with nature has been marketed as so unappealing in anthropocenic terms that it has been transformed into a hero vs. monster narrative to the point of parasitic horror.

NATURE AS COMMUNISTIC PARASITE

Another interpretation of this Mind Flayer scene, as *Stranger Things* makes continual references to The Cold War, is reading the parasitic, hive-mind monster as a demonized version of communism. The show constantly displays nature working together to overwhelm and trap humans. One could argue that the struggle between the cult of the individual and communism is at the heart of the story. Animals, plants, and fungi unite and threaten anthropocenic human civilization with the power of their collaboration. Indeed, nature as a communistic enemy is a perfect antithesis to Western capitalist overconsumption. Jason W. Moore argues that instead of labeling the modern western era as the 'Anthropocene', the term 'Capitalocene' is more fitting when considering the current environment crises as the result of the capitalist system rather than human advancement more generally (Moore 2017). The communist threat of the Upside Down can be seen throughout the three seasons, such as in Season Two as Hopper is overpowered by multiple vines and later when Demodogs combine their power to break the polycarbonate glass in the lab (*Stranger Things,* 2017). This, then, culminates in Season Three whereby the Mind Flayer is made flesh thanks to the sacrifice of its brainwashed followers as an analogy to the threat of communism in America. It is no accident, therefore, that this monstrous manifestation of communism, battles the heroes of *Stranger Things* in Starcourt Mall which serves as a metaphor of Western individualism, consumerism and, of course, capitalism. It is no accident that Season Three aired on the 4th of July, however, as in the final battle, the Mind Flayer is defeated thanks to the use of fireworks, a form of weaponized patriotism, which are explicit metaphors for American exceptionalism.[6] The trope of Ecohorror and Nature and communistic threat can be seen as far back as 1954's *Them!* featuring giant irradiated ant monsters.

Similar to what we observe in this *Stranger Things* Season Three finale, the ants represent a wider, Americanized fear of communism as, like the monster network of the Upside Down, they are portrayed as "an aggressive collectivist society" that must be destroyed, or indeed obliterated with fireworks (Rogin 1992, 263–264.)

However, *Stranger Things* also blurs the binary between capitalism and communism as while individuals are continuously overwhelmed and defeated during its three seasons, it is only through the sacrifice of one individual in each season that the heroes are able to triumph (Eleven in Season One, Bob in Season Two and Billy/Hopper in Season Three). This act of sacrifice and selflessness for the survival and greater good of the community is arguably a communistic principle, not in keeping with the overt capitalistic undercurrent of Hawkins. Equally the anti-capitalist reading of the monsters of the Upside Down is undermined by the fact that they, too, are shown to be corrupted by their desire to exploit nature in their quest for power. It is possible, therefore, to offer a different reading whereby the parasite is not the threat of communism but is instead an analogy for late-stage capitalism and its damaging environmental practices.

CONCLUSION

To conclude, *Stranger Things* expertly creates a feeling of cosmic and otherworldly horror in our own backyard. After all, the monsters and the Upside Down itself are never revealed to be from outer space, but enemies born from within us in a nightmarish but ever-present dimension. The show, therefore, raises a mirror to our own suffering ecosystems, giving them agency and the capacity for revenge. This culminates in how nature-as-parasite invades human bodies and transforms the struggle between nature vs. humans into corporeal horror. The abjection provoked by the parasite neatly encapsulates anthropocenic anxieties surrounding the infiltration of man-made barriers and the blurring of outside vs. inside. The use of the sentient parasite in *Stranger Things* reveals the fragility of humanity in the wake of the more-than-human as shown by the Demogorgon and MindFlayer's on screen victims being children and thus infantilizing the human race. This infantilization effectively positions children as representations of the future which ensure the proliferation of the human race. Children who face the monster signify limitless possibility and potential as their choices will either cause them to continue the damaging cycle and be corrupted or make change and inspire hope for a symbiotic future as seen with Dustin and Dart. As well as showing preference to child victims, the emphasis on female victims (i.e. Barb, the young women in the Mind Flayer scene of Season Three; Episode Four, and even Nancy and

Eleven) adds a gendered quality to the invasion horror. I argue that the show's concern surrounding female purity and how it depicts the existence of female bodies as something to be protected or consumed reveals the long tradition of the male gaze and fear of women's bodies within the horror and science-fiction genres. In addition, the struggle between life and decay forces the viewer to confront the transient reality of humans in the face of nature's ability to endure and overcome. This fear of transience can be seen most keenly when viewing the Upside Down as an empty, futuristic, nightmarish realm of Hawkins that is overwhelmed by nature (or indeed, the Microbiocene). In this regard, *Stranger Things's* Nature serves as an agent of chaos, rallying against humanity's concept of order and as the seasons progress, the battles become more elaborate as humans and nature fight to the death to restore the separation between civilization and wilderness. Specifically, the borders of Western civilization. Indeed, as I have touched upon earlier in the chapter, *Stranger Things* uses the metaphor of nature-as-parasite to exploit real world fears such as child abuse/cancer, women's bodies and communism. As a final thought, although the show refuses to allow its viewers to restore the comfortable boundaries between human spaces and monstrous wilderness, it is not all hopeless. While it may have had a tragic ending, Dustin's relationship with Dart the Demodog offers a silver lining for the Anthropocene and the Upside Down, as once we stop pathologizing nature as an evil parasite, coexistence is possible thanks to the compassion and hope within the future generation.

NOTES

1. The simplistic and child-like naming of this alternate dimension is reminiscent of The Other World featured in Neil Gaiman's *Coraline* (Gaiman, 2002). The Upside Down and The Other World are both spaces of the uncanny and specifically dangerous to children. The Demogorgon and The Other Mother from *Coraline* are both agents from other worlds who attempt to lure, trap and assimilate their young victims, whether that's by absorbing them into nature with vines down their throats or sewing buttons into their eyes.

2. The specifically parasitic horror of fungi is seen clearly in William Hope Hodgson's "A Voice in the Night" (1907) where shipwrecked humans are overwhelmed by a strange gray fungus and compelled to eat it in an act like cannibalism

3. In another nod to the 1980s and environmental themes, this sympathetic reading of Dart bears striking resemblance to that of Studio Ghibli's *Nausicaä* (1984), where lethally toxic plants and rampaging giant insects live in the forest close to the boundaries of human civilizations. Trees are burnt if seen to be infected by the forest's spores, but Nausicaa learns that the poisonous plants and insects are just misunderstood due to the water being polluted and humans upsetting the balance of the eco-system (*Nausicaä*, 1984.)

4. In addition, *Stranger Things* being set in a nostalgic and retrospective 1980s world means the modern viewer is continuously haunted by the present technological age (Heise-von der Lippe, 2017). Thus, the aptly named Mind Flayer nature as a parasitic hive-mind monster (that is characterized by its interconnectedness) and the master-slave relationship it has with its victims is analogous to social media in relation to its pervasive, surveillant and mind rotting aspects.

5. It is also worth noting that, although there may be male victims among the mob, the two victims that we see disintegrate on screen in this scene are young women. Not only does this imply that young women are expendable and there to be consumed and assimilated by others, but (like the aforementioned scenes with Barb and El) it reveals horror's fetishization of (young) women's bodies. This cyclical spectacle of decay is analogous to the female reproductive cycle from menarche through to (post) menopause. A young woman steps up, she decomposes, and all that remains is waste product thus symbolizing attitudes towards women's fertility and value. This rapid aging reveals the contrast between the fetishized young and beautiful female form with the nightmarish, withered and infertile hag. The use of female bodies for this horrific spectacle, therefore, is no accident as it is merely a recent example of the ways in which horror often perpetuates patriarchal obsession with the condition of women's bodies and the male gaze.

6. If the reader of this chapter is interested in similar literary depictions of literal battles between humans and nature, I would recommend two of my favorite examples (Meritt, *The Woman of the Wood*) and the more recent (Novik, *Uprooted*)

WORKS CITED

Addiss, Jeffrey (creator). 2019. *The Dark Crystal: Age of Resistance.* Season One, Episode Nine, "The Crystal Calls." 30 August. Scotts Valley: Netflix.
Alaimo, Stacy. 2010. *Bodily Natures: Science, Environment, and the Material Self.* Bloomington: Indiana University Press.
Desmarais, Jane. 2018. Monsters under Glass: A Cultural History of Hothouse Flowers from 1850 to the Present. London: Reaktion Books
The Duffer Brother (creators). 2016. *Stranger Things,* Season One, Episode Eight, "The Upside Down." 15 July. Scotts Valley: Netflix.
———. 2016. *Stranger Things.* Season One, Episode One, "The Vanishing of Will Byers." 15 July. Scotts Valley: Netflix.
———. 2016. *Stranger Things.* Season One, Episode Seven, "The Bathtub." 15 July. Scotts Valley: Netflix.
———. 2016. *Stranger Things.* Season One, Episode Three, "Holly, Jolly." 15 July. Scotts Valley: Netflix.
———. 2016. *Stranger Things.* Season One, Episode Two, "The Weirdo on Maple Street." 15 July. Scotts Valley: Netflix.
———. 2017. *Stranger Things.* Season Two, Episode Eight, "The Mind Flayer." 27 October. Scotts Valley: Netflix.

———. 2017. *Stranger Things.* Season Two, Episode Five, "Dig Dug." 27 October. Scotts Valley: Netflix.

———. 2017. *Stranger Things.* Season Two, Episode Four, "Will the Wise." 27 October. Scotts Valley: Netflix.

———. 2017. *Stranger Things.* Season Two, Episode Six, "The Spy." 27 October. Scotts Valley: Netflix.

———. 2017. *Stranger Things.* Season Two, Episode Three, "The Pollywog." 27 October. Scotts Valley: Netflix.

———. 2019. *Stranger Things.* Season Three, Episode Eight, "The Battle of Starcourt." 4 July. Scotts Valley: Netflix.

———. 2019. *Stranger Things.* Season Three, Episode Four, "The Sauna Test." 4 July. Scotts Valley: Netflix.

———. 2019. *Stranger Things.* Season Three, Episode Seven, "The Bite." 4 July. Scotts Valley: Netflix.

———. 2019. *Stranger Things.* Season Three, Episode Six, "*E Pluribus Unum.*" 4 July. Scotts Valley: Netflix.

———. 2019. *Stranger Things.* Season Three, Episode Two, "Suzie, Do You Copy?" 4 July. Scotts Valley: Netflix.

Estok, Simon C. 2020. "Corporeality, hyper-consciousness, and the Anthropocene ecoGothic: Slime and Ecophobia." *Neohelicon* 47, (June), 27–39.

Finney, Jack. 1955. *Invasion of the Body Snatchers.* New York: Dell Books

Gaiman, Neil. 2002. *Coraline.* London: Bloomsbury Publishing

Garland, Alex (dir.). 2018. *Annihilation.* Los Angeles: Paramount Pictures.

Hanson, Kristi L., Nicolau, Dan V., Filipponi, Luisa et al. 2006. "Fungi Use Efficient Algorithms for the Exploration of Microfluidic Networks." *Wiley Online Library* 2(10), 1212–1220. https://onlinelibrary.wiley.com/doi/abs/10.1002/smll.200600105. Accessed October 1, 2021.

Heise-von der Lippe, Anya, 2017. *Posthuman Gothic.* Cardiff: University of Wales Press.

Hodgson, William Hope. 2020. "A Voice in the Night" in *Evil Roots: Killer Tales of the Botanical Gothic,* edited by Daisy Butcher. London: British Library Publishing, 163–180.

Hughes, David, P., Andersen, Sarah B., Hywel-Jones, et al. 2011. "Behavioral mechanisms and morphological symptoms of zombie ants dying from fungal infection." *BMC Ecology,* 11, 13.

Knudsen, Eric. 2010. "Slenderman." *Creepypasta.* https://www.creepypasta.com/slenderman/. Accessed October 1, 2021.

Kristeva, Julia. 1982. *Powers of Horror: An Essay on Abjection.* New York: Columbia University Press.

McMain, Emma M, and Judith T. Torres. 2021. "Understories and Upside-Downs: The Pedagogical Misanthropy of *The Overstory* and *Stranger Things.*" *Interdisciplinary Studies in Literature and Environment.* (February), 1–22.

Merritt, Abraham. 2020. "The Woman of the Wood" in *Evil Roots: Killer Tales of the Botanical Gothic,* edited by Daisy Butcher. London: British Library Publishing, 239–273.

Miyazaki, Hayao (dir.). 1984. *Nausicaä of the Valley of the Wind.* Japan: Studio Ghibli.

Moore, Jason W. 2017. "The Capitalocene, Part I: On the Nature and Origins of Our Ecological Crisis." *The Journal of Peasant Studies.* (March), 1–37.

Novik, Naomi. 2015. *Uprooted.* New York: Del Rey Books.

Parker, Elizabeth. 2020. The Forest and the EcoGothic: The Deep Dark Woods in the Popular Imagination. London: Palgrave Macmillan.

Rogin, Michael. 1992. Ronald Reagan, the Movie: And Other Episodes in Political Demonology. Berkeley: University of California Press.

Scott, Ridley (dir.). 1979. *Alien.* Los Angeles: 20th Century Fox.

Tidwell, Christy and Carter Soles. 2021. *Fear and Nature: Ecohorror Studies in the Anthropocene.* Pennsylvania: Penn State University Press.

Yong, Ed. 2017. "A journey into the microbiome." *The Lancet.* (March), 273.

Chapter 15

After the End

The Post-Anthropocene Future of Endzeit

Lars Schmeink

There are a variety of explanations as to the cultural importance of the zombie. Depending on how we portray the living dead, they can be a reflection of us, the human, in its continuous and mindless consumption, in its terrifying spread across the world, in its dehumanizing of the Other to colonize, to exploit, or to kill without prejudice. Our impulse is to keep them out, the stave off the inevitable decay and destruction that they represent. Yet, since the turn of the century, the zombie has become ever more present in our contemporary cultural imagination, proliferating in a wide array of forms and stories. Furthermore, as Sarah Juliet Lauro points out, they are the reminder of a looming end, our call "for catharsis and to reconcile ourselves to an impending disaster, one that is shared by all those that inhabit this planet: namely, global climate change" (2016, 19).

Zombies and humans are thus closely related; they are ontologically just one bite removed from each other, the viral spread of zombiehood already inherent in its human form. As Gerry Canavan has pointed out, zombies represent the monstrous side of human economic exploitation: "Remorselessly consuming everything in their path, zombies leave nothing in their wake besides endless copies of themselves, making the zombie the perfect metaphor not only for how capitalism transforms its subjects but also for its relentless and devastating virologic march across the globe" (2017, 414). The image of the virus is the most potent imaginary of twenty-first-century zombies, best exemplified in the shift from shambling decaying corpses to rushing virally infected ever since Danny Boyle's *28 Days Later* (2002). Sherryl Vint argues that this shift in representation signals a closing of the ontological divide: "zombies emerge more clearly as our possible selves, as abjected and expelled parts of the body politic" (2017, 173). Zombies represent the human potential to instantly change by infection—metaphorically via capitalist culture or literally via a deadly virus or bacterium. But humans are not just *infected*; they are *the infection* itself. Moving up in scale, then, the human is a virus radically changing its host body: the Earth.

In his book *Dark Ecology*, Timothy Morton (2016) argues that the human as a species is so massively distributed across and complexly interwoven with other objects, it is itself a hyperobject, an object that can't be grasped empirically, cannot fully be comprehended in its scale. This position rejects the subject-object divide of humanist thought in favor of thinking about object relations more generally, with humans as "elements, but not the sole elements of philosophical interest. [. . . It] contends that nothing has special status, but that everything exists equally" (Bogost 2012, 6). This is part of a philosophical project called object-oriented ontology and Levi Bryant, one of its central theorists, has described it aptly as "an ontology where humans are no longer monarchs of being but are instead among beings, *entangled* in beings, and *implicated* in other beings" (2011, 40). It is this entanglement that brings the human into relation with its surroundings, and when viewed on a larger scale implicates us with issues of climate change. For Morton, every one of us is part of a larger object, the human species, which needs to be understood as "an entity that is now *a geophysical force on a planetary scale*" (2016, 9). Understanding this, he continues, will require "the task of thinking at temporal and spatial scales that are unfamiliar, even monstrously gigantic" (25). We will need to think new relations with other objects around us. We will need a new ecology based in "disanthropocentrism," as Jeffrey Jerome Cohen suggests: a grey ecology that "propels us beyond our own finitude, opens us to alien scales of both being (the micro and the macro) and time (the effervescent, barely glimpsed; the geologic, in which life proceeds at a billion-year pace)" (2017, 382–383). Within the scope of this grey ecology, as I have argued elsewhere (Schmeink 2022), zombie fictions become a way to disengage from thinking the human as center of being and instead see the potential for thinking "the larger implications that what we are really witnessing in a zombie narrative is a form of violent, transformative renewal" (Christie 2011, 62). As most zombie fictions stick to a group of surviving humans, though, thinking through the alien scales of the Anthropocene is not front and center for them.

With *Endzeit* (eng. *Ever After*, 2018) director Carolina Hellsgård and screenwriter Olivia Vieweg take a different approach to the representation of zombies and the end of the human. In the film—as in the comic by Vieweg it is adapted from—a virus has turned humans into zombies, while only two settlements of human survivors remain. The story follows two young women, Vivi (Gro Swantje Kohlhof) and Eva (Maja Lehrer), on their way from Weimar to Jena through the woods and hills between the two cities, focusing less on encounters with the undead and instead exploring questions of community, growth, and change—between the two women and between humans and surrounding nature. Unwilling to conform to genre conventions, *Endzeit* shifts discourse away from horror tropes and toward an element of fantasy. In their wandering, Vivi and Eva encounter "the Gardener" (Trine Dyrholm) a woman that is part human, part plant and who acts as a personification of Nature. As Beatrice Behn (2019) comments, the film is able to use "folkloristic metaphors to reveal the delusions of grandeur that humans have upheld for so long."[1] The film reveals to us, that we are not "at the center of being, organizing and regulating it like an ontological watchmaker" (Bogost 2012, 5). In the following, I want to explore the film's depiction of zombies and Nature through the disanthropocentric lens of grey ecology, to show how *Endzeit* proposes a radical new beginning of life on Earth after the end of the human species.

NATURE AS REFUGE

Most zombie fictions are based on the idea of categorial difference and the policing of these boundaries: life/death, human/animal, inside/outside, order/chaos. Zombies are the Other that eliminates those categories, the monsters that threaten "a stable, human-centered world [. . .] from the perspective of anthropocentric separation and dominion" (Wallis 2016, 57). We keep the zombie out, we destroy it, because it is categorically not human, not "us." Accordingly, most zombie fictions play with the idea of a literal or metaphorical *cordon sanitaire*, a barrier to stop the spread of the infection, that gives the illusion of control over one's bodily integrity and purity, as well as over socio-political security (Bashford and Hooker 2001).

Endzeit similarly picks up on this idea, by explaining that the surviving humans are locked down in the cities' safe zones and no one is allowed to leave. Importantly, the cities have different policies toward the contagion: while in Weimar all infected are immediately killed, Jena attempts to research and cure the infection. Weimar, then, is enacting a strict policy of separation (the fence) and dominion (killing of infected). The opening scene shows the border in Weimar: a ramshackle fence, barbwire on top and patched up with boards and makeshift barricades in many places, separates two distinct spaces from each other. One shot tracks the fence from above, revealing a noticeable difference between inside and outside. While the outside is green, grassy, and with blooming wildflowers, the inside of the fence is packed dirt, spots of grass trampled down. Workers are shown, patching up holes, mending the broken fence links, checking that the barrier is strong and cannot be breached. The next scene shows the city, deserted and desolate: wooden crosses mark the dead and fire pits with wood stacked next to them can be found all over

the city for light and warmth. A decorative fountain in the central square
has become a water refill station with plastic canisters for transport. The
lower windows of buildings are barricaded with wood. The famous statue
of Goethe and Schiller—symbol of Germany's intellectual heritage of the
Enlightenment and of humanism—has become a solar charging station, a
selection of electronic devices sitting at its foot.

These first few minutes of the film set up the dichotomy, separating the
city and nature around it, yet also reverses its standard interpretation. While
the outside seems oddly alive and beautiful—rabbits play in the grass, rays
of sunshine glimmer through the sparse woods—the city and its civilization
are shown as dying and broken. The old world has crumbled. Both nature
and the zombies press onto the barrier, forcing the remaining humans to vigilance and constant upkeep. But as Alison Bashford and Claire Hooker make
clear, contagion is a threat that defies "fantasies of control, corroding internal
integrity, and ignoring the borders that define and defend identity" (2001,
1). The film reveals this loss of control and integrity in an early scene, when
Vivi and Eva first meet on work duty. While repairing a hole in the fence, a
zombie grabs another woman's arm and bites her. Vivi, who spent the last
years traumatized in a psychiatric facility, is overwhelmed and unable to
react. She screams and collapses, while Eva kills the zombie and then hacks
off the woman's arm to stop the spread of the infection. But Weimar's zero-
tolerance policy forces her to kill the woman, to keep the *cordon sanitaire*
intact and not allow any infected in the city. Keeping up the separation from
the outside is thus revealed as a power fantasy, a task that will inevitably fail,
and both Vivi and Eva realize this. In defending the barrier, Eva has been
scratched and will now be excised from the "healthy body" of the population.
If she does not flee, she will be killed. Vivi is also not fit for life in the city,
unable to participate in the "separation and dominion" policy that is required
to keep up Weimar's integrity. She is haunted by the death of her little sister
and cannot bring herself to violence against the zombies, which she sees as
living creatures. Both women wish to run away from their life in Weimar and
decide to hide in an automated train that connects the two cities—but they
get stranded on their way.

When the train breaks down, Vivi and Eva have to continue on foot and
soon realize both the beauty and uncanniness of their surroundings, the film
engaging in a "study of romantic viewing—'romantic' in the 'history of
thought'—sense of the word" (Platthaus 2019). Nature around them, close
to home and well-known, is made strange by the loss of human agency,
which used to define it. The cinematography provides a new and uncanny
view of the world as "*subjectless* object, or an object that is for-*itself* rather
than an object that is an opposing pole before or in front of a subject"
(Bryant 2011, 19). Cinematographer Leah Striker takes her time panning

over the rolling hills, colored in yellow-orange light of the setting sun, contrasting it with the dark lush greens of the woods. The last remnants of the human world have become overgrown and reclaimed by nature. Mossy cars and vine-grown buildings becoming home to animals and plants, providing shelter to the lone humans. The world does not need a human eye to behold it or a human hand to manipulate it; it is teeming with life nonetheless. To Vivi this abundance of life is startling: a large colony of butterflies emerges from the train's toilet and a pack of wild boar roam the fields at dusk. When the human is not at the center any longer, all things are realized to be "vibrant matter," as Jane Bennett (2010, x) writes, "stretch[ing] received concepts of agency, action, and freedom." Within just two years of human absence, life has grown into a world without us. And both the human and the zombie appear misplaced in this landscape. Nature and not the remaining "civilized" space of Weimar is revealed as a refuge for life, the arrested human city instead becoming a symbol for the death of the old—turning the dichotomies around and vividly pushing for a disanthropocentric reading of the zombie plague.

NATURE'S REVENGE

Pushing the point of a world that will be better off without the human even further, the film introduces a fantastic element into its storytelling, thus shifting its genre context from horror to "eco-fairytale" (Knoben 2019), echoing another aspect of romantic thought. In its interest in using fantastic elements as metaphor for philosophical inquiry, the film reminds of the "Kunstmärchen," as perfected by romantic authors such as Ludwig Tieck or E. T. A. Hoffmann. The film's first words provide an entry point into the fantastic, poetic, romantic view of objects as alive and entangled with the human. After the opening scene described above, the next scene shows Vivi watering plants in her home, the psychiatric facility. She is very attentive of them, caring for them, while reciting the words to a poem:

A brook a-burbling in my ears,
There is no room for you.
The grass a-growing in my eyes,
There is no room for you.
A woodpecker's nest within my heart,
There is no room for you.
I am a rock.
I have seen life and death.
Know, you evil spirits, I don't sleep. (*Endzeit* 2018) [2]

Later in the film, she explains that these words were invented by her sister
for her own belief system of Gods of the Earth. They function as prayer to
the Earth and her many forms to keep you save from harm. Vivi recites them
as a form of penance to her sister and as a traumatic working through of the
events that killed her. But in their poetic form they also signal, right at the
beginning of the film, that humanist boundaries segregating the human from
nature will be dissolved, that nature is full of life to keep the evil spirits at
bay. And it already hints, though with a very different discursive register, at
a posthuman becoming, at a change in the way that integrity and identity will
work in the film.

The film picks up this prayer and its meaning of transcendence in a later
scene, which sets the stage for the fairytale element; the philosophical idea
is teased out when Vivi and Eva take shelter in a hunter's perch, spending
the night under the open sky. They see a couple of giraffe's grazing, the film
subtly highlighting its move from the uncanny to the fantastic. The following
scene shows the two women talking about the past, interspersed with flash-
backs, and picking up the theme of the prayer. The close-up shots also subtly
reveal a closeness of the two women, sharing an intimate moment, enjoying
music together and forgetting for a minute their surroundings. Changing the
musical cues from intra- to extradiegetic further stresses the removed nature
of this moment. The scene turns to night; Vivi is having a vision of her dead
sister and a group of zombies walking through the high grass when she asks
Eva what the apocalypse means for her. Eva then basically vocalizes the
film's message: "I believe the Earth is a wise old lady and humans haven't
paid her any rent for a long time. And out there, that is our eviction order."
She believes there are advantages to the apocalypse, staring up the clear sky,
enjoying the stars now finally visible again—the end of the human allows for
a different perspective, for a disanthropocentric viewpoint.

This viewpoint is then provided with the personified voice of Mother
Nature, as the film introduces the character of the "Gardener," a woman who
seems to have *become-plant*, not a zombie and not human either. A variety
of twigs, leaves, and mosses seem to grow out of the side of her face, giving
the appearance of ornaments or a one-sided tiara. Even though she claims
not to need humans around her anymore, she rescues Vivi from an attack by
a zombie and welcomes her to the orchard and garden, which she tends. She
explains: "What's happening is necessary. It should have happened a long
time ago. The unwelcome guests must leave." For the Gardener, the humans
have not treated their existence and their surroundings with respect and the
virus is the necessary step to assure a renewal for Earth. Vivi, believing she
has no place in this new world, tries to kill herself with an empty gun. The
Gardener invites her to live instead, to live with her and under her protection. Vivi has proven that she is no longer clinging to her old life, instead

seeking a way to be relieved of her guilt for her sister's death. Finally, the Gardener shows Vivi the abundance of life in the garden and invites her to eat from the plentiful rows of tomatoes in the green houses. She continues her explanation: "Humankind is disappearing from Earth. Only just arrived and already finished. The blink of an eye in nature's history. What destroyed humankind we have been carrying with us for millions of years. The virus was lying in wait. Now it is time to take the chance this downfall is giving us."[3]

The Gardener does identify with humanity and includes herself in its entanglement, yet she remains outside of its time scale and perspective. She points out how humans are hosts to micro-organic life, how "we evolve with our symbionts, our most intimate partners, and we cannot survive without them. Shockingly our evolutionary partners proliferate as species more successful than our own" (Rackham 2001, 222). And how that life has the potential to kill the human host body. She holds up a rotten piece of fruit at this point, teeming with larvae and thus highlighting the idea that death and life, destruction and renewal are closely tied to each other, and neither is inherently good or bad. "Everything changes," she exclaims, "there is peace in chaos. Neither destruction nor pills will save the people. Something new will arise." This comment stresses the two human strategies to circumvent their own demise, as Jena pushes science to heal, while Weimar opts to kill any infected. Neither way will actually be right. What is right, though, is a new perspective, "something new" that can be shaped from the objects that once were. During this monologue, the Gardener stands in front of a row of self-drawn portraits of posthuman becomings, zombies that are being taken over by plant life. Having lost their chance of living with nature, nature reclaims the humans' bodies and energy to form a new beginning.

It is important to note that while the film here pushes an object-oriented ontology and a grey ecology beyond the human scale of being, the extended metaphor of the Gardener, her personification of the concept of Nature, or maybe of the hyperobject of planet Earth, is problematically human centered. But as Bogost has pointed out, an understanding of these alien scales of being will only work by analogy: "anthropocentrism is unavoidable, at least for us humans" (2016, 64). Giving objects a human voice forces us to consider differently the ethical decisions involved and weigh the value of things as if they were human. Bennett argues, that especially with ecological thinking, "the risks associated with anthropomorphizing (superstition, the divinization of nature, romanticism)" might be worth it, "because it, oddly enough, works against anthropocentrism: a chord is struck between person and thing, and I am no longer above or outside a nonhuman 'environment'" (2010, 120). In this sense then, the Gardener is not just a fantastic figure to drive home an important eco-critical message, but also an anthropomorphized perspective on issues such as climate change and the destruction of natural habitats by humans. In the Gardener we see a critical reflection of the Anthropocene.

ZOMBIE BECOMINGS

But not just a different view on Nature and its relation to the human are focused in the film. *Endzeit* also reimagines representations of zombies both as an indistinct threat and as the final stage of categorial transgression. Whereas other zombie fictions display zombies as a faceless mass, their individuality and agency usurped by inhuman animality (Lauro and Embry 2008, 90), *Endzeit* takes the time to stage a few longer encounters with specific zombies, highlighting their individuality and personal history even in zombiehood. Zombies in the film are not the shambling horde of corpses but embodied in and haunted by their human selves. When Vivi and Eva visit an old estate house, they find the place set up for a survivor colony. It feels like the survivors are just out for daily chores: food is growing in the courtyard, rain is collecting in big tubs, the rooms are cozy and inviting, toys are strewn across the living room. No one is there. Yet, next to the moat, twelve pairs of shoes stand in a neat row. When Eva falls into the moat, she discovers zombies tied with chains to big rocks sunk to the ground, still "alive." The suicide that was meant to keep them from becoming zombies did not work as imagined. The unfortunate turned under water and there slowly deteriorate into water plants, which does not stop them from trying to attack Eva. The personal history and tragic situation of the zombies is meant to help our understanding, to remove them from our anthropocentric viewpoint of being dehumanized Others. We realize that the space between fighting to survive and becoming part of the threat is getting rapidly slimmer—especially given the fact that Eva is hardly grasping on to her humanity, the zombie virus changing her body.

Toward the end of the film, in an abandoned house, Vivi discovers the remnants of the former tenant's life, food and drink gone bad, furniture overgrown with his house plants, and a book written in Braille. The blind man has turned into a zombie and, startled by Vivi's noise, relies completely on his hearing for his attack, listening intently for sounds and then pouncing on his prey. Vivi is able to fend him off but loses an eye to the attack—a powerful symbol of partially turning into that which attacked her. The zombie's movement and hunting strategy are adapted to his embodied identity, he does not run at a target, but orients himself by listening before moving. The depiction as an individual with alternative cognitive processes and a form of embodied agency provides a disanthropocentric interpretation of the zombie as posthuman, an object (beyond the subject-object dichotomy) of vital materiality, whose agency is not limited to "impede or block the will and design of humans," but instead has its own "trajectories, propensities, or tendencies" (Bennett 2010, viii).

Lastly, the film embraces the idea that human bodies have never been purely human, that the *cordon sanitaire* of our skin, unpenetrated by the zombie's bite, is an illusion of the anthropocentric boundary that keeps me from being part of nature. As Jason Wallis has pointed out, "the vaunted celebration of the uncontaminated human marks a failure to acknowledge that we have never been humans proper by fact of our constitution by microbial and amoebic intelligences that are not our own" (2016, 64). Through the zombie figure, then, *Endzeit* explores a disanthropocentric view of reality, "in which the categories of human, animal, and nonhuman are radically deterritorialized" (64.). In the film, one zombie becomes exemplary for the development of human bodies once they zombify. Early in their journey, Vivi and Eva see a figure clad in a white wedding dress hunting through the grassy hills, a white dove clinging to her shoulder and moss and weeds growing from her skin. The bride is portrayed as slowly decomposing and *becoming-plant*, yet her actions are full of agency and vitality. She reminds us that the bodies' "[d]ecay is a process of transformation. It seems final, fatal, and terminal, but this activity is future directed, creative, and uninterested in our mourning" (Cohen 2017, 389). The image of the bride, with her white dress, is uncanny and jarring, yet it connects human culture with natural transformation. It is fitting that Vivi is not able to kill her—or any other zombie—because she cannot fully dehumanize the bride: "Vivi's empathetic viewpoint cannot distinguish the living from the dead, just as the world of the film is fluid and cannot really ever be grasped" (Kienzl 2009). The fluid categorization, the trajectory of human-zombie-compost shows that human(ist) categories of ethics are no longer clear-cut and easy to apply. What is considered good or bad, right or wrong is not based on the human as a measure anymore. As Ian Bogost argues: "'Preservation' turns out to be an object-relative concept. If a unit is a system, then objects appear, generate, collapse, and hide both within and without it with great regularity" (2012, 75). A decomposing body is the site of transformation, of renewal, of growth—just not from a human perspective.

The film emphasizes this idea of object-relative ethics via Vivi's personal trajectory, which hinges on the trauma of Vivi's perceived guilt in her little sister's death. Not having been able to save her from the zombies, Vivi is haunted by traumatic visions of her dead sister returning as a zombie or by dreams reliving the moment of leaving her sister behind to hide on the roof of her house. A nostalgic longing for the past is blocking Vivi from seeing the world around her, acting upon it. Vivi understands her sister's death as an ending, both to life and her connection to humanity. In a sense, her world died with her sister, and she has been a liminal figure ever since, neither human any longer nor yet zombie. When she finally frees herself and sees clearly for the first time—literally, from a zombie attack that took one eye—she can work through the ethics of death in this posthuman world. She encounters her sister's corpse, overgrown with moss and flowers, snails and bugs moving on the dead matter, decomposing by a river. Vivi makes peace with the situation, lays down beside her sister for the night, and accepts the new reality. The scene is shown from above, focusing on the two sisters, side by side, with a time-lapse effect showing Vivi herself *becoming-plant*, her body overgrowing with moss and leaves. When she wakes up, twigs grow from her skin and the empty wound of the eye socket. Here, the film signals that her ontological status has shifted, that she has moved over to the new world and its grey ecology.

A similar shift in ontology is presented in Eva's development over the film, focusing on her toughness and resilience, her will to survive and finally her transition to zombie-status. Eva is introduced as a hardened survivor, having secured her own survival by shutting out others from safety and letting them die. She has no quarrels about killing zombies and does what needs to be done—she completely enacts the "separation and dominion" doctrine. But while the zombie scratch slowly starts the process of physical change and prompts her to leave Weimar, it is her relationship with Vivi that changes her understanding of the world. It is Vivi's empathy for the zombies that challenges her distanced view, questions the dehumanization of the Other. When Eva dies and lies buried in a grave, Vivi makes a deal with the Gardener to grant her more time to get to Jena. Eva returns human, yet still infected, and flees with Vivi. The two women bond further, recognizing their support and care for each other. During their escape, they encounter a large mass of zombies and Eva saves Vivi by pushing her through a gate, closing it, and sacrificing herself to the zombies—she realizes that she is one of them, though not yet turned, and that Vivi will not be able to move on with Eva at her side. At the end of the film, all ontological categories are dissolved. When Vivi finally reaches the fence surrounding Jena, she hesitates, realizing that she does no longer belong there. In that moment, Eva returns with plants growing out of her body, not human but reborn *becoming-plant*. Neither of them will be welcome in the old world, but the new world is a promise. The two posthuman beings, hybrid and entangled with other objects, realize that their future lies outside. Standing at the border, they turn away from the old and set out into a new world.

In its depiction of a grey ecology of zombies that are entangled with plant life, the film opens up the possibility of a disanthropocentrism, a posthuman world-not-for-us. Other scales of being become important, as the Gardener points out. Human existence, the blink of an eye for the rest of the world, needs to be valued for what it is. By providing a fantastic metaphorical figure to voice this message, the film strays from its horror genre, yet gains an eco-critical perspective beyond the human. *Endzeit*, then, is a creative intervention into the question of what comes after the human, in a truly post-anthropocene world.

NOTES

1. All translation of German texts are mine, LS.
2. Transcript of the English subtitles taken from the Amazon Prime release.
3. The whole scene—as well as some others—has a Christian undertone, with the orchard as Garden Eden, Vivi eating the tomato (a "paradise apple" [Paradeiser] as it is called in some German dialects), and being asked to stay, as humanity has lost its place in paradise. It might be well worth exploring this aspect, but a full reading of the film as religious analogy is not within the scope of this paper.

WORKS CITED

Bashford, Alison and Claire Hooker. 2001. "Introduction: Contagion, Modernity and Postmodernity." *Contagion: Historical and Cultural Studies*, edited by Alison Bashford and Claire Hooker. New York: Routledge, 1–12.
Behn, Beatrice. 2019. "Das Ende der Menschen, der Anfang der Frauen," in: *Kino-Zeit*, n.d., available online: https://www.kino-zeit.de/film-kritiken-trailer-streaming/endzeit-2018. Accessed October 1, 2021.
Bennett, Jane. 2010. *Vibrant Matter: A Political Ecology of Things*. Durham: Duke University Press.
Bogost, Ian. 2012. *Alien Phenomenology, or What It's Like to Be a Thing*, Minneapolis: University of Minnesota Press.
Bryant, Levi R. 2011. *The Democracy of Objects*. Ann Arbor: Open Humanities Press.
Canavan, Gerry. 2017. "'We are the Walking Dead': Race, Time, and Survival in Zombie Narrative." *Zombie Theory: A Reader*, edited by in: Sarah Juliet Lauro. Minneapolis: University of Minnesota Press, 413–432.
Christie, Deborah. 2011. "And the Dead Shall Walk." *Better Off Dead: The Evolution of the Zombie as Post-Human*, edited by Deborah Christie and Sarah Juliet Lauro. New York: Fordham University Press, 61–65.
Cohen, Jeffrey Jerome. 2017. "Grey: A Zombie Ecology." *Zombie Theory: A Reader*. Edited by Sarah Juliet Lauro. Minneapolis: University of Minnesota Press, 381–394.
Hellsgård, Carolina (dir.). 2018. *Endzeit* [Ever After]. Erfurt: Grown Up Films.
Kienzl, Michael. 2019. "Die Filmkolumne," in: *Perlentaucher*, 21 August. https://www.perlentaucher.de/im-kino/filmkritiken-zu-endzeit-von-carolina-hellsgard-und-okko-s-inn-von-kitaro-kosaka.html. Accessed October 1, 2021.

Knoben, Martina. 2019. "Ökomärchen mit Zombie-Feminismus," in: *Süddeutsche Zeitung*, 22 August. https://www.sueddeutsche.de/kultur/endzeit-zombiefilm -rezension-1.4568433. Accessed October 1, 2021.

Lauro, Sarah Juliet. 2016. "Preface Zombies Today." *Generation Z: Zombies, Popular Culture and Educating Youth*, edited by Victoria Carrington et al. Wiesbaden: Springer, 11–19.

Lauro, Sarah Juliet and Karen Embry. 2008. "A Zombie Manifesto: The Nonhuman Condition in the Era of Advanced Capitalism," in: *Boundary 2*, 35 (1), 85–108.

Morton, Timothy. 2016. *Dark Ecology: For a Logic of Future Coexistence.* New York: Columbia University Press.

Platthaus, Andreas. 2019. "Neuer Deutscher Unheimlichkeitsheimatfilm," in: *Frankfurter Allgemeine Zeitung*, 21 August. https://www.faz.net/aktuell/feuilleton/ kino/video-filmkritiken/mehr-als-zombies-filmkritik-zu-endzeit-von-carolina-hell sgard-16343020.html. Accessed October 1, 2021.

Rackham, Melinda. 2001. "Carrier—Becoming Symborg." *Contagion: Historical and Cultural Studies*, edited by Alison Bashford and Claire Hooker. New York: Routledge, 217–226.

Schmeink, Lars. 2022. "A World not for Us: The Grey Ecology of Zombie Fiction." *The Handbook of Medical Environmental Humanities*, edited by Swarnalatha Rangajaran, Vidya Sarveswaran, and Scott Slovic. Cambridge: Bloomsbury. In print.

Vint, Sherryl. 2017. "Abject Posthumanism: Neoliberalism, Biopolitics, and Zombies." *Zombie Theory: A Reader*, edited by Sarah Juliet Lauro. Minneapolis: University of Minnesota Press, 171–181.

Wallin, Jason J. 2016. "Into the Black: Zombie Pedagogy, Education and Youth at the End of the Anthropocene." *Generation Z: Zombies, Popular Culture and Educating Youth*, edited by Victoria Carrington et al. Wiesbaden: Springer, 55–69.

Index

About the Contributors

Simon Bacon is a writer and film critic based in Poznań, Poland. He has edited books on various subjects including *Gothic: A Reader* (2018), *Horror: A Companion* (2019), *Monsters: A Companion* (2020), *Transmedia Vampires* (2021), and *Nosferatu in the 21st Century* (2022), *The Palgrave Handbook of the Vampire* (forthcoming), and co-edited *Undead Memory* (2013 with Katarzyna Bronk) and *Growing Up with Vampires* (2019 with Katarzyna Bronk) and *Spoofing the Vampire* (2022 with Ashley Szanter). He has also published a series of books on vampires in popular culture: *Becoming Vampire: Difference and the Vampire in Popular Culture* (2016), *Dracula as Absolute Other* (2019), *Eco-Vampires* (2020), *Vampires From Another World* (2021), and is working on the next *1000 Vampires on Screen* (forthcoming).

Kyle William Bishop is a third-generation professor at Southern Utah University, where he teaches courses in film and screen studies, American literature and culture, and fantasy/horror literature. He has presented and published a variety of articles on popular culture and cinematic adaptation, including *Night of the Living Dead*, *Fight Club*, *Buffy the Vampire Slayer*, *The Birds*, *The Walking Dead*, *Frankenstein*, and *Dracula*. He received a PhD in English from the University of Arizona and has published two monographs on zombies in popular culture—*American Zombie Gothic* (2010) and *How Zombies Conquered Popular Culture* (2015).

Mikaela Bobiy is a faculty member of the Humanities Department at Dawson College, Montreal. She completed a PhD in art history at Concordia University, where her research focused on performance art and masochism. Her current research focuses on the intersections between psychoanalysis, art and film, and she is co-creator of the Psychoanalysis and Film lecture series (Montreal, Quebec).

Aaron Bradshaw is a postdoctoral researcher working at the intersection of microbial ecology and the environmental post-humanities. He is particularly interested in microbial agency and the relationship between humans and microbes with a particular focus on the theory and practice of bioremediation. In his current research he is attempting to develop methodologies for human-microbe communication and collaboration in the context of responding to pollution and ecological devastation.

Nils Bubandt is professor of anthropology at Aarhus University. Publications include *The Empty Seashell: Witchcraft and Doubt on an Indonesian Island* (2014), *Arts of Living on a Damaged Planet. Ghosts and Monsters* (with Anna Tsing, Heather Swanson and Elaine Gan (2017) and *Rubber Boots Methods for the Anthropocene. Curiosity, Collaboration and Critical Description in Multispecies Fieldwork* (with Astrid O. Andersen and Rachel Cypher, 2022). He is currently working on a multispecies ethnography about corals, dive tourists, and the Second Coming of Christ in West Papua.

Daisy Butcher is a scholar attached to the *Open Graves, Open Minds Project* at the University of Hertfordshire. She is the editor of *Evil Roots: Killer Tales of the Botanical Gothic* (2018) and co-editor of *Crawling Horror: Creeping Tales of the Insect Weird* (2021). She has spoken across Europe at numerous conferences and her research looks at the EcoGothic, Postcolonial and Gendered implications of Plant Horror and Egyptian Gothic with particular emphasis on body horror and feminine archetypes.

Elana Gomel is the author of six academic books and numerous articles on subjects such as narrative theory, posthumanism, science fiction, Dickens, and Victorian culture. She is currently working on a book about narrative representations of post-utopia and editing a Palgrave Reader of International Fantasy, along with several other projects. She is also a fiction writer who has published three novels and more than ninety science fiction and fantasy stories. Several of her stories won international awards and were featured in "Best of Year" anthologies.

Steffen Hantke has edited *Horror*, a special topic issue of *Paradoxa* (2002), *Horror: Creating and Marketing Fear* (2004), *Caligari's Heirs: The German Cinema of Fear after 1945* (2007), *American Horror Film: The Genre at the*

Turn of the Millennium (2010), and, with Agnieszka Soltysik-Monnet, *War Gothic in Literature and Culture* (2016). He is also author of *Conspiracy and Paranoia in Contemporary American Literature* (1994) and *Monsters in the Machine: Science Fiction Film and the Militarization of America after World War II* (2016).

Johan Höglund is professor of English at Linnaeus University and member of the Linnaeus University Centre for Concurrences in Colonial and Postcolonial Studies. He has published extensively on imperial Gothic and horror, climate crisis fiction, and US, British and Nordic (neo)colonialism. He is the author of *The American Imperial Gothic: Popular Culture, Empire, Violence* (2014), and the co-editor of several scholarly collections and special journal issues, including *Dark Scenes from Damaged Earth: The Gothic Anthropocene* (2022), *Nordic Gothic* (2020), "Nordic Colonialisms" for *Scandinavian Studies* (2019), *B-Movie Gothic* (2018), and *Animal Horror Cinema: Genre, History and Criticism* (2015).

Sarah Lewison is an artist and writer concerned with political ecology. Her artistic research employs media, performance, text, and convivial events to explore how the relationships between humans and other-than-human species are shaped by law, history, and materiality in the Anthropocene. Working at the intersection of social practice and environmental media, her practice taps the possibilities inherent in the play of the speculative imagination. She teaches in the media arts at Southern Illinois University, Carbondale.

Lars Schmeink is vice president's research fellow at the Europa Universität Flensburg and project lead "Science Fiction" for the "FutureWork" research project funded by the Federal Ministry for Education and Research. He is the author of *Biopunk Dystopias* (2016) and co-editor of *Cyberpunk and Visual Culture* (2018), *The Routledge Companion to Cyberpunk Culture* (2020), *New Perspectives on Contemporary German Science Fiction* (2022) and *Fifty Key Figures in Cyberpunk Culture* (2022).

Conrad Scott holds a PhD from and is an instructor in the University of Alberta's Department of English and Film Studies, on Treaty 6 / Métis lands. He researches contemporary sf and environmental literature, and his current project examines the interconnection between place, culture, and literature in a study of environment and dystopia in contemporary North American fiction. His reviews and essays have appeared in *Science Fiction Studies*, *Extrapolation*, *Paradoxa*, *Transmotion*, *Environmental Philosophy*, *The Goose*, *UnderCurrents*, and *Canadian Literature*. He is also the author of *Waterline Immersion* (2019).

Rebecca Stone Gordon holds a BA in American history, an MS in audio technology and communication studies, and is an MA student in biological anthropology at American University. She has been an adjunct professor in both audio technology and anthropology and volunteers in a forensic anthropology research laboratory in the Anthropology Department at the Smithsonian Institution in Washington, DC. Recent publications include the essay "'A Lady of Undeniable Gifts but Dubious Reputation': Reading Theodora in The Haunting of Hill House" in *Shirley Jackson: A Companion*, edited by Kristopher Woofter (2021).

Kevin J. Wetmore Jr. is the author of over a dozen books, including *Post-9/11 Horror in American Cinema, Eaters of the Dead: Myths and Realities of Cannibal Monsters*, and *The Theology of Battlestar Galactica*, as well as over a hundred book chapters, journal articles, and essays, on topics from ghosts on the Japanese stage to African adaptation of Greek tragedy to Shakespeare in graphic novels. He is also the twice-Bram Stoker Award-nominated editor of books such as *Uncovering Stranger Things* and *The Streaming of Hill House*. He is an actor, director, and fight choreographer who lives and works in Los Angeles.

Gheorghe Williams is a PhD candidate in theatre studies at the University of Birmingham, UK. His primary research focus is the modern theatrical Gothic, with his doctoral thesis—supported by the Arts and Humanities Research Council (AHRC)—examining the prevalence of Gothicism in contemporary British political drama. He has presented internationally on topics ranging from Ecogothic performance to contemporary feminist stage adaptations of Gothic fiction, and has reviewed academic publications for peer-reviewed journals including *Revenant* and *Gothic Nature*. His further research interests include scenography and theories of affect, particularly where these intersect with the aesthetics and politics of Gothic performance.

Andrew J. Wilson is a writer, editor, and academic publisher. He graduated from the University of Edinburgh, one of the ancient universities of Scotland, as a Master of Arts with Honors. His essays, interviews, reviews and obituaries have been published on both sides of the Atlantic. The primary focus of his critical interests is on literature and film. His short stories and poetry have also appeared all over the world, sometimes in the most unlikely places. With Neil Williamson, he co-edited *Nova Scotia: New Scottish Speculative Fiction*, a critically acclaimed original anthology that was nominated for the World Fantasy Award.

Kristopher Woofter, PhD, teaches on horror, the Gothic and the weird traditions in literature and the moving image in the English department at Dawson College, Montréal, Québec. His recent publications include the edited collections *Shirley Jackson: A Companion* (2021) and *American Twilight: The Cinema of Tobe Hooper* (co-edited with Will Dodson) (2021). He is also editor of the peer-reviewed journal *Monstrum*.

www.ingramcontent.com/pod-product-compliance
Lightning Source LLC
Chambersburg PA
CBHW050634280326
41932CB00015B/2646

9 781793 625847